Island China

Ralph N. Clough

Island China

A Twentieth Century Fund Study

Harvard University Press

Cambridge, Massachusetts, and London, England

1978

Library of Congress Cataloging in Publication Data
Clough, Ralph N., 1916–
  Island China.
  "A Twentieth Century Fund Study."
  Bibliography: p.
  Includes index.
  1. United States—Foreign relations—Taiwan.
2. Taiwan—Foreign relations—United States.
3. United States—Foreign relations—China.
4. China—Foreign relations—United States.
I. Twentieth Century Fund. II. Title.
E183.8.T3C56   327.73′051′249   78–9483
ISBN 0–674–46875–9

The Twentieth Century Fund, founded in 1919 and endowed by Edward A. Filene, is an independent research foundation which undertakes policy studies of economic, political, and social institutions and issues.

To **Awana**

Foreword

When the Board of Trustees of the Twentieth Century Fund first considered Ralph Clough's proposal for a study of United States policy toward Taiwan and China three years ago, it was a time of officially inspired euphoria, stimulated by the opening to Peking as well as the imperatives of great power politics. Clough's proposal took a more skeptical view, suggesting that the transfer of US diplomatic recognition from Taipei to Peking would prove to be a more vexatious problem than was then anticipated. After vigorous debate of his view by the Board, his project was approved.

Subsequent events, of course, justified Clough's viewpoint. The reluctance of the United States to abandon a traditional ally, especially one with a long history of popular support, was bolstered by President Carter's initiative in making human rights an essential element of our foreign policy. Although free expression and democratic practices in Taiwan are restricted, the freedom of Taiwanese citizens—especially relative to the situation in China—is extensive. In addition, the possible repercussions of a modification or elimination of American commitments to Taiwan for our other allies in Asia now seem less favorable. Relations with our Asian allies have been particularly strained by the withdrawal from Vietnam and by US proposals to reduce the American military presence in other areas of Asia. These constraints on changing US policy are balanced, in large part, by the potential benefits—trade, political, and military—of improving relations with Peking through official recognition. Mao Tse-tung's successors have refused to moderate Peking's position on the Taiwan issue or to establish more normal relations with the United States until this issue has been resolved.

Clough offers no quick or painless answers to the problem posed by Taiwan. He examines the political evolution of Taiwan from a refuge for a discredited and defeated regime to a government integrating the native population and dealing with the interests of a new generation that has never known mainland China. The impressive economic achievements of Taiwan have facilitated these adjustments while, in a sense, complicating the problem for both China and the United States. Clough analyzes the political and military positions taken by the two Chinas and evaluates the ways in which both view their inextricably linked futures.

Although Clough is primarily concerned with the triangular relationship of China, Taiwan, and the United States, he regards the problem as one that must be considered in the broader framework of American policy in Asia. He focuses on the close but informal ties between Taiwan and Japan and weighs the hard choices facing the United States in seeking to normalize its own relations with Peking. In the end, he defines a policy approach that he believes will lead to normal relations with Peking while preserving the substance of our ties with Taiwan.

The members of the Fund staff who worked with the author found him a thoughtful, conscientious, and dedicated scholar. His careful and lucid analysis of this important issue makes a positive contribution, one that we are proud to sponsor.

M. J. Rossant, Director
The Twentieth Century Fund

Preface

In the outpouring of books and articles on China since President Nixon's trip to Peking, Taiwan has been neglected. Those proposing that the United States adopt this or that formula in order to normalize its relations with the People's Republic of China frequently offer judgments as to the resultant effect on Taiwan but rarely support such judgments by more than superficial analyses of conditions and attitudes in Taiwan. In this book I have analyzed political, economic, and military trends in Taiwan and the evolving interaction between Taiwan and mainland China and between Taiwan and its close neighbor, Japan, in the hope of providing a more informed basis on which to reach judgments as to future United States policy toward the People's Republic of China and Taiwan. I have also stressed the long-term nature of the Taiwan problem. It will not be resolved by an agreement between Washington and Peking on the normalization of their relations. Final resolution of the relationship between Taiwan and mainland China may take, as Teng Hsiao-p'ing has said, "five, ten, or a hundred years."

I am grateful to the Twentieth Century Fund for understanding and generous support for the research and writing of this book and to the Brookings Institution for providing me with a congenial place to work. I am indebted to my colleagues at Brookings, A. Doak Barnett and Joseph A. Yager, to Murray Rossant and Carol Barker of the Twentieth Century Fund, and also to Alan S. Whiting and Theodore Draper for their perceptive comments on the manuscript. Colonel Angus Fraser (USMC, ret.) was helpful with advice in the military field. Officials of the State Department and other specialists on China in the Washington area and elsewhere have been generous with their time. I owe a special debt of gratitude to officials of the government of the Republic of China and to other friends and acquaintances in Taiwan too numerous to list for their advice and assistance.

The views expressed in this book are my own and should not be attributed to the Twentieth Century Fund, the Brookings Institution, or any of the many persons I have consulted in its preparation.

Ralph N. Clough

Contents

Island China

United States Interests in Taiwan

1

Since the defeat of Japan in World War II, the central problem of United States policy toward East Asia has been how to deal with China. Initially the United States attempted to bring about a compromise between the contending Nationalists and Communists so that our policy toward the region could be based on a close association with a peaceful, united China. When this attempt failed and the Chinese Communists took over the China mainland, the United States ended its support of President Chiang Kai-shek's beleaguered refugee government on Taiwan, resolved to "wait until the dust settled" before formulating a new policy toward a Communist-controlled China formally allied with the Soviet Union. But the outbreak of the Korean war and the resultant conflict between American and Chinese Communist forces caused the resumption of large-scale military and economic aid to the Republic of China (ROC) on Taiwan and convinced the United States that a prime purpose of its East Asian policy should be the military and political containment of the People's Republic of China (PRC). This containment concept dominated US policy in the region for the next twenty years, until President Richard M. Nixon set it on a new course in 1972 by opening relations with Peking.

Implicit in the overture to Peking was the assumption that the expanding power and influence of the Soviet Union posed the greatest threat to US interests throughout the world and that a détente with the PRC, itself now caught up in a tense confrontation with the Soviet Union, would strengthen the US position. Moreover, the failure of US policy in Indochina discredited the concept that the military containment of China should be the principal foundation on which to build a stable structure of peace in the Pacific. Today, the more complex and fluid international relations developing in the region require new methods of dealing with China. Many fundamental differences on international politics continue to separate the United States and the PRC, but the two governments have enough interests in common to offer hope that skilled and sophisticated diplomacy may enable them to manage the differences between them and to improve the prospects for a lasting peace in Asia.

The US effort to cultivate constructive relations with Peking is greatly complicated by the relations that the United States has developed over twenty-five years with Taiwan. The PRC continues to claim the right to "liberate" the island, which it considers to be an integral part of its territory, but millions of Americans would strongly oppose on moral grounds simply abandoning the 17 million people on Taiwan to conquest by the PRC. So abrupt a termination of the close association between the United States and Taiwan would also severely damage US relations with its principal Asian ally, Japan, as well as with South Korea and other countries in the region. Consequently, the China problem faced by the United States today is how to improve relations with the PRC in order to further its broad global and regional purposes, without paying too high a price in its relations with Taiwan. Failure to modify US relations with Taiwan would reverse the promising start made in improving US relations with Peking, while too rapid and far-reaching changes in US-Taiwan relations could provoke turmoil on the island, military intervention by the PRC, and other serious repercussions that would dim prospects for a stable peace in the region. The ROC itself can to some extent affect the policies of the larger powers. Miscalculation of the way it would react to particular steps taken by Washington, Peking, or Tokyo could cause the policies of these powers to miscarry.

For many years, disagreement over US relations with the ROC blocked any improvement whatsoever in US relations with the PRC. During the first couple of years of ambassadorial talks between the two powers, which began in Geneva in 1955 and shifted to Warsaw in 1958, the PRC was more flexible than the United States in contemplating steps to expand bilateral relations, but from 1958 on, whenever the American ambassador proposed some small step, the Chinese ambassador monotonously responded that relations between Peking and Washington could not be improved until the Taiwan problem had been resolved. Finally in 1971, deeply worried by the military threat from the Soviet Union,

2

the PRC modified its adamant stand, agreeing in effect to put the Taiwan issue to one side for the time being and to engage in intercourse with the United States.

The PRC did not, however, retreat from its claim that Taiwan is an integral part of its territory. On the contrary, it reiterated its long-held position in the joint communiqué issued at Shanghai on February 27, 1972, at the end of Nixon's visit to China:

> The Taiwan question is the crucial question obstructing the normalization of relations between China and the United States; the Government of the People's Republic of China is the sole legal government of China; Taiwan is a province of China which has long been returned to the motherland; the liberation of Taiwan is China's internal affair in which no other country has the right to interfere; and all U.S. forces and installations must be withdrawn from Taiwan. The Chinese Government firmly opposes any activities which aim at the creation of "one China, one Taiwan," "one China, two governments," "two Chinas," an "independent Taiwan," or advocate that "the status of Taiwan remains to be determined."

The statement by the United States in the same communiqué, while not agreeing with the PRC view, shifted perceptibly in that direction:

> The United States acknowledges that all Chinese on either side of the Taiwan Strait maintain there is but one China and that Taiwan is a part of China. The United States Government does not challenge that position. It reaffirms its interest in a peaceful settlement of the Taiwan question by the Chinese themselves. With this prospect in mind, it affirms the ultimate objective of the withdrawal of all U.S. forces and military installations from Taiwan. In the meantime, it will progressively reduce its forces and military installations on Taiwan as the tension in the area diminishes.[1]

By this declaration, the United States virtually disavowed any interest in encouraging an independent Taiwan. It did not repeat earlier statements that sovereignty over Taiwan was an unsettled question subject to future international resolution, although it did not explicitly repudiate them either.[2]

---

1. Foreign Broadcast Information Service (FBIS), *Daily Report, People's Republic of China* (Special Report: President Nixon's Visit to China), Mar. 9, 1972, p. 28.
2. See e.g. *Washington Post*, May 2, 1971.

In addition to stating their positions on Taiwan, the parties to the Shanghai communiqué agreed on certain general principles to govern their relations, expressed interest in opening trade and exchanging visitors, and pledged to undertake "concrete consultations to further the normalization of relations between the two countries." During the following five years, within the framework established by the communiqué, the United States and the PRC expanded trade, carried on a program of visits back and forth, and established in each other's capitals "liaison offices" to perform some of the functions of diplomatic missions until such time as relations might be normalized.

Taiwan remains "the crucial question obstructing the normalization of relations." Senior PRC officials in conversation with foreign visitors have laid down as conditions for normalization: the breaking of diplomatic relations between the United States and the ROC, the termination of the mutual security treaty between the two governments, and the withdrawal of all US military personnel from Taiwan. If these conditions were met, they say, the United States could continue to maintain relations with Taiwan comparable to those maintained by Japan since September 1972 when it established diplomatic relations with Peking and broke diplomatic relations with Taipei. That is, the United States could retain extensive economic relations with the island and handle intergovernmental relations through an ostensibly private body staffed by government officials.

What the United States will do about its relations with Taiwan requires a number of difficult judgments. Must the United States make concessions to the PRC on the Taiwan issue soon in order to maintain momentum in improving relations with the PRC and to further its purpose of creating a more stable international system is East Asia? Or will Sino-Soviet rivalry cause the PRC to feel the need of improving relations with the United States even in the absence of progress on the Taiwan issue? If the United States should decide that its broader interests require concessions on the Taiwan issue, how far should it go to meet the PRC's conditions? What would be the effect on Taiwan and the repercussions in Japan and among other US allies in East Asia of meeting some or all of the PRC's conditions? What reciprocal actions or pledges might the United States require from the PRC in order to help to preserve Taiwan's security and stability?

As the above questions suggest, the tacit agreement to lay the Taiwan problem aside represented by the Shanghai communiqué did little to resolve the issue. Even if the United States were to accept the PRC's conditions and normalize relations with Peking in accordance with the Japanese model, the issue would be far from resolved, for the government and people of Taiwan show little inclination to accept PRC control of the island, and the PRC would almost certainly persist in its determination to gain ultimate control. Thus, for the indefinite future the United States is likely to be confronted with further decisions on Taiwan —in broad terms whether to tilt its policy toward helping the people of the island to remain free of PRC control or to tip the scales in the other direction, facilitating the PRC's effort to take over the island. Each decision will have to be made not only in light of the broader considerations imposed by global US objectives—especially in its relations with the Soviet Union, China, and Japan—but also in relation to US interests in Taiwan itself.

Noninvolvement Before 1950

Until the association with the island that developed as a result of the Korean war, the United States perceived no intrinsic interests in Taiwan. To the extent that the country saw any interest, it was that the island not be used by others in ways injurious to the US interests in the region.

In the middle of the nineteenth century, some American officials, frustrated by the inability or unwillingness of Chinese officials to prevent aboriginal tribesmen in Taiwan from pillaging grounded American ships and murdering their crews, and also keen to expand their country's trade and influence in the western Pacific, proposed that the United States acquire Taiwan. The island would be useful, they thought, as a coaling station and as a base from which the United States could pursue its commercial interests along the China coast and in Japan, as the British did from Hong Kong, the Portuguese from Macao, and the Dutch from the Netherlands East Indies. Commodore Matthew C. Perry, after his success in "opening" Japan, recommended to President Franklin Pierce the establishment of an American settlement in Taiwan that could ultimately lead to an American protectorate over the island. Townsend Harris, the first American consul general to Japan, recommended that the United States purchase Taiwan from China. Peter Parker, the American commissioner to China in the 1850s, urged that the United States take over Taiwan, not shrinking from the use of military force should that be necessary. But all such suggestions were coldly received in Washington. Parker's successor, William B. Reed, was instructed to bear in mind that "the whole nature and policy of our government . . .

5

deprived us of all motives either for territorial aggrandizement or the acquisition of political power in that distant region."[3]

Before the end of the century, however, both the status of Taiwan and the US government's view of its role in the western Pacific had changed radically. Japan acquired Taiwan in 1895 as a result of the Sino-Japanese war, thus joining the ranks of the imperialist powers competing to extract concessions from China. Soon thereafter, clashing American and Japanese interests in the Hawaiian islands provided the first test of strength between these expanding Pacific powers, resulting in the annexation of Hawaii by the United States in 1898. The acquisition of the Philippines, almost by inadvertence as the result of a war with Spain over Cuba, soon installed the United States as a colonial power next door to Japan's colony, Taiwan. Many years later, culminating the history of sharpening disputes between the United States and Japan over the Japanese expansionist policies in East Asia, Taiwan became the base from which the Japanese military launched their attack on the Philippines and their advance into other parts of Southeast Asia.

Determined to strip Japan of the power to make war, the United States joined Britain and China at the Cairo Conference in 1943 to declare that Taiwan would be taken from Japan and restored to China. Prior to the conference no thought appears to have been given by senior American officials to the possibility of annexing Taiwan or of offering its inhabitants the choice of independence. The intention to return Taiwan to China was confirmed in the Potsdam Proclamation of July 26, 1945, which was later concurred in by the Soviet Union and France and accepted by Japan. In October 1945, officials of the ROC formally accepted the surrender of the Japanese forces in Taiwan and took the island over from Japan, declaring it to be once more incorporated into the territory of China.

In turning Taiwan over to the ROC, the United States acted on the assumption that its postwar policy in East Asia would be founded upon close cooperation with a strong, united China. Japan, stripped of its colonies, was to remain disarmed and weak. But within four years, US policy was in disarray. The Chinese Communists had gained control of mainland China and were soon to enter into an alliance with the Soviet Union directed against both Japan and the United States.

The conquest of the China mainland by the Chinese Communists and Mao's declaration of July 1949 that his government would take the Soviet side in the global power struggle aroused concern in Washington

---

3. Sophia Su-fei Yen, *Taiwan in China's Foreign Relations* (Hampden, Conn.: Shoestring Press, 1965), pp. 77–78. See also Tyler Dennett, *Americans in Eastern Asia* (New York: Macmillan, 1922), pp. 276, 284–291.

as to the strategic consequences for the United States should Taiwan come under Peking's control. The Joint Chiefs of Staff (JCS) foresaw serious damage to the strategic position of the United States in that event, but they were unwilling to recommend US military intervention to keep Taiwan out of Communist hands because of the potentially more urgent needs elsewhere for limited US forces. There was general agreement within the US government that it would be highly desirable for Taiwan to remain under a friendly, non-Communist regime. Various proposals to achieve this end, short of military intervention, were considered, including an appeal to the United Nations, US support of the Taiwan independence movement, and provision of large-scale economic and military aid to the Nationalist government, which had withdrawn to Taiwan in December 1949. The continuation of a modest economic aid program was approved, but massive economic aid was rejected as likely to be ineffective. President Harry S. Truman also decided against reinstituting a military aid program in Taiwan, despite recommendations to that end by the JCS and demands by prominent Republican members of Congress.[4]

In January 1950, Truman announced that "the United States has no desire to obtain special rights or privileges or to establish military bases in Formosa at this time. Nor does it have any intention of utilizing its armed forces to interfere in the present situation. The United States Government will not pursue a course which will lead to involvement in the civil conflict in China. Similarly, the United States Government will not provide military aid or advice to Formosa."[5]

The Department of State two weeks earlier had issued a confidential policy memorandum to information officers abroad informing them that the fall of Taiwan was widely anticipated and giving instructions intended to minimize the damage to US interests that would result.[6] Thus, at the highest level, the United States had decided in early 1950 that US interests in Taiwan were not important enough to warrant intervention to prevent its conquest by the Chinese Communists. Chiang Kai-shek and his remaining forces would have to fend for themselves.

Reversal of Policy During Korean War

The surprise attack by North Korean forces against South Korea in June 1950 and the decision to intervene with American forces caused

---

4. See *Foreign Relations of the United States, 1949,* vol. IX, *The Far East: China* (Washington, D.C.: US Government Printing Office, 1974).
5. *Department of State Bulletin,* Jan. 16, 1950, p. 79.
6. Hungdah Chiu, ed., *China and the Question of Taiwan* (New York: Praeger, 1973), pp. 217–220.

an urgent reassessment of US interests in Taiwan and a reversal of the hands-off policy. This blatant use of force by a Soviet proxy, coming soon after the formation of the Sino-Soviet alliance, raised serious questions about possible future Soviet and Chinese Communist actions in this region or elsewhere. Under the circumstances, particularly in light of the views already prevalent in the government concerning the strategic importance of Taiwan, it seemed only prudent to keep the island for the time being out of Chinese hands. Moreover, it would be difficult to justify continued rejection of Republican pressures for US assistance in the defense of Taiwan while seeking public support for the decision to intervene militarily in Korea. Consequently, Truman declared:

> The occupation of Formosa by Communist forces would be a direct threat to the security of the Pacific area and to United States forces performing their lawful and necessary functions in that area. Accordingly, I have ordered the Seventh Fleet to prevent any attack on Formosa. As a corollary of this action, I am calling upon the Chinese Government on Formosa to cease all air and sea operations against the mainland. The Seventh Fleet will see that this is done. The determination of the future status of Formosa must await the restoration of security in the Pacific, a peace settlement with Japan, or consideration by the United Nations.[7]

Thus, the attack in Korea and the American reaction to it brought about a fundamental reassessment of US policy toward China and Taiwan, causing that policy to veer sharply from the direction it had taken prior to June 1950. The attack set in motion a series of developments that linked Taiwan more and more firmly to the United States in a connection that would become the main issue between Washington and Peking in the years to come.

The Korean war was instrumental in radically changing US relations with Taiwan, not only because it impelled Truman to adopt emergency measures to protect Taiwan from attack, but also because by the end of the war the United States and the PRC had come to regard each other as implacable enemies. From the US viewpoint, the Chinese had intervened in Korea in order to back an unprovoked Soviet-supported North Korean aggression against South Korea. From the Chinese viewpoint, they had intervened to counter an imminent threat to their industrial heartland by a government that had just resumed its support of the defeated Chiang Kai-shek forces in Taiwan. The need of both nations to mobilize public support for their forces

---

7. *Department of State Bulletin,* July 3, 1950, p. 5.

engaged in combat in Korea caused each to depict the other in the darkest colors. The United States came to perceive the PRC as an aggressive power prepared to use military force to extend Sino-Soviet hegemony over East Asia. The PRC saw the United States as a continuing military threat that had even hinted at its possible use of nuclear weapons against China to end the war in Korea.[8] Angrily rebutting Truman's assertion that the status of Taiwan was undetermined, Peking accused Washington of seeking to gain control over Taiwan and sever it from the motherland.[9]

Once China, strongly backed by the Soviet Union, began to be viewed as a serious menace to US interest in the western Pacific, Taiwan took on a new importance. It came to be regarded as a vital link in the US defense line, whose loss to Communist forces would imperil the US position in Japan and the Philippines. As early as the summer of 1950, General Douglas MacArthur, after a visit to President Chiang Kai-shek, stressed the importance of defending Taiwan, that "unsinkable aircraft carrier."[10] In an address to the Congress following his dismissal MacArthur expressed the extreme view that the loss of Taiwan "might well force our western frontiers back to the coasts of California, Oregon, and Washington."[11] The concept was gaining support that, by strengthening the government of the ROC on Taiwan, the United States could pose a continual threat to the PRC, tie down large numbers of forces opposite Taiwan, provide an alternative focus of loyalty for overseas Chinese in Southeast Asia, and perhaps ultimately help the government on Taiwan to recover the mainland from a weakened and beleaguered Communist regime.

Not all Americans agreed that the PRC was an aggressive power that had to be contained by military force, but the opposition was a minority, inhibited in public debate by the emotional atmosphere created by Senator Joseph R. McCarthy's trumpeted accusations against alleged Communists in the US government. Moreover, Peking's abusive propaganda attacks on the United States could not be ignored. The PRC's aid to the Vietminh and its attacks on the Nationalist-held offshort islands soon after the cease-fire in Korea also strengthened the view that the PRC would further the spread of communism through violence wherever it did not encounter superior force.

While the conflict in Korea was hardening the attitudes of the two

---

8. Foster Rhea Dulles, *American Foreign Policy Toward Communist China, 1949–1969* (New York: Crowell, 1972), pp. 136–137.
9. See Chiu, *China and the Question of Taiwan*, p. 232–236.
10. Dulles, *American Foreign Policy Toward Communist China*, pp. 99–100.
11. Akira Iriye, *Across the Pacific: An Inner History of American-East Asian Relations* (New York: Harcourt, Brace, and World, 1967), p. 292.

sides, the United States was engaged in cementing its relations with Taiwan. A military mission from General MacArthur's headquarters in Tokyo arrived in Taiwan in the summer of 1950 to survey the military needs of the Chinese forces there. By the middle of 1951, $50 million had been allocated for military equipment and supplies and $42 million for economic aid. A Military Assistance Advisory Group (MAAG) had arrived, headed by a major general who immediately asked Washington to expand his small staff to 777 persons. The Mutual Security Appropriations Act, passed in October 1951, envisaged aid totaling some $300 million for Taiwan in fiscal 1952. By April of that year Karl L. Rankin, the American chargé d'affaires in Taiwan and a vigorous advocate of strong US support for Nationalist China, was able to inform the members of his staff that the policy of the United States was not merely to provide minimal military and economic aid to Taiwan until its future could be decided by international agreement. On the contrary, he declared, the actual US program for Taiwan was "now on a comprehensive, medium to long-term basis which foresees making the island economically self-supporting except for such assistance as may be required to maintain a larger-than-normal military establishment until peace and security are re-established in the Far East." By the time the shooting stopped in Korea in July 1953, the American official community in Taiwan administering these ongoing military and economic aid programs had grown to 1200 persons, exclusive of dependents, a tenfold increase over the 119 officials present in April 1951.[12]

Consolidation of Relations

The conclusion of the Korean conflict diminished but did not end the tension between the United States and the PRC. Peking watched with growing concern as the relations between the United States and Taiwan grew closer. Within two weeks after assuming office, President Dwight D. Eisenhower had withdrawn the order to the Seventh Fleet to prevent military operations by the ROC against the mainland, but he continued its mission to protect Taiwan. For its part, Washington was much disturbed by the PRC's support for the Vietminh's war against the French in Indochina. The collapse of French resistance in 1954 and the partition of Vietnam at the Geneva Conference seemed like a threatening advance by the Sino-Soviet bloc into Southeast Asia. Secre-

---

12. Karl Lott Rankin, *China Assignment* (Seattle: University of Washington Press, 1964), pp. 105, 122–123, 174.

tary of State John Foster Dulles set about organizing the Southeast Asia Treaty Organization (SEATO) to resist the Communist threat. He also stated at a press conference in early August 1954 that the United States was considering both a northeast Asia security pact and a bilateral defense treaty with the ROC.

Chou En-lai, premier of the PRC, in a major policy speech on August 11, 1954, denounced US efforts to build a chain of alliances around China. A series of increasingly explicit statements on Peking's determination to liberate Taiwan culminated on September 3 in the opening of a heavy bombardment of Quemoy, the largest of the Nationalist-held offshore islands. A few months later, Americans were outraged when a military court in Peking imposed long prison sentences on eleven US airmen and two civilians shot down during the Korean war.

By this time, negotiations on a mutual defense treaty with the ROC were well advanced. Both President Chiang Kai-shek and Ambassador Rankin had pressed for a formal US commitment to the defense of Taiwan as a means of solidifying the steadily expanding relationship between the United States and the ROC.[13] Dulles saw such a pact as an essential link in the chain of bilateral and multilateral treaties that the United States had concluded in the western Pacific, from the Republic of Korea and Japan in the north to SEATO and the security treaty with Australia and New Zealand in the south. Making Taiwan an integral part of this US-backed security system was a momentous further assumption by the United States of responsibility for Taiwan's destiny. The PRC bitterly denounced the treaty as an attempt to legalize the occupation of Taiwan by the United States. In January 1955, a month after the signing of the treaty, PRC forces in a well-coordinated amphibious assault overwhelmed one thousand Nationalist defenders and occupied Yichiang Shan Island, near the Ta Chen group, well to the north of Taiwan.

Conclusion of the mutual defense treaty vindicated Ambassador Rankin's judgment of more than two years earlier that the United States had entered into a "medium to long-term" relationship with Taiwan.[14] It provided a stable framework within which the programs

---

13. Ibid., p. 186.
14. Rankin arrived in Taiwan as chargé d'affaires in August 1950 and was appointed ambassador in February 1953. During his seven and one-half year assignment he played an important part in strengthening US-Taiwan relations, with the firm backing of Walter S. Robertson, Assistant Secretary of State for Far Eastern Affairs from 1953 to 1959. For Rankin's basic view of China policy, see a letter of July 7, 1953, to Ambassador George V. Allen in New Delhi: "The Nationalists are convinced—and I share that conviction—that unless mainland China can be liberated in due course from

to strengthen Taiwan militarily and economically could go forward. The treaty had no expiration date, although it could be denounced by either party on one year's notice. By undertaking a formal, open-ended commitment to help defend Taiwan, the United States in effect created an interest that did not previously exist. It now had the obligation to live up to the formal pledge, lest failure to do so undermine confidence in similar US pledges to other allies in the region and elsewhere.

In negotiating the treaty and deciding how to react to PRC attacks on the offshore islands, which occurred both just before and after its signing, the United States had to face up to the differences in interests and policy objectives that existed between Washington and Taipei. The ROC's fundamental policy was to overthrow the PRC and regain authority over the mainland. It clung to the offshore islands in large measure as a political symbol of its dedication to this goal. But the United States did not wish to be committed to assist in such an enterprise. Hence, the application of the treaty was carefully limited to the defense of Taiwan and Penghu, and in an exchange of notes accompanying the treaty the ROC agreed that, except for "action of an emergency character which is clearly an exercise of the inherent right of self-defense," it would launch its forces from Taiwan, Penghu, or the offshore islands only in "joint agreement" with the United States.[15] The exchange of notes constituted, in effect, a "releashing" of Chiang Kai-shek's forces.

Attacks on the offshore islands by the PRC during the fall and winter of 1954–1955 created a perplexing dilemma for the United States. It did not want to commit itself to help defend every islet off the China coast occupied by the Nationalists. But the United States had assumed a degree of moral responsibility for some of the islands by encouraging the ROC in 1953 to strengthen their defenses.[16] Conquest of the larger islands would inflict a severe defeat on Nationalist forces and seriously weaken defenses on Taiwan itself. Eisenhower considered the ROC army indispensable to the free world position in the western Pacific— especially after the departure of the French army from Indochina. In a letter to Prime Minister Winston Churchill in early February 1955, he wrote that the ROC forces were held together by a conviction that some

communism, whether of the Moscow or Peking variety, the rest of Asia will eventually go down the same drain." Rankin, *China Assignment*, p. 172.
15. See Chiu, *China and the Question of Taiwan*, pp. 250–253. Penghu, also known as the Pescadores, is a group of islands in the Taiwan Strait lying closer to Taiwan than to the mainland.
16. Rankin, *China Assignment*, pp. 168–169.

day they would go back to the mainland. To surrender Quemoy and Matsu, their stepping-stones to the mainland, would destroy the reason for their existence, which "would mean the almost immediate conversion of that asset [Taiwan] into a deadly danger, because the Communists would immediately take it over."[17] The ROC made certain that the stakes in this international poker game remained high by placing one-third of its forces on Quemoy and Matsu, where they remain today.

The United States resolved its dilemma for the time being by three means: getting the ROC to allow the evacuation of civilians and troops by the US Navy from the more distant and less defensible Ta Chens, apparently in return for an informal pledge to help defend Quemoy and Matsu; hinting that the United States would, if necessary, employ nuclear weapons against the PRC; and securing passage by the Congress of the Formosa Resolution authorizing the President to employ US forces to defend Taiwan and Penghu against armed attack and "such related positions and territories of that area now in friendly hands" as he might find necessary to assure the defense of Taiwan and Penghu.[18] Thus, the probability of US intervention was increased enough so that the PRC accepted the half loaf of the Ta Chens and refrained for a time from pressing its attack on the two more important islands. Shifting to a moderate approach to the United States, Chou En-lai proposed at the Bandung Conference of Asian Nations in April 1955 that the United States and the PRC open direct negotiations with each other about their differences. After the tension in the Taiwan Strait had somewhat subsided, Eisenhower also tried but failed to persuade Chiang Kai-shek, in exchange for a promise to station US Marines and an air wing in Taiwan, to withdraw the bulk of the civilian population and troops from Quemoy and Matsu, converting them into outposts rather than strongly defended territories whose loss would severely damage the ROC's morale and prestige.

The first offshore island crisis left the United States more firmly committed to the defense and support of Taiwan. The provision in the defense treaty granting the United States the right to station forces on the island strengthened the view of Taiwan as a vital link in the chain of US bases or potential bases in the western Pacific. The crisis also, however, highlighted the conflict of interest between the United States and the ROC over the offshore islands, which was to arise again in more

---

17. Dwight D. Eisenhower, *Mandate for Change* (New York: Doubleday, 1963), pp. 470–471.

18. J. H. Kalicki, *The Pattern of Sino-American Crises* (London: Cambridge University Press, 1975), p. 149; Eisenhower, *Mandate for Change,* p. 477; Chiu, *China and the Question of Taiwan,* p. 257.

acute form in the second offshore island crisis in 1958. Despite the nearly unanimous approval by the Senate of both the defense treaty and the Formosa Resolution, the Senate majority leader, Senator Lyndon Johnson, and other prominent Democratic senators questioned the wisdom of risking war with the PRC over the offshore islands, as did some of our European allies.

It is important to recall that the consolidation of relations between the United States and Taiwan in 1954–1955 took place during the brief honeymoon in Sino-Soviet relations, when those two countries appeared to be cooperating closely and coordinating their efforts to expand the area of Communist control in Asia. The slogan "Learn from the Soviet Union" was in vogue in China. Thousands of Chinese students were studying in the Soviet Union. The PRC had embarked on its first five-year plan, based on the Soviet model, and Moscow had committed itself to a massive transfer of technology to China. The People's Liberation Army was being modernized with large quantities of Soviet weapons. Hidden strains existed between the Communist allies even then, but to the outside observer the preponderance of evidence at that time showed that the Sino-Soviet alliance was solidly established.

Start of US–PRC Talks

Three years passed before the United States and the PRC again clashed over the offshore islands. In the meantime, the two governments had opened a channel for direct communication through a series of bilateral meetings at the ambassadorial level in Geneva. The ROC, fearing a sellout of its interests by its ally, did not hesitate to voice opposition to this gain in prestige by the PRC. However, the United States had important interests in entering into the talks, which were not shared by the ROC. It hoped to reduce the risk of conflict with the PRC and to obtain the release of the eleven airmen and some forty American civilians imprisoned in China. The talks got off to a good start in August 1955 with the PRC announcement that the airmen would be released. Hard bargaining for five weeks brought agreement on the return of civilians, but when the PRC failed to release all the civilians held, the talks bogged down. The United States rejected the PRC proposals for a bilateral foreign minister's conference, for removal of the US embargo on trade with China, and for an exchange of journalists. The efforts by the United States to persuade the PRC to renounce the use of force in the Taiwan area were rebuffed. The talks were suspended in December 1957, and less than nine months later, in August

1958, the PRC's heavy artillery began a massive bombardment of Quemoy.[19]

While the United States and the PRC were feeling each other out through the dialogue in Geneva, the programs aimed at strengthening Taiwan militarily and economically continued. Within the national security bureaucracy in Washington Taiwan was acquiring a constituency committed to making it a stronger link in the chain of alliances forged to contain Sino-Soviet expansion. Ongoing programs tended to gain momentum as it became increasingly evident that long-term planning would improve the effectiveness of both military and economic aid.

The US military aid program had brought about striking improvements in the ROC's armed forces. Old and disabled soldiers were retired with the help of a $42 million contribution from the United States, and through a conscription system their places were taken by young men serving two to three years. Obsolete weapons and equipment were replaced with modern rifles, machine guns, tanks, trucks, artillery, jet aircraft, destroyers, and minelayers. In early 1958, about one-third of the cost of the ROC's military establishment of 650,000 men, one of the largest in the world, was being met by US aid.[20] Ambassador Rankin, in a dispatch to the State Department, declared: "By 1957 the re-equipped military establishment of Free China once more constituted a large and vital part of the free world's might in the Western Pacific. Taiwan became indeed a position of strength, where United States military bases were unnecessary; the substantial military capabilities of Free China itself constituted an important deterrent to Red aggression elsewhere in East Asia."[21]

Although the United States had established no military bases on Taiwan, it had taken steps to facilitate US military operations there, should such become necessary. Twenty-five million dollars was made available for runway extension and other improvements of Kung Kuan airfield in central Taiwan so that it would be able to serve as a recovery base for B-52 bombers of the Strategic Air Command. In 1957 a Matador missile unit, manned by Americans and capable of hitting the China mainland with nuclear warheads, was stationed in Taiwan. US Air Force fighter squadrons from Okinawa or the Philippines were rotated into Chinese air bases in Taiwan for a month or two at a time on familiarization visits. A US Taiwan Defense Command, headed by a vice admiral, was established in Taipei with a skeleton staff charged

---

19. See Kenneth T. Young, *Negotiating with the Chinese Communists* (New York: McGraw-Hill, 1968).
20. US Mutual Security Agency, *Report to Congress on the Mutual Security Program for the Six Months Ended June 30, 1958,* p. 40.
21. Rankin, *China Assignment,* p. 322.

with developing contingency plans for US cooperation in the defense of Taiwan and Penghu, pursuant to the mutual defense treaty. Intelligence operations based on Taiwan, including overflights of the mainland by ROC pilots, became an important source of information on PRC forces which, like the ROC forces, were being modernized and strengthened.

Taiwan was also receiving substantial amounts of economic aid in the form of surplus agricultural commodities and loans and grants for development, averaging $114 million annually in the three years 1955–1957.[22] Such aid was considered essential in order to maintain at least the existing standards of consumption for a population increasing at over three percent annually and thus to prevent any impairment of morale and political stability on the island. US aid also supported a program for attracting overseas Chinese students from Southeast Asia to study in Taiwan, in order to help the ROC compete more effectively with the PRC for such students. By 1958, nearly 8000 overseas Chinese students were in Taiwan under this program, as compared to about 100 studying there in 1951.[23] In summing up the US accomplishments in Taiwan in the spring of 1957, Ambassador Rankin reported that since mid-1950 the United States had given military and economic aid to the ROC amounting to $2 billion and that some 5000 official Americans, excluding dependents, were stationed on the island, or more than four times the number in 1953. Moreover, although only a handful of American businessmen lived in Taiwan, the American missionary community had increased to over 700 by 1958.[24]

High Point of Confrontation

The PRC, having made no progress in the Geneva talks toward diplomatic recognition by the United States and failing to weaken the US commitment to Taiwan, decided in 1958 to engage in another test of strength over the offshore islands. Chairman Mao Tse-tung apparently believed that conditions were unusually favorable. The orbiting of Sputnick by the Soviet Union, which increased public concern in the United States over the presumed missile gap between the United States and the Soviet Union, as well as other developments that seemed promising from the viewpoint of the PRC, caused Mao to declare on his

22. ROC Economic Planning Council, *Taiwan Statistical Data Book 1976* (Taipei, June 1976), p. 215—hereafter referred to as *TSDB*.
23. US Mutual Security Agency, *Report*, pp. 40–41.
24. Rankin, *China Assignment*, pp. 288, 315.

visit to Moscow in 1957 that "the East wind was prevailing over the West wind." Inside China, the Great Leap Forward was launched in a spirit of exuberant optimism. To leaders in Peking, the balance of forces seemed to be shifting in favor of the Communist camp, and they judged that the time was ripe for probing the strength of the US determination to assist the ROC in defense of the offshore islands. The resort to force by the PRC was to have enduring consequences for Sino-Soviet relations, for US-ROC relations, and for the view on the offshore islands held by the world community.

Quemoy, which had been heavily fortified since the previous PRC attack, could be taken by assault only with severe losses, even if the United States did not intervene. The objective, therefore, of the PRC's heavy shelling of Quemoy beginning August 23, 1958, was not to prepare the way for an immediate invasion of the island, although threats to this effect were made in propaganda broadcasts to its defenders, but rather to interdict resupply. In this goal, the bombardment was initially successful. But the United States quickly deployed powerful naval and air forces nearby and sharply warned Peking that it would not hesitate to use armed forces in the defense of Taiwan, stressing that the defense of Quemoy and Matsu had become increasingly related to the defense of Taiwan.

Chou En-lai then proposed resuming the suspended ambassadorial talks in order to discuss the Taiwan question, to which Eisenhower promptly agreed. Nikita Khrushchev then warned Eisenhower that an attack on the PRC would be an attack on the Soviet Union, but only after Chou's proposal for talks had significantly lowered the risk of conflict between the United States and the PRC.

To assist the ROC in breaking the blockade of Quemoy, the United States began to convoy Nationalist supply vessels. The US destroyers carefully turned back, however, at the three-mile limit off the island, while with equal care the PRC forces avoided attacks on US ships—despite Peking's claim to a twelve-mile territorial sea. By the end of September 1958, although the ambassadors of the two nations had made little progress in resolving the crisis through their talks at Warsaw, it was evident that the US-escorted ROC supply ships, supplemented by air drops by the ROC air force, had succeeded in breaking the blockade. Bombardment of Quemoy gradually diminished, and the PRC finally resorted to firing only on odd-numbered days in order to demonstrate both its rejection of the cease-fire urged by the Untied States and its ability to impede or permit at will the resupply of the islands.[25]

25. See M. H. Halperin, *The 1958 Taiwan Straits Crisis: A Documented History* (Santa Monica: The Rand Corporation, 1966), processed. The bulk of this originally

The ROC emerged from the crisis appreciably stronger. It acquired important new military equipment, notably 8-inch howitzers located on Quemoy, Sidewinder missiles for its jet fighters, and landing craft to facilitate the resupply of the offshore islands. Morale was boosted by the outstanding performance of the ROC air force, which consistently out-fought the PRC air force by a wide margin, and by the success—after a shaky start—of the resupply of Quemoy by sea and air. Although Chiang Kai-shek failed to obtain the outright US commitment to defend the offshore islands that he had sought, he did obtain the strong US statements and decisive action necessary to frustrate the PRC's attempted blockade. Unknown to him at the time, the crisis had forced President Eisenhower and Secretary of State Dulles to the conclusion that the loss of Quemoy to Peking would be so catastrophic in its "domino" effect on Taiwan and subsequently on US influence throughout Asia that it had to be prevented, even at the cost of using nuclear weapons.[26] Throughout the crisis the United States assumed primary responsibility for the air defense of Taiwan, and from October 6 it stationed a Nike-Hercules missile unit on the island to strengthen its air defense.

But the ROC gains were made at a high cost. Differences between Washington and Taipei over how to cope with the crisis imposed un-precedented strains on the alliance. Urgent requests by the ROC for permission to bombard PRC artillery positions on the mainland were turned down. The United States resisted pressure to commit itself without reservation to prevent the conquest of Quemoy, to escort Nationalist ships all the way to the beach instead of to the three-mile limit, and to continue escorts even after the PRC's adoption of odd-day shelling had removed the military necessity for them. Mutual confidence was also undermined by the suspicion engendered among American officials that the ROC had deliberately acted so as to increase the prob-ability of a military clash between PRC and US forces.

Even more harmful from the ROC viewpoint than the disputes with the United States over military tactics were the negotiations con-ducted by the United States with the PRC in Warsaw. The United States sought first PRC agreement to a cease-fire, after which it hoped that arrangments could be worked out to prevent future clashes over the offshore islands. Although records of these talks have never been made public, the United States apparently put forward a number of proposals, ranging from the reduction of forces on the islands to some form of

---

top-secret study was declassified in March 1975, after some material had been deleted. See also Young, *Negotiating with the Chinese Communists;* Kalicki, *The Pattern of Sino-American Crises.*
26. Dwight D. Eisenhower, *Waging Peace* (New York: Doubleday, 1965), pp. 691–693.

demilitarization, neutralization, trusteeship, or judicial settlement.[27] Dulles even hinted in public statements that significant changes in US policy toward the PRC might follow if agreement could be reached on the islands.

Proposals to make the offshore islands less of a potential threat to the mainland were anathema to the ROC, which objected vehemently to any agreement between the United States and the PRC that would run counter to its fundamental policy of being prepared to invade the mainland should an opportunity arise. The ROC recognized that the heavy fortification of the mainland opposite Quemoy and Matsu had made the islands of little value as bases for an invasion force or even for mounting intelligence-collecting raids; nevertheless, it opposed any arrangement that would even symbolically undercut its national policy. The US differences with the ROC over such issues were not put to the final test, however, for the PRC adamantly rejected even the first step of a cease-fire, insisting that the only solution to the problem was for the United States to withdraw its forces entirely from the Taiwan area and to cease its interference in Chinese domestic affairs.

The risk that conflict over the offshore islands might escalate and draw the United States into direct conflict with the PRC and perhaps even with the Soviet Union subjected the US government to an entirely different set of pressures from those affecting the ROC's calculation of its interests. Many Americans who approved of the US commitment to help defend Taiwan strongly opposed US military intervention in defense of the offshore islands. Not only were Democrats in Congress highly critical of administration policy, but support for it among Republican members of the Senate Foreign Relations Committee was only lukewarm. The chairman of that committee, Senator Theodore Green, wrote Eisenhower expressing concern that the policy might "result in military involvement at the wrong time, in the wrong place, and on issues not of vital concern to our security."[28]

There was strong criticism and little support for US policy among allies of the United States and neutral states. Dulles told ROC Ambassador George Yeh that the United States was isolated in world opinion on this issue. Later, in a discussion of the situation with US officials, Dulles said that most UN members supported the withdrawal of ROC forces from the offshore islands, adding that 90 percent of the UN members favored placing Taiwan under a trusteeship and admitting the PRC to the United Nations, and that such a resolution was prevented from passage only by US pressure. Dulles commented privately to his

---

27. Young, *Negotiating with the Chinese Communists,* p. 179.
28. Halperin, *The 1958 Taiwan Straits Crisis,* pp. 392–393.

colleagues that Chiang Kai-shek must be made to realize that the US government had been forced to strain its relations with both Congress and its allies almost to the breaking point in order to save him and that such a situation could not be permitted to arise again.[29]

Seeking to counter criticism of the US policy at home and abroad, Dulles expressed the opinion at a press conference that the ROC had been "rather foolish" to keep so many forces on the offshore islands, adding that the United States would favor a reduction of those forces after a cease-fire. He also emphasized that the United States had no commitment to help the ROC return to the mainland. Reacting indignantly, Chiang Kai-shek rejected any reduction in the garrisons of the offshore islands. Eventually, however, as the result of a visit to Taiwan, Dulles obtained Chiang's agreement to reduce the forces on the islands by 15,000 in exchange for an increase in firepower there. In a joint communiqué issued at the time of the visit, the ROC declared that the "principal means" of achieving its objective of recovering the mainland would be through the implementation of Sun Yat-sen's "three people's principles" and "not the use of force."[30]

The US-ROC alliance was not the only one to suffer strain as a result of the offshore island crisis; the PRC-USSR alliance was even more severely affected, as became apparent in the public exchange of polemics between the two states in 1963. Disagreement over the support that the PRC might fairly call for from its ally in challenging the common foe added much to the rapidly growing burden of disputes that soon caused the alliance to break down.

An unanticipated outcome of the offshore island crisis of 1958 was a lowered risk that the PRC would try again to take them by force. The risk declined not only because the United States had demonstrated its readiness to intervene in 1958 but also because the world reaction to the crisis had shown the PRC that severing the islands from Taiwan would strengthen support for "two Chinas." Many countries clearly favored cutting the link between Taiwan and the mainland, and the United States at Warsaw had pressed vigorously for separate treatment of the offshore islands. From Peking's viewpoint, there was much to be said for leaving Chiang Kai-shek in possession of the islands as a means of perpetuating his commitment to "one China." Thus, when the PRC suspended shelling on even days, PRC Defense Minister P'eng Te-huai broadcast to his "compatriots in Taiwan, Penghu, Quemoy, and Matsu" that he wanted them to be able to ship enough supplies to the islands

29. Ibid., pp. 344, 433–434, 504–505.
30. Chiu, *China and the Question of Taiwan*, p. 288. The three principles expounded by Sun Yat-sen, founder of the Chinese republic, dealt with nationalism, democracy, and people's livelihood.

to be able to entrench themselves "for a long time to come." He appealed to them to enter into negotiations with the PRC in order to foil the US scheme to isolate Taiwan and place it under trusteeship. To remove any doubt about the PRC's intentions, Foreign Minister Ch'en Yi briefed foreign diplomats in Peking on December 16, 1958, to the effect that the PRC's policy was either to liberate all the offshore islands, Penghu, and Taiwan together, or to preserve the present situation.[31]

The ROC has retained possession of the offshore islands, and the PRC has not again attempted to seize or blockade them. The year 1958 proved to be the high point of confrontation between the United States and the PRC. The United States and the ROC have not again been forced to evaluate, while under the stress of critical military decisions in the Taiwan area, the extent to which their interests coincide or differ. But by the end of the 1960s, the American people and government had significantly changed their perceptions of the US interests in relation to the PRC and the ROC.

Changing Views, 1960–1969

In 1962, another crisis arose that threatened to create a new confrontation between the United States and the PRC, but it was quickly defused. The PRC was suffering painful economic shortages and dislocations as the combined result of several years of poor harvests, the miscarriage of the Great Leap Forward, and the withdrawal of Soviet technicians. Sensing an opportunity, Chiang Kai-shek began to ready his forces to support any rebellion that might break out, and the PRC, in response, moved reenforcements into the coastal region. President John F. Kennedy emphasized, both to the press and through the Warsaw channel to the PRC, that the United States opposed the use of force in this area and would not back offensive action by the ROC.[32] The crisis promptly subsided. Thereafter, although the ROC from time to time reiterated its determination to recover the mainland, its military preparations were directed almost exclusively to defense, thus substantially moderating the clash of interests on this issue between the United States and the ROC.

By 1960, it was evident that the Sino-Soviet alliance had been severely damaged. At first the breakdown of the monolithic Communist bloc seemed to offer small comfort, for the Chinese were more

---

31. Halperin, *The 1958 Taiwan Straits Crisis,* pp. 475, 483.
32. Young, *Negotiating with the Chinese Communists,* pp. 250–251.

militant than the Soviets. They denounced Moscow for not standing up more stoutly to the United States, belittled the dangers of nuclear war, and called for more vigorous backing of revolutionary war at a time when the United States was becoming more deeply involved in Vietnam. Peking's nuclear explosion in 1964 and its early progress in developing nuclear missiles further disturbed American policymakers. The expanding US air operations over North Vietnam increased the risk of a military clash with the PRC.

But by the end of the 1960s, a different view had emerged. The PRC was seen to be more cautious in action than in rhetoric. Its progress in nuclear weapons, particularly toward developing an intercontinental ballistic missile capable of hitting the United States, was slower than had been predicted. The cultural revolution had turned the attention of Chinese leaders inward, and a large portion of the People's Liberation Army was occupied in restoring law and order. The extensive purges of party leaders and widespread disorder made China seem much less of a threat to its neighbors than it had seemed earlier. Fear of a military clash over Vietnam subsided as the United States and China exercised reciprocal restraint over their military activities in and around North Vietnam. Most important of all, the growing tension between Peking and Moscow, climaxed by the border clashes at Chen Pao Tao (Damansky Island) in March 1969, placed new military constraints on any inclination that the PRC might have had to use its forces other than in defense of the Sino-Soviet frontier.

While the transformation of the Sino-Soviet alliance into a Sino-Soviet military confrontation was undermining the view of Taiwan as a strategic base essential to US security, support for the ROC as the legitimate representative of China in the world was also eroding, as Dulles had admitted privately during the 1958 offshore island crisis. By 1960, it was no longer possible to muster a majority vote in the UN General Assembly "not to consider" the question of Chinese representation. A majority did agree that any change in Chinese representation could be made only by a two-thirds vote, but that device for excluding the PRC also gradually lost support as the years passed. Sympathy grew in the United States itself for admitting the PRC to the United Nations, while reserving a place for the ROC as well. Following the example of France, which established diplomatic relations with the PRC in 1964, more nations shifted their diplomatic missions from Taipei to Peking.

Although the American view of Taiwan as a strategic position essential to the containment of an aggressive PRC was gradually changing during the 1960s, economic and military assistance to Taiwan continued. By the middle of 1969, total aid extended since 1950 exceeded $4.5 billion.[33]

During this period, ROC forces acquired much additional equipment, including Nike-Hercules and Hawk antiaircraft missiles, as well as more tanks, howitzers, and M-14 rifles. The aging F-86s were replaced by F-100, F-104, and F-5 aircraft. The arrival of C-119 transport aircraft increased the military airlift capability of the forces, and in 1969 a loan was made to the ROC to build a factory for coproducing with Bell Helicopter Co. helicopters for military use. Additional destroyers, LSTs, and various types of landing craft made resupply of the offshore islands easier, although the ROC's total amphibious capability fell far short of what would be needed for a large-scale landing on the mainland. The ROC also made progress toward greater self-sufficiency. By 1969 it was producing M-14 rifles, machine guns, artillery shells, mortars, and a variety of other types of military equipment.

The Vietnam war demonstrated the value of Taiwan for supporting US military oeprations in Southeast Asia. The United States stationed a wing of C-130 transport aircraft and a KC-135 tanker squadron at Ching Chuan Kang (formerly Kung Kuan) airfield, making use of the runway at this Chinese air base that had been extended at US expense in the 1950s for contingency use. The C-130s provided tactical airlift support for US forces in Vietnam, while the tankers refueled B-52s carrying out bombing missions there. US military personnel attached to these two units numbered nearly 6000, bringing total US military personnel stationed in Taiwan in the late 1960s close to 10,000. Beginning in 1962, the United States permanently stationed Detachment One of the 405th Fighter Wing (part of the 13th Air Force, based at Clark Air Base in the Philippines) on the Chinese air base at Tainan and in 1969 added Detachment Two. Taiwan also provided the best overhaul and repair facilities in East Asia outside of Japan for US fighter aircraft, tanks, and personnel carriers.[34]

Unlike US military aid, which continued at a relatively high level during the 1960s, economic aid on concessional terms was phased out in 1965. This was done not because of a decline in US interest in the state of Taiwan's economy, but because the economy had developed to the point where Taiwan could qualify for loans on nonconcessional terms and no longer needed US aid. Aid had constituted 10 percent of

---

33. *United States Security Agreements and Commitments Abroad, Part 4—Republic of China,* Hearings before Subcommittee on US Security Agreements and Commitments Abroad of Senate Foreign Relations Committee, November 1969, May 1970 (Washington, D.C.: US Government Printing Office, 1970), p. 943.
34. See *U.S. Security Agreements and Commitments Abroad,* esp. pp. 1113–1130.

the island's GNP in 1951, but it declined by 1965 to less than 2 percent of a greatly enlarged GNP.[35] Inflation had been checked, and the ROC had shifted the emphasis in its economic policy from stabilizing the economy to expanding it, primarily through increasing the production and export of manufactured goods.

With the phasing out of the aid program, US interest in Taiwan's economy began to change. Despite its continued heavy military burden, the ROC was now in a position to maintain economic stability and growth without a large drain of US resources. The ROC was pointed to with pride by US officials as an example of a nation that had made effective use of economic aid and had become the first developing nation to "graduate" from the US economic aid program. The growth of Taiwan's economy accelerated in the latter half of the 1960s, stimulated by the rapid expansion of exports. Exports to the United States quadrupled between 1964 and 1969, while imports from the United States doubled in the same period. Taiwan became an increasingly attractive location for US investment. By the end of 1968, 23 American firms employed more than 22,000 Chinese employees in plants in Taiwan. Two American banks had established branches there.[36] The US Export-Import Bank continued to make sizable loans to Taiwan to encourage sales of US products. The United States began to have a small but growing economic interest in Taiwan.

Reassessment, 1970–1977

The further consolidation of the bonds between the United States and Taiwan during the 1960s did not deter Nixon from taking a fresh approach to US policies toward Peking and Taipei. In the past, he had been among the harshest critics of the PRC and the staunchest supporters of the ROC. It was therefore ironic that it should fall to him as President to understake a sweeping reassessment of US interests in Taiwan.

Nixon and his national security adviser, Henry Kissinger, were primarily concerned with building a more stable, less dangerous relationship with the chief global rival of the United States, the Soviet Union. Recognizing that public backing for the war in Vietnam was crumbling, they also sought urgently to disengage US forces from the fighting with minimal damage to the prestige and position of the

---

35. Neil H. Jacoby, *U.S. Aid to Taiwan* (New York: Praeger, 1966), p. 39.
36. Data provided by American Embassy, Taipei.

United States in the world. They perceived that an easing of the rigid hostility that had marked relations between the United States and the PRC for so many years would contribute to the accomplishment of these objectives. Moreover, a more constructive relationship between Washington and Peking was fundamental to a long-term policy of reducing the risk of war and increasing international stability in East Asia. Nixon judged correctly that American views of the PRC had changed enough during the 1960s so that an opening to Peking would be generally applauded rather than condemned, despite the strain that this action would place on US relations with the ROC.

In this new perception of American purposes in East Asia, US interests in Taiwan were substantially downgraded. Accommodating to the rising tide of world opinion that favored seating the PRC in the United Nations, the United States withdrew its opposition. It worked to retain a seat for the ROC, but by sending Henry Kissinger to Peking at the climax of the UN debate on the China issue in October 1971, Nixon signaled that he attached a higher priority to promoting the new relations with the PRC than to keeping the ROC in the United Nations. No longer was Taiwan viewed as a vital strategic link in an alliance system primarily aimed at containing the PRC. On the contrary, the United States declared in the Shanghai communiqué its intention ultimately to withdraw all its military forces and installations from the island. It said that it looked forward to the day when the Chinese themselves might resolve the Taiwan question peacefully, at which time the US interest in the island as a political entity separate from China would presumably disappear. By its emphasis on the peaceful settlement of the Taiwan question, however, the United States put the PRC on notice that it would continue to oppose any attempt to use force against Taiwan.

In pledging to work toward a normalization of relations with the PRC, the United States did not indicate when or on what terms it expected normalization to be accomplished. Consequently, there was no immediate change in the substance of US relations with Taiwan, despite the downgrading of US interests there. The ROC was shocked and alarmed by the change in US policy, which it bitterly condemned in an official statement, but recognizing the continuing importance to it of the United States, the government took no further action that would strain their relations.[37]

The United States then proceeded to expand its relations with the PRC, facilitated in early 1973 by an agreement to exchange liaison offices that would provide a temporary substitute for full-fledged diplomatic

---

37. *The New York Times,* Feb. 29, 1972.

missions. Trade grew rapidly, reaching a peak of nearly $1 billion in 1974, but declined to about $460 million in 1975 and $336 million in 1976. Some fifty delegations were exchanged under quasi-official arrangements, and thousands of other Americans visited China, including ten congressional delegations and many Chinese-Americans. Kissinger, first as the President's special assistant for national security affairs and later as secretary of state, visited Peking six times after the Nixon visit, and President Gerald Ford made a second presidential visit in December 1975. There was no visible progress, however, toward the establishment of formal diplomatic relations with the PRC. Peking made known its displeasure when in 1974 the United States, instead of permitting the level of its representation in Taipei to decline, replaced its ambassador there with a senior career diplomat and at the same time authorized the government of the ROC to open three new consulates in the United States. By 1976, PRC officials were telling visitors that a further expansion in its relations with the United States could occur only with normalization.

Early in his administration President Jimmy Carter indicated that he favored the normalization of relations with the PRC if the security of the people of Taiwan could be assured. Secretary of State Cyrus R. Vance undertook an exploratory visit to Peking in August 1977 to sound out Mao's successor, Hua Kuo-feng, and other Chinese leaders on matters of concern to both countries, including the Taiwan problem. Carter described Vance's visit as "a very important step forward in our ultimate goal of normalizing our relations" with the Chinese. But he let it be known that the establishment of full diplomatic relations was "undoubtedly going to be well into the future."[38] Deputy Premier Teng Hsiao-p'ing in an interview with executives and directors of the Associated Press said that, although the meetings with Vance had been cordial and useful, the position he had taken on normalization represented a retreat from the proposals advanced by Ford and Kissinger.[39]

Two trends were apparent in US security relations with Taiwan during the period from 1972 to 1977. The United States was withdrawing its own combat units and military personnel from the island, while continuing to cooperate with the ROC in strengthening its own forces. Even before Nixon's visit, the United States had quietly removed from Taiwan two F-4s, specially equipped with nuclear bombs and prepared to take off on very short notice to attack strategic targets, which had been stationed there as part of the worldwide Quick Reaction Alert force.[40] Later the C-130 wing, the KC-135 squadron, and two

---

38. *Washington Post,* Aug. 28, 1977.
39. *The New York Times,* Sept. 7, 1977.
40. *The New York Times,* Feb. 29, 1972.

squadrons of F-4 fighter-bombers which had been stationed in Taiwan in return for an ROC loan of F-5s to South Vietnam, were withdrawn, the last combat aircraft coming out in June 1975. US military personnel in Taiwan were reduced from 8500 in early 1972 to 1100 by the middle of 1977. The largest group of those remaining was engaged in an electronic eavesdropping and cryptographic analysis operation. The MAAG, which in the late 1950s with over 2000 men had been one of the largest such advisory groups in the world, was down to less than 50. In 1974 Congress, without fanfare and with the acquiescence of the State Department, repealed the Formosa Resolution.

The ROC continued to acquire American military equipment, but almost all of it was purchased on credit or for cash. Grant aid ended in June 1974, except for small amounts of less than $500,000 a year for military training. The ROC was now in a position to maintain its defense program from its own resources, although access to spare parts and new equipment from the United States was still indispensable. Taipei took a small but important step toward greater self-reliance by entering into a contract with the Northrop Corporation for the co-production in Taiwan of F-5E fighter aircraft. The first plane came off the assembly line in October 1974. Other major items acquired by ROC forces during the past few years included two disarmed submarines, additional destroyers, helicopters, F-104G fighters, and C-123 aircraft.

While the United States was loosening its military connections with Taiwan, its economic links were growing stronger. Washington moved promptly after Nixon's visit to Peking to reassure Chinese and American businessmen as to Taiwan's economic future. Within six weeks, the president of the US Export-Import Bank had arrived in Taiwan to announce that the bank expected to approve $350 to $400 million in credits during the next several months and was prepared to extend an unlimited amount of long-term credits for public and private projects on the island.[41] By 1975, the amount of Export-Import Bank loans outstanding exceeded $1.2 billion, with an additional $700 million in guarantees, which was the bank's largest exposure in any country except Brazil. Private American capital also continued to flow into Taiwan's economy. Direct US private investment was over $400 million in 1975, by which time American companies represented in the American Chamber of Commerce in Taipei had increased from sixty in 1972 to two hundred.[42] American private investments in Taiwan continued to

---

41. *The New York Times,* Apr. 5, 1972.
42. The ten largest US investors in Taiwan in mid-1975, each with approved investments of $10 million to $40 million (much still in the pipeline, not yet arrived), were Ford, Ampex, General Instruments, RCA, Gulf Oil, Union Carbide, Timex, Corning International, IBM, and OAK Industries.

receive guarantees from the Overseas Private Investment Corporation (OPIC), a US government agency. As of May 1976, eight American banks maintained branches in Taiwan and 4200 Ameican civilians resided on the island. A US trade center was established in Taipei in 1973, and two-way trade between Taiwan and the United States increased from $1.8 billion in 1972 to $4.8 billion in 1976, when it amounted to more than fourteen times the value of US trade with the PRC.

Questions for the Future

The broad interests of the United States in East Asia are to prevent domination of the region by a single power, to strengthen the US position there relative to the Soviet Union, to consolidate the vital alliance with Japan, to reduce tension and the risk of large-scale war, and to further the economic development and international stability of the region. The progressive expansion of constructive relations with the PRC would aid these interests. Furthermore, the United States has an important interest in preventing any recurrence of military confrontation with the PRC. But whether the United States can continue to improve its relations with Peking without either so disruptive an impact on Taiwan or such adverse repercussions elsewhere as to impair the prospects for achieving overall US objectives in the region is uncertain.

The United States has given up those interests in Taiwan that conflicted most sharply with the PRC interests. It no longer views the island as a strategic base for potential use by US forces against the PRC or as a seat of government blocking acceptance by the international community of the PRC as the government of China. Yet it continues to have important interests there. US economic relations with Taiwan are more substantial than those with the PRC. The ROC's free enterprise system and relatively open society, deeply engaged in foreign trade, can make a significant contribution to the kind of international order in East Asia favored by the United States and Japan. There is a moral issue, too. After so long a period of close cooperation and the establishment of innumerable personal relations between Americans and the Chinese on Taiwan, many Americans would find it repugnant to abandon the people of Taiwan in the face of pressures from Peking. The United States has never broken diplomatic relations with a friendly government.

The interests of the PRC in Taiwan are more deeply rooted than American interests there, for they involve a claim to national territory unsatisfied because of foreign intervention in a Chinese civil war. Territorial claims everywhere are capable of arousing the most intense nationalistic emotions. In China, they may be felt even more deeply than in most countries because of the "century of humiliation" suffered by China at the hands of foreigners. Chinese leaders now declare proudly that China has "stood up" and can no longer be pushed around by others. Concessions to foreigners on the sensitive issue of Taiwan could make leaders vulnerable to denunciation for having sold out China's interests. Consequently, the "principled" positions taken by the PRC, which to Americans sometimes seem excessively rigid, lacking a spirit of compromise, and even out of tune with reality, have deep historical roots.

Although the PRC adamantly opposes any compromise of its position that Taiwan is part of China, the fact that the ROC holds firmly to the same position makes the unresolved problem of Taiwan easier to live with. China's long history is a testament to the essential unity of the Chinese people. As long as the Chinese on both sides of the Taiwan Strait embrace this view, the prolonged temporary division can be endured and practical compromises are not inconceivable.

In seeking a compromise with the PRC on the Taiwan issue, one that would keep the door open to further improvement of bilateral relations with Peking, the United States must be conscious of the effects of its actions on other friendy nations in East Asia, especially on its principal ally, Japan. The United States has an important stake in maintaining close and friendly relations with Japan, the second largest economy in the non-Communist world. The commitment of the United States to Japan's defense has enabled Japan to prosper as a lightly armed, nonnuclear power, which in turn has contributed to peace and stability in East Asia.[43] Japan has many connections with Taiwan resulting from the island's fifty years as a Japanese colony, and it has sought to maintain as extensive relations as possible with both the PRC and Taiwan. Hence, the Japanese are extremely sensitive to US actions toward mainland China and Taiwan.

Conscious of their own dependence on the United States for security, the Japanese have watched with some concern as the United States has reduced its military deployments in the western Pacific after the Vietnam war. The decision of the Carter administration early in 1978 to withdraw US ground forces from South Korea evoked uneasiness in Japan. Termination of the security treaty with the ROC, as demanded by the PRC as a condition for normalization, would be seen in Japan as a

---

43. See Ralph N. Clough, *East Asia and U.S. Security* (Washington, D.C.: Brookings Institution, 1975).

further step in a perhaps continuing US withdrawal from the western Pacific. Unless offset by actions that convincingly demonstrate US concern for the security of the people of Taiwan, many Japanese would wonder how confidently they could rely on the US commitment to their own security.

The Republic of Korea, already upset by the decision to withdraw US ground forces, would be more disturbed than the Japanese by an end to the security treaty between the United States and Taiwan. The Filipinos would also be concerned, although less so than the peoples of Northeast Asia. Accustomed to the predictable US policies of the era of containment, the allies of the United States are becoming uncertain how to protect their interests as US policies toward China become more flexible.

Thus, the policy followed by the United States in the future toward Taiwan, including the terms agreed upon with the PRC for normalization, will affect other US interests in the region. A policy that led to an attack on or a blockade of Taiwan, or one that precipitated internal conflict or collapse on the island, inviting PRC intervention, would greatly reduce the prospects for achieving the objective of a more stable, peaceful region. So also would a US policy that caused the ROC in an act of desperation to declare formal independence of the mainland, to seek a deal with the Soviet Union, or to develop nuclear weapons. Any one of these drastic moves would substantially increase the probability of armed conflict between the PRC and the ROC. Were US policy to result in any of these consequences, Japan's confidence in the United States would be seriously undermined, and prospects for a stable peace would be much diminished.

Extreme consequences appear less likely, however, to the extent that the US and PRC interests overlap. Each has, up to the present at least, regarded the Taiwan issue as secondary to the need to fortify its own position relative to the Soviet Union. Each would consider the emergence of an association between Taiwan and the Soviet Union as damaging to its own interests, and both recognize that a continued association between the United States and Taiwan, until the people of the island are prepared to accept reassociation with the mainland, serves to forestall a Soviet-Taiwan link. A continued association between the United States and Taiwan also reduces the risk that the ROC will be driven to develop nuclear weapons or to declare its independence, both of which acts would be contrary to PRC interests. The economic development of Taiwan serves US interests and will also serve those of the PRC in the long run if Taiwan and the mainland are ever reassociated. Washington and Peking also appear at present to share an interest in seeing the Taiwan issue managed in a way that will neither cause their relations with each other to deteriorate sharply nor drive Japan to large-scale rearmament. The extent of interests in common as perceived by the two governments may change with changes in leadership. A more radical, more xenophobic group of leaders in Peking than those confirmed in power by the Party Congress of August 1977 would be likely to see a sharper conflict of interests with the United States over the Taiwan issue. An improvement in Sino-Soviet relations would ease the constraints on Peking with respect to pressing for resolution of the Taiwan problem on its own terms. Nevertheless, some coincidence of interests between the United States and the PRC—by no means total, but substantial—may make it possible for the Taiwan issue to drag on for a long time unresolved but unexplosive, provided only that Peking does not become convinced that the United States is determined to sever Taiwan from the mainland permanently.

To the extent that the United States reevaluated its interests in the region so that they conflicted less sharply with those of the PRC, its conflict of interest with the ROC increased. The differences now related to a more vital issue than the offshore islands; they concerned US relations with Taiwan itself. The United States had not only failed to keep the PRC out of the United Nations, but it was perhaps on the verge of shifting its formal diplomatic relationship from Taipei to Peking and ending the security treaty. The threat confronting ROC leaders was no longer confined to their fundamental national policy of recovery of the mainland, which had long been more a slogan than a guide to their current policy toward the mainland, but concerned the future security and prosperity of Taiwan. Consequently, although they were gratified that the economic bonds between the United States and Taiwan continued to strengthen and that US military equipment for ROC forces was still available, they were deeply worried.

In spite of the anxiety on Taiwan, the United States has a strong, long-term national interest in pursuing a more constructive relationship with the PRC. As the PRC's industrial base and military strength grow, so will both the advantages of being able to cooperate with it toward common ends and the dangers of reverting to a military confrontation. It is essential to seek unremittingly for ways of further improving relations with Peking while at the same time remaining sensitive to the effects of US actions on Taiwan and on PRC policies toward Taiwan. For economic crisis, political turmoil, or acts of desperation by ROC leaders could present difficult problems for the United States and threaten the achievement of its regional objectives. Therefore, the United States must analyze trends and attitudes on Taiwan in order to assess the possible effects of alternative policies. Judgments must be made with regard to such questions as: What is the outlook for negotiation, or conflict, between Taiwan and the PRC? Are Taiwan's economic and political systems sturdy enough to bear the shock of the severance of diplomatic relations by the United States? Can the ROC carry on in the unprecedented international status of having diplomatic relations with no influential state? What continuing military and economic relations are essential to Taiwan's security and prosperity? Under what circumstances might the government on Taiwan declare the island independent from China, go nuclear, or establish a link with the Soviet Union?

The Political System
of Taiwan

2

The ROC has been exceptional among developing countries for its political stability. With the exception of the Taiwanese uprising in 1947, before the Nationalist government had moved from the mainland to Taiwan, the island has not been plagued with the political disorders, insurgencies, and military coups common among developing countries. The question is how a government whose corruption and inefficiency had permitted the Chinese Communist party to win on the mainland managed to establish effective control and to gain a wide degree of popular acceptance in Taiwan.

The Nationalist government, headed by Chiang Kai-shek, had arrived in Taiwan in 1949 purged and chastened. Although the number of government and party officials who fled to Taiwan was large in relation to the territory that remained for them to govern, they were only a small fraction of all Chinese officials. The flight to a refuge that most of the world expected would soon be overrun by the victorious Communist armies automatically purged the Nationalist party, army, and government of large numbers of corrupt, wavering, and ineffective officials. Most of those who had the money to do so fled to Hong Kong or more distant places of safety. The officials who chose Taiwan had either strong personal loyalty to Chiang or no place else to go. Many of the less competent senior officials who reached Taiwan were shunted into sinecures that gave them a modest living but little influence. Chiang and his principal lieutenants, recognizing that they bore a significant share of responsibility for the debacle on the mainland, knew that their only hope for the future was to make radical improvements in their methods of governing. Taiwan was their last chance.

Conditions in Taiwan favored a new start. It was a small area with good transportation and communications. Its population was relatively well educated and accustomed to authoritarian rule. There was no entrenched provincial leadership that had to be catered to, for the Japanese had kept the reins of authority firmly in their own hands. Taking advantage of the absence of the kind of connections between landlords and government officials that had prevented land reform on the mainland, the government redistributed agricultural land, thereby weakening the local political power of landlords and making large numbers of farmers beholden to the new government for title to their land and improvement in their economic position.

From mid-1950 on, the government also benefited from the support of the United States. The amount of economic and military aid per capita was much larger than that received by other countries getting US aid. Perhaps even more important to the ability of the government to administer the island effectively during the early years was the US commitment to prevent a Communist attack. The public confidence in the security of the island engendered by US protection gave the government the breathing spell it needed to create an effective economic and political system. The deep involvement of the United States in the defense and economic development of the island also gave the modernizing technocrats in the government, many of whom were American-educated, far more influence on decisions than they had possessed on the mainland.

Although conditions in Taiwan were relatively advantageous for the Nationalist government, its political system has been beset by severe strains, arising particularly from Taiwanese resentment at mainlander domination and from the restiveness of intellectuals under the tight security controls imposed to prevent Communist subversion and Taiwanese opposition activities. The methods used by the government to cope with these political strains in the system, which have proven successful so far, must now prove their effectiveness in the face of the international uncertainties of the future.

It is difficult to reach judgments on the political system in Taiwan, for data on political attitudes are scanty, and conclusions must be based to a considerable extent on scattered impressions derived over the years from interviews dealing with sensitive political subjects not freely debated in the press or scholarly journals. The effectiveness and stability of the political system must be evaluated from the viewpoint of the people of Taiwan, whose attitudes toward authority, civil rights, and democratic processes differ from those of the average American. Many tolerate or even approve of government behavior that most Americans would find unacceptable. For the people of Taiwan, comparisons with their own past are likely to be more meaningful than comparisons with the United States.

The Structure of Government

The national government of the ROC was established in accordance with a constitution adopted on the mainland in 1946. The constitution provides for a National Assembly to elect the president and vice-president and amend the constitution, a Legislative Yuan to pass the laws, an Executive Yuan to carry out the laws, a Judicial Yuan to interpret the constitution and serve as a court of last resort, a Control Yuan to supervise officials, and an Examination Yuan to conduct civil service examinations. Members of the three elective bodies—the National Assembly, the Legislative Yuan, and the Control Yuan—were elected on the mainland in 1947 and 1948 from all the provinces of China.

All these government bodies moved to Taiwan in 1949, although some of their members remained behind. Because the government of the ROC has never relinquished its claim to be the legitimate government of all China, the constitution and government structure have been retained essentially unchanged. The membership in the elective bodies has gradually declined, because over the years as members died, it was not possible to hold new elections throughout China, so the terms of the original members were extended for the duration of "the period of Communist rebellion." By 1969, it was evident that new members would have to be added. Consequently, special elections were held in Taiwan in 1969, 1972, and 1973, adding new members to all three bodies as follows:[1]

National elective body	Original membership	Remaining original members	Members elected 1969	Members elected 1972–1973	Total membership 1974–1975
National Assembly	2961	1281	15	53	1349
Legislative Yuan	760	376	11	51	438
Control Yuan	180	57	2	15	74

---

1. *China Yearbook, 1975* (Taipei: China Publishing, 1975), pp. 81, 82, 98, 111. Totals for National Assembly and Control Yuan are for December 1974; total for Legislative Yuan is for March 1975.

The original members of all three elective bodies are old, and their death rate is continuing to rise. Consequently, more new members will have to be elected before long. With each new election, these bodies will become increasingly representative of Taiwan province. Even in 1976, the new members elected in Taiwan were more influential than their numbers would indicate, for many of the original members were too old or ill to be active. For example, in the Legislative Yuan only about 200 of the 438 members attended sessions regularly, and of these, 63 were new members elected since 1969.

Far more important than the Legislative Yuan is the Executive Yuan, the principal decision-making body of government. Because its members are appointed, not elected, its membership has been continually renewed. The president of the Executive Yuan, or premier, and the ministers and heads of commissions who constitute the Executive Yuan are all appointed by the president of the nation.

In addition to the national government, with its panoply of ministries and commissions responsible for the entire range of governmental functions, from defense and foreign affairs to finance, economics, education, and justice, there is a Taiwan provincial government, which has a variety of subordinate functions under the direction of the national government. The provincial government is headed by a governor appointed by the president. There is also an elected provincial assembly, which approves the budget of the provincial government and has other limited, mostly advisory, powers.

County magistrates, city mayors, and county and city councils, all of which are elected, have wide powers in local affairs. The city of Taipei is an exception, having been made a special municipality under the Executive Yuan in 1967. Its mayor is appointed by the president, but the Taipei city council is still elected by popular vote.

The electoral process in Taiwan is dominated by the ruling party, the Kuomintang (KMT), established by Sun Yat-sen in 1919 as the successor to earlier revolutionary parties which he had also founded. The KMT moved its headquarters to Taiwan along with the government. The party was headed by Chiang Kai-shek until his death in 1975 and subsequently by his son, Chiang Ching-kuo. It is a pyramidal structure, topped by a 130-member Central Committee elected by the Party Congress, which convenes at approximately six-year intervals. A 22-member Central Standing Committee serves as executive body between plenary sessions of the Central Committee. Below the Central Committee are provincial, county, and district committees, heading the party cells of 3 to 15 members each.

A large proportion of government officials and local politicians belong to the party. The KMT has a wide range of functions, including backing candidates for national, provincial, and local office, monitoring the press and cultural activities, sponsoring youth and women's organizations, and maintaining the ROC's connections and influence among overseas Chinese. It operates a number of profit-making enterprises and also has access to government funds to support its operations. The two minor parties in Taiwan, the Young China party and the China Democratic Socialist party, have little prestige or influence. The political system in Taiwan is essentially a one-party system.

A prominent feature of government in Taiwan is the security system, designed to protect the government from subversion by Communist agents or by Taiwanese opponents of KMT rule. Since 1949 martial law has been in effect, suspending constitutional guarantees for those accused of political crimes and empowering the Taiwan Garrison Command, a military organization responsible for internal security, to try political suspects secretly in military courts. Although the Taiwan Garrison Command has the primary responsibility for internal security, the KMT, the military forces, and the Ministry of Justice all have investigative units that supplement it in particular areas.

Animosity between mainlanders and Taiwanese has been a principal cause of political strain in Taiwan. The ill will arose partly because of differences of language and customs, but primarily because the minority mainlanders had reserved to themselves the controlling position in the government, party, and military. Mainlanders clung to the myth that the government of the ROC was the legitimate government of all China, while Taiwanese inclined toward separatism for Taiwan. The PRC threat to Taiwan compelled mainlanders and Taiwanese to cooperate in the face of the common peril, but it also resulted at times in the imposition of excessive controls by both the KMT and the security agencies, which tended to heighten political strain. The protection extended to the island by the United States has moderated the impact of the PRC threat, but it has also stimulated resentment at Taiwan's dependence on the United States and fear that the US support might one day be withdrawn. Lesser strains, which may become more severe in the future, have arisen from the social changes brought about on the island by the process of modernization.

Mainlander-Taiwanese Differences

Of Taiwan's population of 17 million, about 14 percent, or more than 2 million, are those who came over from the China mainland since

1945 or their descendants.[2]   There are marked differences of dialect and custom between these recently arrived mainlanders and the Taiwanese. But there are also divisions within each group.   The ancestors of most Taiwanese emigrated from Fukien Province on the mainland during the eighteenth and nineteenth centuries, but there is a large minority, the Hakkas, whose forebears came from Kwangtung Province during this same period and who speak a distinctive dialect.[3]   The so-called mainlanders, who came from various parts of China after 1945, speak a variety of other dialects.   Thus, although the division between Taiwanese and mainlanders is the most important one for political purposes, the differences within each group, not only in spoken dialect but also in social and economic status, tend to blur and soften the clash of interests between the two major groups.

Friction and tension between mainlanders and Taiwanese developed early.   The newcomers were initially welcomed by the Taiwanese, who expected that the reunion of Taiwan with China and the departure of their Japanese colonial rulers would give them a greater part in running the island.   Unfortunately, the first wave of mainlanders under Governor Ch'en Yi, a corrupt and inept Nationalist general, was more interested in making fortunes out of the assets confiscated from the Japanese than in restoring the island's war-damaged economy.   Instead of moving up into administrative and technical positions vacated by the departing Japanese, the Taiwanese saw these positions taken over by mainland officials and their relatives.   Some Taiwanese were even ousted from their jobs and houses by arriving "carpetbaggers."   The rising resentment of the Taiwanese boiled over on February 28, 1947, when the arrest by government agents of a Taiwanese woman accused of peddling untaxed cigarettes set off sporadic rioting against mainlanders which soon spread throughout the island.   The Taiwanese hastily organized to demand reforms, but Ch'en Yi temporized until large numbers of troops had arrived from the mainland and brutally suppressed all opposition.   Thousands of Taiwanese were killed, including many of the island's political elite.[4]

---

2. Precise figures on Taiwanese and mainlanders are not easy to come by, as government policy is to minimize the distinction and official publications giving population data do not show this breakdown.   Estimates of the proportion of mainlanders in the population range from 14 to 16 percent.   Yung Wei, "Political Development in the Republic of China," in Chiu, *China and the Question of Taiwan*, p. 91; Hung-mao Tien, "Taiwan in Transition: Prospects for Socio-Political Change," *China Quarterly*, no. 64, December 1975, p. 626.

3. The aboriginal tribes, residing in Taiwan when the Chinese immigration began, living mainly in the mountains, and descended from Malay stock, number only about 200,000 and have little political influence.

4. See George H. Kerr, *Formosa Betrayed* (Boston: Houghton Mifflin, 1965).   Kerr, who was American vice-consul in Taipei when the rebellion and its suppression occurred, was an eyewitness to some events and had firsthand accounts of others.   He had many

The February 28 uprising left behind a lasting legacy of hostility and suspicion between mainlanders and Taiwanese. Although Ch'en Yi was replaced soon afterward by Governor Wei Tao-ming, who made a serious attempt to repair the damage, the collapse of the Nationalist government on the mainland and the arrival of a flood of refugees in Taiwan made the improvement of relations between mainlanders and Taiwanese difficult. A few of the Taiwanese who had been active in the uprising escaped to Hong Kong, where they founded the Taiwan independence movement, which advocated an independent state of Taiwan governed by Taiwanese and drew on the memory of the uprising to stimulate Taiwanese antipathy to KMT rule.[5]

Aside from the February repression, the primary source of tension between the two groups was the dominant position of mainlanders on the island. All the higher level positions in the government, party, and army were initially occupied by mainlanders, except for a few token positions held by Taiwanese who had spent much of their lives on the mainland and had returned to Taiwan with the mainlanders. The mainlanders constituted the great majority in the elective bodies, since they were chosen to represent all the provinces of China. By holding tenaciously to recovery of the mainland as the government's primary objective, Chiang Kai-shek perpetuated the unrepresentative character of the national government on Taiwan. To make the national government representative of the majority of people on Taiwan—the Taiwanese— would have amounted to abandoning this cherished national goal. Moreover, personal interests strongly motivated the mainlanders to hold on to their positions in the national government. Most had no other way of making a living. They owned no land or businesses in Taiwan. Thrust into an environment where they lacked the local personal ties and connections so essential to making one's way in Chinese society, they clung to the only means of livelihood they had, government jobs.

Thus, personal and national objectives intertwined. For the mainlanders, the goal of mainland recovery, however illusory it might come to seem as the years passed, justified the perpetuation of a national gov-

---

friends among the Taiwanese, some of whom were killed, and his account is openly partisan. For another account sympathetic to the Taiwanese, see Douglas Mendel, *The Politics of Formosan Nationalism* (Berkeley: University of California Press, 1970). Even detached observers such as General Albert Wedemeyer were strongly critical of the conduct of the Nationalist government during the rebellion. See US Department of State, *United States Relations with China* (Washington, D.C., August 1949), p. 309. For an official Nationalist report, see *The Truth about the February 28, 1947 Incident in Taiwan* (Taichung: Historical Research Commission of Taiwan Province, 1967).

5. See Kerr, *Formosa Betrayed;* Mendel, *The Politics of Formosan Nationalism;* Ong Jok-tik, "A Formosan View of the Formosan Independence Movement," *China Quarterly,* no. 15, July–September 1963, pp. 107–114; Tien, "Taiwan in Transition."

ernment that represented all China and therefore should not be dominated and staffed by Taiwanese. So long as mainland recovery seemed a credible possibility, the policy also held potential benefits for Taiwanese, through the return of the national government to the mainland, the departure of large numbers of mainlanders from Taiwan, and the elimination of the military threat posed to the island by the PRC. But as mainland recovery increasingly appeared to be a mirage, the policy came to be viewed by most Taiwanese as principally a device for ensuring the retention of power in mainlander hands.

The handful of Taiwanese exiles who had fled to Hong Kong after the February 28 uprising soon split into two factions, pro-Communist and anti-Communist. The pro-Communists went to the China mainland after the Communist victory there, while the principal anti-Communist leaders moved to Tokyo. The Taiwanese in mainland China organized a Taiwan Democratic Self-Government League, which took the view that Taiwan was an integral part of China and should be "liberated" from the control of the Nationalist government and brought under Peking. The Tokyo group, however, called for overthrowing the Nationalist government and setting up an independent state of Taiwan to be governed by Taiwanese. Their publications elaborated the historical and legal arguments for regarding Taiwan as a political entity separate from China.

In 1956, Taiwanese exiles in Tokyo announced the establishment of a Provisional Government of the Republic of Formosa, with Liao Wen-yi (Thomas Liao) as its first president. There was much internal bickering and factionalism among the Taiwanese exiles, however, and in 1965 Liao himself abandoned the movement to return to Taiwan, soon followed by others active in the movement. Other organizations advocating independence for Taiwan sprang up in Tokyo, including the Formosan Association, first headed by Ong Jok-tik and later by Richard Koo, and the United Young Formosans for Independence, led by Ng Yu-zin. In 1970, a more broadly based organization appeared, known as the World United Formosans for Independence. It has a chapter in the United States headed by George T. Chang, which has solicited members mainly among the large community of Taiwanese students, as well as chapters in Japan and Europe.

All organizations favoring Taiwanese independence were strictly proscribed by the government in Taiwan which, not unreasonably, regarded actions aimed at its overthrow as treasonable. Secret supporters of the Taiwan independence movement were sought out just as assiduously by security agencies as were agents of the PRC. In fact, ROC officials charged that the Taiwan independence movement was backed by the PRC, despite the obvious inconsistency between the goals of that movement and the PRC's insistence on "one China." The PRC, in turn, accused the United States of backing the Taiwan independence movement, perhaps in the hope of creating friction between the United States and the ROC. The weakness of the independence movement and its tendency to split into warring factions suggested that it had no powerful backer. Its limited funds probably were provided principally by Taiwanese or Japanese businessmen in Japan.

The Taiwan independence movement was unable to create an effective underground organization in Taiwan, but occasional arrests of Taiwanese for carrying on antigovernment activities in support of Taiwan's independence demonstrate that the concept has had enough attraction for some Taiwanese to inspire them to take grave risks to promote it. The relatively few arrests on security charges reported in the press (although most such arrests are not so reported) indicate that Taiwanese were more likely to be arrested for Taiwan independence activities than for acting as agents of the PRC. A case which attracted international attention was that of Professor Peng Ming-min, former chairman of the political science department at National Taiwan University, who in 1965 along with two associates was sentenced to eight years in prison for having had secretly printed a manifesto calling on Taiwanese to unite to overthrow "Chiang's dictatorial regime."[6] Peng's sentence was subsequently commuted, and he escaped from Taiwan via Sweden to the United States. Although the vast majority of Taiwanese have not been directly affected by the government's suppression of the Taiwan independence movement, the constant surveillance by main-lander-dominated security agencies of Taiwanese suspected of engaging in such activities and the arrests of some of these have contributed to mainlander-Taiwanese tension.

Other causes of tension have grown out of the differing status and outlook of mainlanders and Taiwanese. Corruption in government, although far less pervasive than in some other Asian developing countries, has created resentment among Taiwanese, as has favoritism toward mainlanders by mainlander bureaucrats. Taiwanese are more likely than mainlanders to take exception to the size of the tax burden to support the military forces and the requirement of military service for all young men. Even land reform, which created a large group of new landowners beholden to the national government for their gains, incurred costs for the government in the alienation of many of the in-

---

6. See Mendel, *The Politics of Formosan Nationalism,* pp. 117–119; Peng Ming-min, A *Taste of Freedom* (New York: Holt, Rinehart, and Winston, 1972).

fluential local gentry who were forced to give up their land. This group of former landlords recalls most fondly the "good old days" under the Japanese.

Internal Security and External Dependency

The ever-present PRC threat to Taiwan is a fundamental source of political strain. Although the military threat has seemed less imminent since the offshore island crisis of 1958, the danger of infiltration and subversion has not receded. This danger is associated in the minds of ROC security officials with Taiwanese disaffection, but it has a broader compass, potentially affecting mainlanders as well. In fact, mainlanders are more susceptible than Taiwanese to being recruited by the PRC because of their past association with the mainland and the presence of their relatives there.

To cope with the subversive danger, the government declared martial law in 1949, which remains in effect today. The Taiwan Garrison Command and other agencies responsible for internal security maintain an extensive network of informants and watch carefully for any suspicious activities. Political officers in each unit of the armed forces are responsible for the detection of any evidence of disloyalty there. The KMT, through campus cells of the Youth Work Committee and the China Youth Corps, as well as the military instruction personnel, or *chiao kuan,* at the universities, monitor student attitudes and behavior. The KMT also supervises the media to guard against the appearance of material helpful to the enemy. So extensive a security system inevitably commits errors and abuses. Consequently, there is a constant tension between the need for security measures that nearly everybody recognizes are necessary and the tendency to carry them to excessive lengths, resulting in the arrest of innocent people and the smothering of healthy debate on government policy.

The government of the ROC had ample reason to be worried about Communist subversion when it withdrew from the mainland to Taiwan in 1949. The civilian bureaucracy and the army on the mainland had been riddled with Communist agents, and the number and importance of defections to the Communist side rose rapidly as it became increasingly evident that the Nationalists were losing the civil war. In late 1948, Chiang Kai-shek sent one of his most competent and trusted generals, Ch'en Ch'eng, to take over as governor of Taiwan, assisted in the field of internal security by Chiang's older son, Chiang Ching-kuo. An

American observer, writing from the perspective of 1952, described the actions they took to weed out the subversives:

> The Nationalists acted hurriedly and sometimes ruthlessly to stamp out Communist activities, arresting and interrogating some thousands of suspects. They captured and executed some real Communist agents and frightened others off the island, but they also intimidated and imprisoned many individuals who appeared to be innocent. At present several thousand persons are in jail, where many of them have been held for more than a year and a half without benefit of public trial.
>
> For the great majority of Chinese on Formosa the fearful feature of this situation is the lack of legal protection for the ordinary citizen. He can be arrested at night by a squad of military police, tried by a military court-martial and sentenced, with little opportunity for appeal. Once taken into custody, the ordinary Chinese is in effect at the mercy of the garrison headquarters. A person may be arrested because he actually is subversive. He can also be picked up because someone who wants his job or property has denounced him as a Communist to the authorities.[7]

As confidence grew that Taiwan would not come under early Communist attack, security measures were eased somewhat and procedures regularized. In 1952 security regulations had already been modified to require a civil police warrant for the arrest of a civilian, to allow defense counsel in military courts, and to permit the accused the presence of family and material witnesses during trial.[8] Nevertheless, close surveillance of suspects and arrests and trials continued. A recent official publication states: "the tasks of searching for Communist agents and uncovering their plots [have] been vigorously pursued and a number of arrests and executions have taken place over the years."[9]

The workings of the security system brought about the downfall of several prominent mainlanders. Wu Kuo-chen (K. C. Wu), an American-educated, liberally inclined politician who had been mayor of Shanghai, succeeded Ch'en Ch'eng as governor of Taiwan in 1949, when the latter was made premier. Wu found the political atmosphere in Taiwan stifling and the security agencies abusive of their powers.

7. Albert Ravenholt, "Formosa Today," *Foreign Affairs* 30 (July 1952): 620. See also Hollington K. Tong, *Chiang Kai-shek* (Taipei: China Publishing, 1953).
8. Ibid.
9. Han Lih-wu, *Taiwan Today* (Institute of International Relations: ROC, 1974), p. 20.

Resigning in 1953, he left for the United States where he denounced Taiwan's lack of democracy and security excesses in open letters to the National Assembly and Chiang Kai-shek.[10] Sun Li-jen, commander-in-chief of the army, was removed from his position in 1955, charged with responsibility for the demands presented to Chiang at a military review by disaffected officers under his command. He was placed under house arrest, where he remained in 1977.[11] Lei Chen, editor of the political journal *Free China*, who attempted to organize an opposition party in 1960, was charged with harboring a Communist agent on his staff and sentenced to ten years in prison.[12] As these cases indicate, opposition to the leadership or attempts to bring about fundamental change in the political system were severely repressed, even when there was no evidence that the individual was a Communist agent. Although over the years the balance gradually shifted within the government from those who favored harsh and strict security measures to those who were more lenient, the problem of striking the right balance between the demands of security and the requirements of a modernizing society remains a principal source of political strain in Taiwan.

Overdependence on any outside power over a long period of time cannot fail to produce resentment. Taiwan is no exception to this rule. As early as 1957, resentment boiled over in the sacking of the US embassy by a mob infuriated by the acquittal in a US military court of an American serviceman who had shot and killed a Chinese. The government quickly presented apologies and repaired the physical damage. But the knowledge that Taiwan's security and prosperity are so much at the mercy of the United States will continue to cause strain.

The submerged feelings of the people of Taiwan come to the surface from time to time in bitter comments in the Taipei press about the United States, particularly since President Nixon's 1971 announcement of the change in US policy toward the PRC. The government's dilemma has been how to reconcile its reliance on the United States for the principal support for Taiwan's survival as an autonomous political entity with its need to satisfy the people that it is acting in a manner that upholds the national dignity and self-respect of the ROC. The strain imposed by this dilemma will inevitably increase as the United States moves closer to the normalization of its relations with the PRC. And Peking will no doubt do its utmost to increase the strain by its accusations that the government in Taiwan is a US puppet.

---

10. Kerr, *Formosa Betrayed*, pp. 421–424, 480–486.
11. Rankin, *China Assignment*, pp. 272–273.
12. Kerr, *Formosa Betrayed*, pp. 446–447; Mendel, *The Politics of Formosan Nationalism*, pp. 114–115.

Problems of Modernization

For many years, there was a continual tug-of-war between those who placed prime emphasis on the goal of recovering the China mainland and those who favored concentrating on the development of Taiwan. For convenience, the two groups might be dubbed the ideologues and the pragmatists. The distinction between them was not always clearcut, for the two groups overlapped to some extent. The pragmatists did not openly reject the goal of mainland recovery; they argued that the best hope of achieving this goal was to develop and modernize Taiwan as rapidly as possible in order to improve its capacity to serve as a base for the future recovery of the mainland, rather than to divert attention and resources to quixotic attempts to act before the time was ripe. The ideologues did not oppose the development of Taiwan, but deprecated allowing it to detract from the struggle with the PRC. Both groups strongly opposed accepting domination by Peking; yet they all were staunch Chinese nationalists, deeply influenced by China's long history as a unified state, who found it difficult to conceive of the permanent separation of Taiwan from China.

Chiang Kai-shek himself headed the ideologues. More than any other single person, he was responsible for asserting and perpetuating the concept of mainland recovery, rejecting either compromise with the PRC or a separate status for Taiwan. He insisted on tighter authoritarian controls and a greater diversion of resources to military and security purposes than the pragmatists would have preferred, and he sometimes distressed his foreign policy advisers of the pragmatic school by his lack of flexibility in foreign affairs. Despite his dedication to the goal of mainland recovery, however, he was not impervious to the arguments of the pragmatists. On the contrary, he decided time and again in their favor, thus permitting the rapid economic development of Taiwan to go forward. As the final authority in Taiwan, he determined how the balance should be struck between ideologues and pragmatists, and with the passage of time and the fading of prospects for mainland recovery, the balance tilted increasingly in favor of the pragmatists.

The ideologues had lost most of their political influence long before Chiang's death in 1975. The return-to-the-mainland theme persisted in official rhetoric but carried little weight. As Brian Crozier noted, "It had begun as a fierce resolve; it became an aspiration, then a myth, then a liturgy."[13] Military officers no longer pressed for enough landing

---

13. Brian Crozier, *The Man Who Lost China* (New York: Charles Scribner's Sons, 1976), p. 351.

craft to transport an army corps to the mainland. The government was no longer deterred from publicly supporting family planning by the insistence of party elders that birth control would reduce the number of soldiers that Taiwan could provide for the mainland recovery effort. Mainlanders and Taiwanese agreed, particularly after the ROC lost its UN seat and the United States changed its policy toward the PRC, that all their resources and efforts should be concentrated on the development and defense of Taiwan.

Twenty-five years of rapid economic growth have introduced new strains into the body politic. With the waning of differences over mainland recovery, the context of the internal debate over military issues changed. Questions began to be raised about Taiwan's political system and even about its basic political structure. People became preoccupied with problems arising from shifts in income distribution, urbanization, the changing attitudes of youth, a rising crime rate, and the quality and relevance of education.

Taiwan shares these problems of social change and political response with much of the rest of the world, but their presence raises special questions in view of Taiwan's unique situation. Do they add to the strain imposed on the society by the PRC threat, or does the existence of this external threat make them easier to manage than elsewhere? Do they exacerbate mainland-Taiwanese differences, or do they create interest groups transcending this basic division, thus moderating its effect?

Despite inevitable differences over the amount of resources to allocate to the military, a consensus on what needed to be done was easier to achieve once the focus of military preparedness turned exclusively to defense. Both mainlanders and Taiwanese have long accepted the need for a strong defense. The prospect that the US defense commitment to the ROC might be withdrawn has tended to draw the two groups together. In the future, however, they could split over the defense of the offshore islands. Although a case can be made that holding the islands contributes to the defense of Taiwan, their primary significance has long been to symbolize the ROC's determination to recover the mainland. In some circumstances the wisdom of keeping so large a proportion of Taiwan's defense forces there could become the subject of sharp and divisive dispute in Taiwan, with some mainlanders, particularly within the armed forces, adamantly rejecting any weakening of the offshore islands' defenses.

The political strain caused by Taiwanese resentment at mainlander domination of the national government may be aggravated by modernization. Pressures to reform the KMT and to modernize the political system so as to make it more responsive to the people appear

46

to have increased, not only among the Taiwanese, but also among younger mainlanders. The influx of ideas from the United States and Japan, the increasing contact with those countries, and the return to Taiwan of greater numbers of young people educated overseas have contributed to a growing tendency to question the traditional practices of the KMT. Demands made from time to time for greater freedom of political debate, greater respect for the rule of law, and greater freedom for opponents of the KMT to contest elections have been responded to or contained by the leadership, but such pressures seem certain to continue and perhaps increase as the modernization of Taiwan's society proceeds.

Keeping crime and corruption in check has been a continuing problem for the government. It has succeeded reasonably well so far, and public dissatisfaction over such issues has not seriously detracted from the government's effectiveness. But modernization has brought a rise in crime, especially among youth. The growing affluence of the society, urbanization, and unemployment among teenagers has contributed to the problem. Although such problems are less serious in Taiwan than in many other countries, they will require continuing effort by the government if they are not to aggravate the political tensions arising from other causes.

Despite the severity of these political strains, a number of factors have allowed the government of the ROC to maintain political stability on the island and to proceed successfully with its economic development. The government's control of a large military establishment and a pervasive internal security apparatus has certainly helped. But outside observers who have lived on the island and studied its political system testify that the employment of a variety of other political techniques has permitted the government's resort to military and police controls to be highly selective and relatively moderate.

Leadership

From the time that Chiang Kai-shek assumed control of the Nationalist government on Taiwan, the general acceptance of his legitimacy as the national leader was an important stabilizing factor. Chiang had been the most powerful figure in China ever since he had led the Northern Expedition in 1926–1927. During the war of resistance against Japanese aggression, even the Chinese Communist party nominally accepted his leadership for a few years. He had been elected *tsung ts'ai,* or party leader, of the KMT in 1938, and in 1948 he was elected president of China by the National Assembly in accordance with the new constitution. He was also commander-in-chief of the armed forces.

Despite the damage to Chiang's prestige suffered as a result of the loss of the mainland to the Communists, and Taiwanese dissatisfaction under Nationalist rule, when he arrived in Taiwan in 1949 as head of the government, party, and army, no one was in a position to challenge his authority. Many of the most powerful military and political figures on the mainland did not go to Taiwan. There were no warlords on the island with their own armies and local sources of revenue. The generals were dependent on Chiang for money to pay their troops. He reorganized the army so that commanding officers no longer had a claim on particular units. He instituted a two-year term for the chief of the general staff and the commanders of the services to prevent any individual from entrenching himself in a powerful position. Retaining in his own hands broad powers to appoint, dismiss, or transfer officials, both military and civilian, Chiang employed a system of checks and balances in his assignment of personnel, as he had on the mainland, to prevent any individual or agency from becoming too powerful. By his control of the chains of command in government, party, and military forces, as well as of the separate security agencies that kept a watchful eye on the personnel in these main branches, he placed himself in an impregnable position.

But Chiang's authority as a leader derived not only from his skill at political maneuver but also from his selection of able officials for key positions. He was far more effective in this respect in Taiwan than he had been on the mainland, where a glaring weakness of the Nationalist government was his tendency to value loyalty above ability. Loyalty was important in Taiwan, too, and Chiang could be ruthless with those he suspected of disloyalty, as he demonstrated in Sun Li-jen's case. His military and civilian officials in Taiwan therefore had to be loyal, but many were also able.

Ch'en Ch'eng, who served for many years as vice-president and premier, was a key figure. Although a military man without a modern education, he played an important role in pushing through land reform and was a strong backer of the brilliant group of economic officials, such as K. Y. Yin, C. K. Yen, and K. T. Li, who shaped Taiwan's economic development program. He also had a large part in reorganizing and modernizing the armed forces.

Chiang's style of leadership, while out of tune in some respects with the modernizing trends over which he presided, served reasonably well for managing a society at Taiwan's stage of development. He ruled in the Confucian tradition of paternalistic government, in which the ruler had an obligation to look after his subjects, while they owed loyalty to the ruler so long as he did not depart from the expected norms of right conduct. This tradition of leadership was widely accepted among the Chinese in Taiwan, both mainlanders and Taiwanese, and continued to be inculcated in the rising generation through the school system.

Chiang, whose personal life and habits were austere, sought with considerable success to enforce similar austerity on his subordinates. He was not a popular leader in the American sense of one who is close to the people. It is hard to imagine Chiang out "pressing the flesh." Nor was he an electrifying public speaker. On those rare occasions when he made a public address, many in the audience found his strong Chekiang accent hard to understand. But oratorical skill has never been an important qualification for Chinese leaders. To the people of Taiwan, Chiang was an aloof, rather remote figure, but one who was conceded the authority to make all major policy decisions. As Taiwan's circumstances improved from 1950 on, his hold on power became increasingly secure, and he was reelected to successive terms as president without significant opposition until his death in 1975.

By the time Chiang died, he had already transferred active leadership to his son, Chiang Ching-kuo, whom for years he had carefully groomed for the position. Therefore, the succession to power was accomplished smoothly. Chiang Ching-kuo has been widely accepted as Chiang Kai-shek's legitimate successor.

One-Party System

The KMT has also played an important role in maintaining political stability in Taiwan. It has had the primary responsibility for establishing and controlling the limits of public debate, for broadening political participation, especially by integrating the Taiwanese into the political system, and for providing a link between the leadership and the people.

The views of the leaders and party ideologues have been disseminated principally, although not exclusively, through KMT channels. The party owns and operates the Central News Agency with its worldwide network for collecting and distributing news, the *Central Daily News* (*Chung Yang Jih Pao*) in Taipei and other newspapers, the Broadcasting Corporation of China (operating seventy transmitters and broadcasting six hundred hours daily in seventeen languages), the Central Motion Picture Corporation, and the Chung Cheng Book Company. The party organs for disseminating information are supplemented by the Government Information Office, an official body under the Executive Yuan.

The party does not hold a monopoly on the dissemination of news and opinion, having to compete with numerous privately owned newspapers, magazines, book publishers, radio and TV stations, and motion picture studios.[14] But the party has a special responsibility for monitoring the output of these private companies to ensure that subversive material is excluded. News management in the ROC is rather sophisticated, in that a wide range of material appears, some of it quite critical of government officials, agencies, and policies. Dispatches from foreign news agencies supplement those of the Central News Agency to provide the reading public with a broad coverage of international news. Certain topics, however, are taboo, such as personal attacks on the leader, favorable comments on the PRC, and any questioning of the basic political system in the ROC or its mainland recovery policy. Over the years, a number of political journals have been suspended, shut down, or forced to change management for having overstepped the permitted bounds.

Since the introduction of local self-government in Taiwan in 1950, the KMT has had the responsibility of putting forward and supporting candidates for election as city mayors, county magistrates, provincial assemblymen, city and county councilmen, and village and township chiefs. Candidates backed by the KMT have had a substantial advantage over independents or those KMT members who sometimes ran without party approval. During the elections held between 1964 and 1968, for example, the proportion of KMT-backed candidates elected at all levels ranged from 78 percent to 92 percent.[15]

Because only Taiwanese candidates stood any chance of being elected in these local elections by the predominantly Taiwanese electorate, it was essential to bring Taiwanese in large numbers into the KMT party organization. Initially, Taiwanese occupied only the lower rungs of the party hierarchy, but as their numbers in the party increased, they moved up into the middle grades and a few senior positions. Although party jobs generally carried less prestige than government appointive or elective positions of an equivalent level, they did provide a means of co-opting thousands of Taiwanese into the political system. Taiwanese now constitute 70 percent of the party membership, although the top positions remain in mainlander hands.[16] Of the

---

14. See J. Bruce Jacobs, "Taiwan's Press—Political Communications Link and Research Resource," *China Quarterly*, no. 68 (December 1976): 778–788.
15. *The Kuomintang, A Brief Record of Achievements* (Taipei, n.d.), p. 59.
16. Figure supplied by Hsueh Jen-yang, deputy secretary-general of the KMT, in May 1976.

twenty-two members of the Central Standing Committee in 1976, only five were Taiwanese.

Another major function of the KMT is to provide a link between the leadership and the people. Professional party workers work closely with and have significant influence on leaders of farmers' associations, fishermmen's associations, labor unions, cooperatives, and women's organizations. They operate 400 service centers throughout the island, providing assistance to people ranging from free medical care to vocational training and job procurement. They direct the China Youth Corps, which carries out recreational and educational programs for 200,000 participants each year, and through party cells on college campuses they keep in close touch with student opinion and activities. They maintain contact with overseas Chinese around the world. Thus, the KMT touches the lives of the people in many ways. The leadership relies on the party's intricate network of connections with mass organizations throughout the country as an important means of indoctrinating and influencing people and winning sufficient support to enable them to go on governing effectively.

Although the KMT seems omnipresent in Taiwan, it is not dominant as the party is in Communist countries. As an organization, it has relatively little influence on military, economic, and foreign policy decisions. Except in those areas where it has primary responsibility, such as the management of local elections and the monitoring of the media, it does not normally initiate action. In most areas, action is initiated by the government department concerned or by the leader himself, and decisions are made by the leader in consultation with his principal economic and military officials. Major decisions are then ratified by the Central Standing Committee of the KMT, of which the leader and the chief economic and military officials are members.

In Taiwan, unlike the practice in Communist states, few party careerists have made their way into the top ranks of government. One reason may be that the KMT is not a small, elite organization with stiff requirements for admission, designed to train future leaders. Anyone can join who is at least twenty years old, subscribes to KMT principles, and submits to party discipline. As of 1976, membership was 1,570,000, or about 20 percent of all persons over nineteen years of age. Party members probably number over one-third of all adult males, since as of 1970 only about 10 percent of party members were women.[17] Samuel Huntington argued that one indicator of the strength of a one-party system is the premium placed on party membership, and that if member-

---

17. *Introduction to the Kuomintang* (Taipei: Department of Information, Central Committee, KMT, 1971), p. 67.

ship becomes universal, it becomes meaningless.[18] Thus, the KMT's mass membership policy has probably tended to weaken the influence of the party.

It is instructive to compare the results of Taiwan's one-party system with those of another non-Communist one-party system, that of Mexico. Both Taiwan and Mexico have enjoyed remarkable political stability for the past twenty-five years and have achieved impressive records of economic growth. In both, the leader has enormous power: in Mexico, the leader is the president; in Taiwan, the leader was the president while Chiang Kai-shek lived and has been the premier since Chiang Ching-kuo took over. Both countries have carried out land reforms and are governed by parties that style themselves "revolutionary." But there are significant contrasts between the results produced by the two systems, particularly in their agricultural policies and the trends in income distribution.

After its land reform, Taiwan limited landholdings to small parcels, while Mexico did not. Consequently, as of 1960, landownership in Mexico had become highly concentrated, with 1 percent of farm units occupying 50 percent of the land, while 77 percent of private owners held only 11 percent.[19] Most of Mexico's increase in agricultural production has come from large commercial farms, which have received the lion's share of government investment in the agricultural sector, while in Taiwan the increase in production has come from the mass of small farmers as the result of the broad impact of government measures to aid agriculture.

The fact that income inequality has declined in Taiwan while it has increased in Mexico probably can be attributed largely to the differences in their treatment of the farm population. In Mexico, the standard of living of the farm population has declined because the underemployed labor force increased in size as the average number of days worked per year decreased from 194 in 1950 to under 100 in 1960. In Taiwan, although the number of agricultural workers increased by 20 percent from 1946 to 1965, the average number of days worked increased from 90 to 156, and thus the standard of living of the farm population has risen.[20] Taiwan has also had the advantage of a population policy that helped to reduce the annual rate of population growth

18. Samuel P. Huntington, "Social and Institutional Dynamics of One-Party Systems," in Huntington and Clement H. Moore, eds., *Authoritarian Politics in Modern Society: The Dynamics of Established One-Party Systems* (New York: Basic Books, 1970).

19. For all data on Mexico see Roger E. Hansen, *The Politics of Mexican Development* (Baltimore: Johns Hopkins University Press, 1971).

20. You-tsao Wang, "Technological Changes and Agricultural Development of Taiwan, 1946–65," in *Conference on Economic Development in Taiwan* (Taipei: Academia Sinica, 1967), p. 167.

from 3.5 percent in the 1950s to 1.9 percent in 1975, while in Mexico the rate was at 3.2 percent in 1976.[21]

Mexico's one-party system has succeeded in institutionalizing the leadership succession. Mexican presidents are elected for a single six-year term, and their successors are chosen by a few men in the top ranks of the party, ultimately by the outgoing president. Election then becomes a formality, as the party's nominee runs unopposed. Whether Taiwan's present leader can be replaced without disorder by means of the existing political machinery remains to be tested.

Corruption appears to be far more prevalent and on a larger scale in Mexico than in Taiwan. Thousands of elective and appointive officials hold office in Mexico for six years only, being replaced by a new group when a new president takes over. Hence, there is great pressure to accumulate as much money as possible during the term of office. No top officials are jailed for corruption, and conspicuous consumption among them is common.[22] In Taiwan, senior officials live modestly, and from time to time convictions of highly placed persons for corruption do occur. On the other hand, there are fewer restrictions on political and civil rights in Mexico than in Taiwan. Freedom House ranked Mexico and Taiwan in this respect on a scale of one to seven, with one representing the greatest freedom for political and civil rights:[23]

One-party system	Political rights	Civil rights
Mexico	4	3
Taiwan	6	5

Despite Mexico's greater freedom, brutal military suppression of student oposition has occurred there twice in recent years, with some three hundred demonstrating students killed in 1968 and thirty in 1971.[24] No comparable incidents have occurred in Taiwan since the Taiwanese uprising in 1947.

These two cases illustrate that non-Communist one-party systems can have very different results in different places. In its population policy, its drive against corruption, and its egalitarian treatment of rural and urban populations, Taiwan seems to have prepared itself better than Mexico to extend its record of political stability and eco-

---

21. *The New York Times,* Sept. 2, 1977
22. *The New York Times,* June 29, 1976; Alan Riding, "Mexico Elects a Symbol," *The New York Times Magazine,* June 13, 1976, p. 19.
23. *Freedom at Issue* (New York: Freedom House, 1976), p. 15.
24. Riding, "Mexico Elects a Symbol," pp. 14–15.

nomic growth, provided that it can institutionalize the succession process as successfully as Mexico.[25]

The KMT has become a huge bureaucracy and suffers from the defects of bureaucracies: inefficiency, rigidity, and excessive conservatism. Its top levels are overloaded with ideologues reluctant to adjust to changing circumstances. Nevertheless, the record shows that the party has made important contributions to stability without preventing substantial growth and social change. Its performance provides some support for the view expressed by Samuel Huntington that "a strong one-party system appears to meet certain functional needs for a society in the early to middle phases of modernization ... the single party is the functional equivalent of the absolute monarchy of seventeenth century Europe."[26] Robert Ward also concluded from a study of modern Japan that authoritarian forms of government may be superior to democracy in the early stages of political development.[27] A young Taiwanese lawyer who was not particularly complimentary of the KMT nevertheless expressed the opinion that the party was essential to Taiwan's present stage of development; if it did not exist, some other mechanism would have to be created to perform its function. He hoped, however, that the quality of the party cadres would gradually improve as the older ones died off.

The question for the future is whether the KMT can creatively adjust to the further modernization of Taiwan's society. Given the crucial role of the leader in shaping politics in Taiwan, much will depend on Chiang Ching-kuo's conception of the future role of the party.

Political Development

Political change has occurred in Taiwan, especially in provincial and local politics, even though the mainlander-dominated political structure brought over from the mainland has not been altered. Political participation has been expanded, the political values inculcated by the government have been widely accepted, and progress has been made in integrating mainlanders and Taiwanese.

Although local politics have been firmly controlled by the KMT, the opportunities to vote and run for local office have been greatly

---

25. See Richard R. Fagen, "The Realities of U.S.-Mexican Relations," *Foreign Affairs* 55 (July 1977): 685–700.
26. Huntington and Moore, *Authoritarian Politics in Modern Society*, p. 12.
27. Robert E. Ward, ed., *Political Development in Modern Japan* (Princeton: Princeton University Press, 1968), p. 590.

broadened since the Nationalist government took Taiwan over from Japan. The Japanese had permitted no island-wide elective body, although in 1935, after years of agitation by the home-rule movement in Taiwan and influenced by Japanese liberals, they had finally agreed to assemblies in each prefecture, county, and town. Half of the assembly members were elected by popular vote and half were appointed by the prefectural governors. They had power to act on local budgets, certain local tax matters, and a few unimportant administrative questions, but the Japanese governors held the veto power. Only males over twenty-five with certain property qualifications could vote. Elections were set up and managed by the Japanese police. Of the 172 persons elected and appointed to the first assemblies, 109 were Japanese and only 63 Taiwanese.[28] Larger numbers of Taiwanese were elected in later elections, but the elective process remained highly restrictive under the Japanese.

Under the Nationalist government, participation in the local elective process has been much expanded, and for the first time an elective provincial assembly has been created. In 1950, counties and cities began electing their councils, mayors, and magistrates, which have important powers in local affairs. The provincial assembly, created in 1951, was at first elected indirectly by the city and county councils, but since 1959 it has been elected by popular vote. All citizens over twenty have the right to vote in local and provincial elections.[29]

Local and provincial elections, which occur every four years, have become an important means of giving the Taiwanese a stake in the political process. They have opened to ambitious Taiwanese hundreds of positions that offer local prestige and in some instances control of patronage. These local offices have served some as stepping-stones to higher positions in the provincial or even the national government. Because of the KMT's dominant influence on the elections, most aspiring Taiwanese politicians join the party. Local elections thus provide a means of co-opting a large number of active and politically minded Taiwanese into the KMT. They also have given voters a degree of influence on local government, for the KMT's control is by no means

---

28. George H. Kerr, *Formosa: Licensed Revolution and the Home Rule Movement, 1895–1945* (Honolulu: The University Press of Hawaii, 1974), pp. 78, 170. Under the Japanese, Taiwan was divided into five large prefectures (*shu*) and three districts (*cho*) under appointed governors. These administrative divisions were eliminated by the Chinese, who designate all of Taiwan and Penghu as a province (*sheng*), with subordinate counties (*hsien*), cities (*shih*), urban and rural townships (*chen* and *hsiang*), and villages (*ts'un*).

29. See Richard L. Walker, "Taiwan's Movement into Political Modernity, 1945–72," in Paul K. T. Sih, ed., *Taiwan in Modern Times* (Jamaica, N.Y.: St. John's University Press, 1973); Wei, "Political Development in the Republic of China"; Han *Taiwan Today;* Mendel, *The Politics of Formosan Nationalism.*

absolute. To ensure election of its candidate, it must put forward one who has voter appeal. The local KMT headquarters is unlikely to back for reelection any mayor or magistrate who is widely regarded as having done a poor job.

Although the appearance of opposition candidates is resented by party bureaucrats, whose job is to get the officially sponsored KMT candidates elected, the fact that some opposition exists adds liveliness and interest to the elections and makes them more credible as an exercise in democracy. Opposition candidates, either independents or KMT members at odds with the party hierarchy, are at a disadvantage relative to the KMT candidates, who can rely on funds and help from party cadres, can campaign more openly before the campaign period officially opens, can get better press coverage, can benefit from the prohibition against speaking at other than authorized campaign forums, and are less likely to be taken to court for illegal practices.[30] Despite these handicaps, some opposition candidates get elected in each election. Criticizing the KMT has proved an effective way to attract the Taiwanese protest vote.

The most successful opposition candidate has been Kao Yu-shu (Henry Kao), a Taiwanese engineer educated in Japan, who twice won the mayoralty election in Taipei, much to the chagrin of KMT bureaucrats. In 1967, before Kao had completed his second term, the government made Taipei a "special municipality" under the Executive Yuan, to be headed by an appointed mayor, thus eliminating the risk that future mayoralty elections in the capital city might accentuate the division between Taiwanese and mainlanders and provoke disorder. In a shrewd political move calculated to diminish the adverse reaction to the ending of mayoralty elections in Taipei, Chiang Kai-shek named Kao the first appointed mayor. In 1964, the year that Kao was elected to his second term as mayor, independents were also elected mayor in Keelung and Tainan. Thus, non-KMT mayors held office in three of Taiwan's largest cities. That year marked a high point in independent electoral successes in the big cities.

In rural areas, where virtually all local officials had been appointed under the Japanese, the Nationalist government initiated elections for township heads and township councils. With the decline in the power of wealthy landlords as the result of land reforms, a new class of rural politicians has arisen, introducing some of the evils of democratic politics, such as corruption and vote buying, but also compelling poli-

---

30. J. Bruce Jacobs, "Taiwan 1973: Consolidation of the Succession," *Asian Survey* 14 (January 1974): 27–28.

ticians to provide services in exchange for votes.[31] Township elections have provided grass-roots experience for Taiwanese politicians ambitious for higher political position. So also have the elections of heads of farmers' associations, although in recent years the national government has reduced local freedom of choice by imposing higher educational and other qualifications for candidates in an effort to reduce nepotism and corruption in these elections and to secure more competent officeholders.

The electoral process in Taiwan, despite its imperfections, has served to involve large numbers of Taiwanese in the management of local affairs, as KMT bureaucrats, as candidates for office, or as voters. Involvement in local government has somewhat relieved Taiwanese frustration at mainlander domination of government at the national level. More important, the mechanism that has been accepted for choosing local officials and the experience being gained in operating it can eventually be applied at the national level. Already elections are being held periodically of small numbers of additional members to the National Assembly, the Legislative Yuan, and the Control Yuan.

The extent to which the KMT dominates the electoral process and some of the methods it has employed to maintain this domination have given rise to much cynicism, particularly among the intellectuals. The KMT is frequently criticized for placing loyalty to the party machine ahead of quality in selecting candidates for local office. Up to the present, however, the workings of the electoral process seem to have met fairly well the demands for political participation on the part of the mass of people in Taiwan. Those demands are likely to rise with modernization, unless held in check by consciousness of the external threat to the island. As a leading non-KMT Taiwanese politician remarked in the spring of 1976, "Right now Taiwan's survival is more important to the people than whether it has more or less democracy."

Essential to the stablity of any political system is widespread acceptance by the people of certain values, norms, and modes of behavior. In Taiwan, an important element in the stability of the political system has been the persistence of certain fundamental Chinese attitudes among both mainlanders and Taiwanese and the continuing reinforcement of these attitudes through the school system.[32] Most important

31. Bernard Gallin, "Political Factionalism and Its Impact on Chinese Village Social Organization in Taiwan," in Marc J. Swartz, ed., *Local Level Politics* (Chicago: Aldine, 1968).

32. See Richard W. Wilson, *Learning To Be Chinese: The Political Socialization of Children in Taiwan* (Cambridge: MIT Press, 1970); Sheldon Appleton, "Taiwanese and Mainlanders on Taiwan: A Survey of Student Attitudes," *China Quarterly*, no. 44

has been the inculcation of respect for authority and conformity to group norms. The great majority of schoolteachers appear to have co-operated in cultivating among children support for the government.

In the schools much emphasis is placed on respect for authority figures, especially parents, school principals, and the national leader. So long as a leader conforms to group norms, to oppose him is to place oneself outside the group—a lonely and shameful place to be. Consequently, open criticism of the leader is inhibited. Dissatisfaction is more likely to be expressed by cynicism and concentration on personal interests than by overt opposition. The low level of political interest and activism in Taiwan's universities can probably be attributed to this early training, as well as to the KMT's close supervision of student activities.

Most Chinese students seem to be more interested in the honesty and capability of government than they are in civil rights or the democratic process. They prefer the Chinese family system and pattern of human relations to the Western. They are moderately satisfied with their future prospects. The minority of discontented students immerse themselves in personal and family concerns, or the more ambitious migrate to the United States rather than challenge the system in Taiwan.[33] There is little difference between the political attitudes of mainlanders and Taiwanese.

The effectiveness of the school system in inculcating respect for authority thus seems to be reasonably well established. There may be latent danger, however, in a system that inhibits any criticism of the leader. Cynicism and discontent may build undetected, to burst out in a moment of crisis.[34]

Not only is the integration of Taiwanese into the political system taking place through their education in school, their admission into the KMT, and their participation in local politics, but there are additional ways in which the two groups are slowly being mixed together to form a single body politic in which provincial origin will no longer be politically significant. By far the most important means of breaking down the barriers between mainlanders and Taiwanese has been the use since 1945 of the national language (*kuo yu,* generally called Mandarin in English) as the medium of instruction in the public schools.

(October–December 1970): 38–65; Appleton, "Regime Support among Taiwan High School Students," *Asian Survey* 13 (August 1973): 750–760; Appleton, "The Prospects for Student Activism in Taiwan," in Yung-hwan Jo, ed., *Taiwan's Future* (Hong Kong: Union Research Institute for Center for Asian Studies, Arizona State University, 1974), pp. 52–62; Yung Wei, "Political Development in the Republic of China on Taiwan," in Jo, *Taiwan's Future,* pp. 11–38.
33. Appleton, "The Prospects for Student Activism in Taiwan," p. 53.
34. Wilson, *Learning To Be Chinese,* p. 137.

An entire generation has now been educated in the national language, and many young Taiwanese speak it with a better accent than older mainlanders, whose Mandarin is heavily accented with their native Cantonese, Hunanese, or Shanghai dialect. Although Taiwanese generally prefer to use their own dialect at home or among themselves, there is no longer a significant communications barrier between the two groups. Not only are Taiwanese learning Mandarin in school, but many younger mainlanders have learned to speak Taiwanese.

Children born in Taiwan of mainlander parents now outnumber the mainlanders who came from the mainland.[35] These young mainlanders have no personal experience on the mainland. Like the Taiwanese, Taiwan is the only home they have known, and their values and attitudes differ little from those of the Taiwanese. Although there is still a tendency for mainlanders and Taiwanese to socialize more with members of their own group than with each other, mainlander-Taiwanese intermarriage has become quite common. As the young mainlanders and their Taiwanese contemporaries move up into increasingly responsible positions in the society, the differences between the two groups will steadily narrow.

Much credit must be given to the school examination system for the successful intermingling of mainlanders and Taiwanese in the schools. To advance into senior high school or college requires passing an examination. Whether a candidate is admitted to a prestigious institution or a mediocre one depends strictly upon the grade he or she receives in the examination. Although the examination system has been widely criticized for the heavy strain it places upon students and their parents, it is generally agreed that the examinations are fairly administered. Not even high officials can secure special treatment for their children if they receive low grades. Critics have been unable to suggest a fairer system. Given the high value placed by mainlanders and Taiwanese alike on providing their children the best possible education, the absence of discrimination between the two groups has made a vital contribution to political stability.

Integration of the two groups has been hindered by their distinct vocational and residential patterns. Mainlanders are concentrated in the cities, where the majority of them hold jobs in government, the KMT, government corporations, or teaching. According to a survey done in 1967, mainlanders held 82 percent of the positions in the military, police, and national security agencies and 34 percent of those in

---

35. Based on fact that as of 1975, 58 percent of Taiwan's total population was under 25 and thus had been born after the great influx of mainlanders into Taiwan in 1949–1950. *TSDB,* p. 13.

public administration and the professions, compared to only 6 percent in commerce and 1 percent in agriculture.[36] While these proportions probably have changed considerably in recent years, the pattern of distribution persists.

Over the years, the tension between mainlanders and Taiwanese has gradually declined, a process that Chiang Ching-kuo has made a special effort to further. Taiwanese continue to resent their political subordination, seeing little chance that the mainlanders will relinquish to them the commanding heights in the critical areas of defense, internal security, foreign affairs, finance, or the KMT. Nevertheless, because most of the land and the majority of private enterprises are owned by them, they have benefited, perhaps more than the average mainlander, from Taiwan's economic growth and political stability. They may enjoy hearing the occasional fiery Taiwanese politician lash out at the KMT in an election campaign, but few would wish to provoke a showdown with the mainlanders that would disturb the public order. After all, the passage of time will ineluctably bring power into their hands if Taiwan remains free of mainland control.

Adjustment to Change, 1969–1976

Beginning about 1969, the political system, which had successfully absorbed and contained the political strains on it, was subjected to new pressures, particularly after 1971, when Nixon's announcement of his intention to visit Peking struck Taipei like a bombshell. Difficult economic decisions were required in both industry and agriculture. The 1968 extension of free public schooling from six to nine years, although universally popular, demanded a great effort on the part of the government to provide additional schoolrooms and teachers. The weakening international position of the ROC created deep anxieties. New blood was needed in the National Assembly, Legislative Yuan, and Control

---

36. Tung-ming Lee, *A Study on Social Increase of Population in Taiwan* (Taichung: Population Study Center, Bureau of Public Health, 1968), p. 67, quoted in Yung Wei, "Modernization Process in Taiwan: An Allocative Analysis," *Asian Survey* 16 (March 1976): 262. These figures must exclude Taiwanese conscripts in the armed forces, who constitute over 90 percent of the rank and file but serve only two or three years. The proportion of Taiwanese in the police appears to have increased substantially in recent years. According to the director of the Foreign Affairs Department of the National Police Administration, as of 1976, Taiwanese constituted 80 percent of the rank and file and 50 percent of the higher officers in the national and provincial police.

Yuan, as the original members aged or died. And by 1969, Chiang Kai-shek was eighty-two years old, which meant the decision would soon have to be made as to who would be his successor.

By this time, the grooming of Chiang Ching-kuo was far advanced.[37] In the early 1950s, he served briefly as chairman of the KMT's Taiwan Provincial Headquarters and for a longer period as director general of the Political Department of the Ministry of National Defense. Later in the decade, in addition to his duties as chief coordinator of intelligence and security activities, he became chairman of the Vocational Assistance Commission for Retired Servicemen and director of the China Youth Corps. In 1964, he became deputy minister of defense and was moved up to minister in 1965. By 1967, he was ready for broader responsibilities, becoming vice-premier of the Executive Yuan and concurrently chairman of the Commission for International Economic Cooperation and Development.

As defense minister, Chiang Ching-kuo had worked out a program for streamlining the armed forces, which would trim them down from the 600,000 level of the 1960s to close to 500,000 by the mid-1970s. Later, as vice-premier, he took part in the decisions to step up aid to farmers and to begin work on the construction projects that later became known as the Ten Major Development Projects. But it was only after becoming premier in 1972 that he was recognized as the principal decision-maker in all fields and the probable successor to his father, who by that time was failing in health and withdrawing from an active role in government.

Chiang Ching-kuo's personal style differs greatly from that of his father. He has continued the practice he followed as director of the Youth Corps and the Vocational Assistance Commission for Retired Servicemen of getting out into the field and talking with all kinds of people. The newspapers frequently carry pictures of him, typically clad in sport shirt and slacks, conversing with a group of farmers, workers, students, or soldiers in some part of the island. He has effectively created an image of a leader who is concerned about the life of the ordinary man. The contrast with Chiang Kai-shek's aloof Confucian style is striking. He has also not followed his father's practice of balancing factions and personalities against each other. Instead, he has centralized the government more than in the past, establishing clear lines of authority and concentrating decision-making power in his hands.

Chiang Ching-kuo has not departed, however, from his father's adamant opposition to communism and continues to issue ringing

---

37. See Tillman Durdin, "Chiang Ching-kuo's Taiwan," *Pacific Community* 7 (October 1975): 92–117.

declarations of the ROC's determination to recover the mainland.[38] Any slackening in this regard would not only weaken his support among the old guard of the KMT but might also give rise to suspicions among the Taiwanese, if it were interpreted as a sign that he was considering negotiating with Peking. A leader who spent twelve years in the Soviet Union and has a Russian wife must work harder than most to preserve popular confidence in his anti-Communist credentials.[39]

Even before Chiang Ching-kuo took over as premier in June 1972, tension between mainlanders and Taiwanese had diminished as a result of the US change in policy toward the PRC. This unexpected action shocked both groups in Taiwan into realizing that they could not afford internecine quarreling in the face of the dangers and uncertainties now facing Taiwan. Sympathy within Taiwan for the independence movement's campaign to bring down the KMT largely evaporated, and the mainstream of the movement overseas, while still advocating independence for Taiwan, began to urge the reform rather than the overthrow of the Nationalist government. Some leaders of the movement in Japan visited Taiwan to talk with government and party officials. One of them, Ch'iu Yung-han (Kyu Eikan), a wealthy Taiwanese businessman, began conducting groups of Japanese businessmen to Taiwan to investigate investment possibilities.

As premier, Chiang Ching-kuo took a number of actions to demonstate his intention to improve the position of Taiwanese. He appointed as governor of Taiwan, Hsieh Tung-min, the speaker of the provincial assembly; and the first Taiwanese minister of interior in the previous cabinet was named deputy premier, the highest position ever held by a Taiwanese. Other high posts allocated to Taiwanese during Chiang's administration include the deputy governor of the Central Bank, ambassadors to Nicaragua and El Salvador, and the deputy director of the General Political Department of the Ministry of National Defense. At the eleventh KMT Party Congress in November 1976, two Taiwanese were added to the three already on the highest party body, the 22-member Central Standing Committee. Sixteen of the 48 new members brought into the 130-member Central Committee were Taiwanese. Many Taiwanese were appointed to head local KMT headquarters and to hold positions in the government bureaucracy, including some vice-

---

38. See *China Yearbook, 1975*, pp. 660–717.
39. Chiang Ching-kuo went to the Soviet Union in 1925, when he was only 16, to attend Sun Yat-sen University in Moscow and then the Military and Political Institute in Leningrad. Several requests by him to return to China were refused by the Soviets, and he worked in mines and factories until finally allowed to leave in 1937. Howard L. Boorman, ed., *Biographical Dictionary of Republican China* (New York: Columbia University Press, 1967), I, 307–308.

ministers. Moreover, Chiang demonstrated a marked personal interest in the rural development program, begun in 1969 and stepped up in 1972, the benefits of which go almost exclusively to Taiwanese. The Taiwanese, although not totally satisfied by the steps taken, were impressed. Chiang has made notable headway in transforming his image among Taiwanese from that of an oppressor to one concerned about their welfare. Mainlanders are now beginning to complain that the government's policy of increasing the appointment of Taiwanese is reducing their job prospects.

When Chiang Ching-kuo became premier, he announced a ten-point administrative reform program aimed at improving the efficiency of the bureaucracy, cracking down on corruption, and barring government officials from bars, dance halls, and expensive restaurants. He showed that he meant business by promptly arresting forty-five government employees charged with colluding with smugglers, including ten employees of the powerful Taiwan Garrison Command.[40] Later, the former personal secretary of Chiang Kai-shek, Wang Cheng-yi, was sent to jail for accepting bribes.[41] These actions created a favorable impression of the premier as one who would try hard to maintain honest and efficient government. The government's determination to prevent corruption was further demonstrated in November 1976, when the Taipei District Court imposed harsh sentences ranging from eight months to life on twenty-two officials, bankers, and businessmen convicted of giving or taking bribes in a case involving the government-owned Farmer's Bank, the Taiwan Tobacco and Wine Monopoly Bureau, and a group of private companies.[42]

Travel regulations were eased to permit group sightseeing tours abroad, whereas previously a traveler had to have some other reason, such as visiting relatives, business, or study. Passport application procedures were simplified, and overseas Chinese were allowed to visit Taiwan for up to three months without having to go through the bothersome process of obtaining an exit permit to leave. In 1972, 80,000 people from Taiwan traveled abroad.[43]

The new Chiang administration paid greater attention to youth, organizing a youth work conference in the spring of 1973, presided over by the energetic new minister of education, Y. S. Tsiang, and attended by other senior officials, including Chiang Ching-kuo himself. Additional funds were allocated to the National Youth Commission, which had been established in 1966 to help young people find jobs and assist

---

40. *The New York Times,* Aug. 23, 1972.
41. Ibid., Sept. 5, 1973.
42. *Far Eastern Economic Review,* Nov. 12, 1976, pp. 62, 67.
43. *The New York Times,* Apr. 15, 1973.

those studying abroad to return to Taiwan on completion of their studies. Higher educational qualifications were established for certain official positions. Younger people were brought into high positions in the government, including Ch'ien Fu (Fred Chien), age thirty-seven, as director of the Government Information Office, Chang Feng-hsu, a Taiwanese and age forty-four, as mayor of Taipei, and Li Teng-hui, a Taiwanese and age forty-eight, as minister without portfolio.[44] Education Minister Y. S. Tsiang replaced the incumbent vice-ministers in his ministry with two Taiwanese, aged thirty-seven and thirty-nine. High rank for such young men, especially for Taiwanese, was unprecedented in Taiwan.[45]

In 1975, responding to public concern over the rising crime rate, the government adopted harsher penalties for ordinary criminals. Those accused of the most serious crimes were turned over to military courts for trial. The government's determination to deal severely with perpetrators of violent crime was dramatized by showing on TV criminals sentenced to death being led off to face the firing squad.

During 1971 and 1972, a political debate unprecedented in openness and scope developed among intellectuals in Taiwan, sparked by students and young faculty members at Taiwan National University, the most prestigious institution of higher learning on the island. Students were initially stirred up by Japanese claims to the Tiao Yu T'ai (Senkaku) Islands, a group of small, uninhabited rocky outcroppings between Taiwan and the Ryukyus, which both the ROC and the PRC regard as Chinese territory. Students, following the example set by Chinese students in Hong Kong and the United States, organized patriotic anti-Japanese demonstrations in Taipei. Later, reacting to the threat to Taiwan's future imposed by the US change of policy toward the PRC and emboldened by a speech by Chiang Ching-kuo urging youth to speak out, young intellectuals began to publish articles calling for greater academic freedom, the curbing of the security police, new blood in government, and a fairer distribution of income. In December 1971, the students of Taiwan National University conducted a public survey of rural problems, the condition of the poor in cities, police-citizen relations, and other social questions.

At first, the KMT tolerated the debate, even offering cooperation with the students who were making the social survey. But as the proposals for change grew bolder, calling for sweeping reforms, including elections for the Legislative Yuan and other national elective bodies

---

44. Three years later, Ch'ien Fu became a vice-minister of foreign affairs.
45. See Jacobs, "Taiwan 1972: Political Season" Jacobs, "Taiwan 1973: Consolidation of the Succession," *Asian Survey* 13 (January 1973): 102–112; 14 (January 1974): 22–29; *The New York Times,* Oct. 31, Dec. 12, 1971.

to make them representative of the people of Taiwan, the party began to move against the most outspoken of the young intellectuals. It did not clamp down abruptly, but through a carefully orchestrated series of moves, including warnings to individuals and newspapers and the dismissal or shifting to other jobs of several faculty members at Taiwan National University, it underscored the limitations on public political discourse. One of the young reform advocates resigned from the KMT and joined three other independents to run for the Taipei City Council in December 1973, carrying to the people their attacks on one-party rule, martial law, and government favoritism. All were defeated by the candidates backed by the KMT machine.[46]

In 1975, a new monthly, the *Taiwan Political Review* (*Taiwan Cheng Lun*), began to publish articles critical of the political system in Taiwan and commenting on highly sensitive issues such as martial law and military spending. One article went so far as to quote the view of an anti-KMT intellectual abroad to the effect that the people of Taiwan had a choice of either overthrowing the government to establish an independent Taiwan or negotiating a peaceful reunification with the PRC. After only five issues, the journal, which had attracted many readers by its outspokenness on issues rarely discussed in the media, was suspended for a year for having disseminated seditious ideas. Late in 1976, the managing editor was sentenced to ten years for sedition and the magazine's license was revoked.[47] During 1975 and 1976, the government also arrested a number of Taiwanese dissidents, including an unsuccessful candidate for the Legislative Yuan. Some of the dissidents resorted to terrorism. A parcel bomb seriously injured the governor of Taiwan, and a letter bomb was mailed to the ROC's ambassador in Washington.

Dissident activity and demands for reform were not met solely by repression, however. Chiang Ching-kuo was responding in some measure to reform demands by his actions to help the farmers, to ease travel regulations, to bring more Taiwanese and young people into government, and to take the lead through personal example in bringing high government officials into direct contact with the people. The government also took actions aimed specifically at countering criticism of its security measures. After Chiang Kai-shek's death in 1975, the government reduced the sentences of political prisoners and released about two hundred of them. In December 1976, Premier Chiang Ching-kuo announced that the ROC was holding only 254 persons imprisoned for sedition, 95 of whom had been convicted during the three years 1974–1976. He emphasized that they had been tried and convicted by legal

---

46. *The New York Times,* Feb. 20, 1972, Mar. 16, Nov. 25, 1973; *Washington Post,* Jan. 3, 1974.
47. *Far Eastern Economic Review,* Jan. 30, 1976, p. 26, Nov. 19, 1976, p. 19.

process and denied that there had been any infringement of human rights by his government. He offered to cooperate with an investigation by any international organization "that is based on goodwill toward us."[48] Observers noted a number of actions by the government during the first half of 1977 showing a cautious easing of curbs on dissenters, which were attributed by some to a sensitivity to President Carter's emphasis on human rights and by others to modernizing trends on Taiwan.[49]

Problems and Prospects

Under the protective umbrella of the US security commitment to Taiwan, the island's political system has been remarkably stable, despite the heavy strains imposed upon it. It has adjusted to and absorbed the impact of rapid social change, economic recession, and the decline of its diplomatic relationships to a handful of countries. But the prospect that the United States may end its formal relations and its security treaty with the ROC in the course of normalizing relations with Peking poses new uncertainties.

The change in US policy toward the PRC in 1971–1972 had a unifying effect on the people of Taiwan. It also, however, tended to strengthen the conservative nature of the government, making it even more reluctant than usual to consider political reforms that would involve risks. Impending external dangers and uncertainties make it difficult for the government to relax significantly its security controls or to permit what would probably be a highly divisive public debate on the basic political changes needed to cope with the problems that will confront the ROC over the next decade.

Increased reluctance to modify the existing political system and practices coincides with a rising demand from young people, including Taiwanese critics of the KMT, for change to meet the unprecedented challenges facing the ROC. Many would like to see a more representative national government, greater freedom for public debate, and a relaxation of security measures. Some of those pressing for change are among the American-educated intellectuals who have returned to Taiwan from the United States in increasing numbers during the past few years. How the government handles pressures for change will greatly influence

48. *The New York Times,* Dec. 26, 1976. See also *Country Reports on Human Rights Practices,* submitted by Department of State to House International Relations Committee and Senate Foreign Relations Committee, Feb. 3, 1978 (Washington: GPO, 1978), pp. 228–233.
49. *The New York Times,* June 27, 1977.

whether these young intellectuals stay in Taiwan and whether the number returning from the United States continues to grow.

In a broad sense, the problem of maintaining political stability on Taiwan in the next few years can be reduced to two issues: how to yield to demands for change rapidly enough to prevent explosive pressures from building up, but not so rapidly that the governing group loses control of the process; and how to transfer power to a new leader when Chiang Ching-kuo dies or becomes incapacitated. The events of 1971–1972 foreshadow the likely increase in demands on the government for change as the new and better-educated generation moves into positions of greater influence in the society. The "Taiwanization" of the government, party, and military forces is bound to accelerate, with mainlanders fighting a rearguard action to keep in their hands the levers of power at the top. The external threat gives both groups a strong motivation for keeping this process orderly. Both would benefit from political stability and continued economic growth.

So far, the mix of repression and reform offered by the Chiang Ching-kuo administration has stayed within limits acceptable to the great majority of people in Taiwan. Taiwanese hotheads and mainlander mossbacks have been kept at the fringes of politics. Chiang Ching-kuo has demonstrated skill as a leader, combining willingness to take decisive action, ability to select and use competent subordinates, and receptivity to advice from a variety of sources. His greatest weakness may be a tendency to control things too tightly from the center, or conversely, an unwillingness to rely sufficiently on local initiative and the often untidy workings of the democratic process in local affairs. Nor is he entirely free from the traditional tendency of Chinese rulers to equate opposition with treason.

Chiang Ching-kuo was sixty-seven in 1977. He is unlikely to be as long-lived as his father, but could be in power for another ten years. A decade could provide the time needed to institutionalize the selection of his successor by a revitalized National Assembly and to confer a more important role on a Legislative Yuan with a majority of members elected from Taiwan. It may not be necessary to restructure the government in order to effect needed change. New Taiwanese wine can be poured into the old mainlander bottles. The Chinese have a talent for altering the substance of institutions without changing their form.

Taiwan has the important advantage of a strong, widely accepted leader, determined to prevent corruption and high living among government officials. It has a well-trained bureaucracy committed to and experienced in both promoting rapid economic growth and widely distributing the fruits of that growth. The defection of a PRC air force squadron leader with his MIG-19 in July 1977 gave a great boost to morale and strengthened the widespread conviction in Taiwan that conditions there are much better than on the mainland.

On balance, prospects for political stability on Taiwan look reasonably good. This optimistic prognostication could be upset, however, by the early death of Chiang Ching-kuo or by an abrupt, drastic change in US relations with the island. The government's efforts to maintain political stability would be much helped by a continuation of Taiwan's outstanding success in maintaining a high rate of economic growth.

The Economy of Taiwan

3

In setting their course through the troubled waters of the future, ROC leaders will benefit from Taiwan's dynamic economy. The economies of few developing countries have grown as rapidly as Taiwan's has over the past twenty-five years or spread the fruits of growth as evenly throughout the population. The emerging economic problems that the island will face during the coming years should be no more difficult than those surmounted in the past, provided Taiwan has continued access to foreign markets, raw materials, capital, and technology. The willingness of the United States, Japan, and other trading partners to maintain economic relations with Taiwan, the possibility of PRC interference, and even the long-range possibility of economic interchange between Taiwan and the mainland are all related to Taiwan's past economic progress, the present state of its economy, and the government's plans for the future .

Past Economic Progress

The island of Taiwan, 240 miles long and 60 to 90 miles wide, is about one-third the size of the state of Virginia. Its population has increased from 6 million in 1945, when the ROC took over the island, to about 17 million in 1977. With 436 persons per square kilometer, it is one of the most densely populated areas in the world, far exceeding the

Netherlands, which has 334 persons per square kilometer.[1]   Moreover, the bulk of the population is crowded into the one-fourth of the island's surface that is relatively level and arable; the other three-fourths, consisting of rugged mountains rising to over 13,000 feet, is sparsely populated.   Except for its fertile soil and favorable climate, Taiwan's only important natural resources are coal, natural gas, and water power, which together supply 29 percent of its commercial energy needs.[2]

Despite the paucity of natural resources, Taiwan's gross national product (GNP) increased in real terms by 8.8 percent annually during the twenty years from 1953 to 1972.   Moreover, the tempo of growth accelerated during the later years.   From 1953 to 1962, it averaged 7.2 percent, picking up to 10.4 percent from 1963 to 1972.   In 1973, growth hit 11.9 percent, then slumped to 0.6 and 2.8 percent in two subsequent years as a result of the worldwide recession.[3]   During the first half of 1976, it regained momentum as economic activity increased in its two principal markets, the United States and Japan, reaching 11.7 percent for the year.[4]

Exceptionally rapid economic growth permitted per capita income to rise also, from $132 in 1952 to $700 in 1975, despite the considerable increase in population.[5]   During the 1950s, the annual increase in population averaged 3.6 percent, but by 1975, it had fallen to 1.9 percent, as urbanization and improvements in public health conditions reduced the incentives to have many children, and the institution of an effective family planning program in the early 1960s made limitation of family size easier.[6]   Taiwan now has a higher per capita income than any other country in East Asia except Singapore and Japan.   Moreover, the increase in income was widely distributed throughout the population.   The ratio between the top 20 percent of income recipients compared to the bottom 20 percent fell from a disparity of 15 to 1 in the early 1950s to 5 to 1 by the late 1960s, at a time when the disparity was increasing to 16 to 1 in Mexico and 25 to 1 in Brazil.[7]

---

1. *TSDB*, p. 273.
2. Domestic production of coal has been declining since 1967, and hydroelectric power cannot be increased much beyond the present level, but production of natural gas, which supplied 9 percent of commercial energy in 1974, has been increasing slowly. *TSDB*, p. 85.
3. ROC Ministry of Economic Affairs, *Economic Development in the Republic of China*, April 1976, p. 7; *China News* (Taipei), May 27, 1976.
4. FBIS, *Daily Report, East Asia and Pacific*, Jan. 27, 1977, p. B1.
5. *Economic Development in the Republic of China*, p. 7. All dollar figures are US currency.
6. *TSDB*, p. 4.
7. James P. Grant, *Growth from Below: A People-Oriented Development Strategy* (Washington, D.C.: Overseas Development Council, December 1973), p. 23.   See also Yuan-Li Wu, *Income Distribution in the Process of Economic Growth of the Republic of*

Although living standards in Taiwan in most respects lag well behind those prevailing in the industrialized world, they have outstripped those in most developing nations, including the PRC. Public health has improved to the point where life expectancy is sixty-seven years for men and seventy-two for women, only slightly below that of the United States. Average daily calorie consumption exceeds that of the Japanese. In 1973, 95 percent of all families on Taiwan had electric lighting, although only 48 percent had piped water. More important, however, to the people of Taiwan than comparisons with other countries is their standard of living compared to ten years ago. For example, TV sets, which numbered 5 per 1000 population in 1965, increased to 60 by 1974. During the same period, the number of telephones per 1000 population increased from 13 to 57, automobiles from 3 to 15, and motorcycles from 5 to 91. Housing investment increased from 1.0 percent of GNP in 1952 to 3.2 percent in 1974.[8]

The high value placed by the Chinese on education is shown by the large proportion of young people in school and by the extension in 1968 of free public education from six years to nine years. In 1975–1976, 99 percent of all elementary school age children attended school. There were 289,000 students in colleges and universities, and the proportion of the total population engaged in acquiring higher education exceeded that of the United Kingdom.[9] The PRC, with fifty times the population of Taiwan, had only 584,000 students in colleges and universities in 1977.[10]

In order to achieve its high rate of growth, Taiwan's economy underwent extensive structural change. At each stage in its development, new problems and bottlenecks appeared, and difficult decisions had to be made by economic policy makers. Basic issues were often involved, such as what proportion of investment should go into agriculture as compared to industry or into government corporations as compared to private enterprises; what should be the relative emphasis on import substitution as compared to exports; what preferences should be given to heavy industry or light industry; or what incentives should be offered to foreign investors. Structural change continues in Taiwan,

---

China, University of Maryland School of Law, Occasional Papers/Reprints Series in Contemporary Asian Studies, no. 2 (Baltimore, 1977).
8. Economic Planning Council, *Social Welfare Indicators, Republic of China* (Taipei, 1975), pp. 31, 46–48, 75.
9. In 1971, Taiwan had 222,000 students in higher educational institutions, or 1.5 percent of the total population, while the UK had 529,000 students, or 0.9 percent of its total population. *TSDB,* pp. 4, 243; *United Nations Statistical Yearbook, 1974,* p. 840.) The difference is explained in part by the more rapid population growth in Taiwan, producing a larger proportion of young people.
10. *The New York Times,* Sept. 2, 1977.

and new problems and decisions lie ahead, which will be complicated by the changes that both have occurred and may yet occur in Taiwan's external political relations. An understanding of the reasons for the high growth rate achieved during the transformation of the economy in the past twenty-five years will contribute to an assessment of the island's uncertain future.

Agricultural Development

Under the Japanese, Taiwan was an agricultural colony, developed primarily to supply additional foodstuffs for the growing population of rapidly industralizing Japan. By carefully surveying land boundaries, registering and guaranteeing farm ownership, and reducing rents, the Japanese introduced greater incentive for the farmers to increase their production. An extensive network of agricultural experimental stations developed improved seeds and techniques. Farmers' associations were established to disseminate the new materials and methods, while flood control and irrigation works made possible a great expansion of irrigated land. The increasing use of fertilizer and pesticides further stimulated agricultural productivity. Improved ports, railways, and roads facilitated the export of Taiwan's agricultural products.

In 1939, Taiwan's highly productive farms were exporting large amounts of sugar, rice, tea, and bananas, mostly to Japan. The per capita value of Taiwan's external trade was thirty-nine times that of China and one and one-half times that of Japan itself.[11] Thus, when the ROC took over the island, its economic well-being already was significantly dependent on the export of agricultural products. The Japanese had begun developing hydroelectric power, petroleum refining, aluminum production, and a variety of light industries in Taiwan, especially during the 1930s, when the island was being converted into a base for Japan's expansion into Southeast Asia, but the economy remained predominantly agricultural. By 1952, after the ROC had repaired wartime damage and restored production to its prewar level, agriculture contributed 36 percent of the net domestic production, whereas industry contributed only 18 percent.[12]

Japan had created the basic mechanism through which the govern-

---

11. George W. Barclay, *Colonial Development and Population in Taiwan* (Princeton: Princeton University Press, 1954), p. 33, quoted in Maurice Meisner, "The Development of Formosan Nationalism," *China Quarterly*, no. 15 (July–September 1963): 95.
12. *TSDB*, p. 32.

ment efficiently managed the agricultural development of Taiwan. The government of the ROC took over the existing rural infrastructure but introduced changes and refinements to make the system respond to Taiwan's own needs rather than Japan's. A key instrument for effecting change was the Joint Sino-American Commission on Rural Reconstruction (JCRR). Established during the final days of the ROC on the China mainland, the JCRR, which originally had two American commissioners and three Chinese commissioners, served both as the de-facto ministry of agriculture of the national government and as the agricultural section of the US aid mission. This unique organization, existing outside the regular bureaucracy of both governments, was able to recruit a well-paid, highly skilled staff. With sizable amounts of US aid funds to disburse, it played an important role in introducing innovations in agriculture, expanding agricultural production, and improving the quality of rural life.[13]

The fundamental government action stimulating agricultural production was land reform, carried out between 1949 and 1957. In the first stage, rents were reduced from an average of 50 percent of the crop to a maximum of 37.5 percent. In the second stage, public land was sold to tenant families. In the third stage, the landlords were compelled to sell to the government all land exceeding 3 hectares of rice paddy or 6 hectares of dry land, and in turn the land was sold to the tenants. Tenants paid for the land in ten annual installments, while the landlords were compensated by the government in part in bonds redeemable in kind and in part by shares of stock in government enterprises confiscated from the Japanese. Cadastral surveys done by the Japanese provided the data necessary to implementing land reform. Politically, it was feasible to push land reform through quickly and smoothly because landowners received compensation for their land and because those who would have preferred not to sell, being Taiwanese, lacked the connections with the mainlander government that would have enabled them to resist, as has happened in other developing countries.

Land reform reduced the proportion of tenant farmers from 39 percent in 1949 to 17 percent in 1957 and to 9 percent by 1974. More than any other single measure it encouraged increased agricultural productivity, as the new owner-operators had strong incentives to increase their incomes by working longer hours, increasing multiple cropping, and adopting technological innovations. The great majority of individual farms were tiny by American standards, averaging less than 3 hectares, and this would present problems later, but in the 1950s and

---

13. Jacoby, *U.S. Aid to Taiwan*, pp. 62–63.

1960s such farms were well suited to the labor-intensive techniques that made effective use of underemployed rural labor, once appropriate incentives had been provided.[14]

Working through the JCRR and expanding the role of the network of farmers' associations, the government created an effective balance between official planning and guidance and the individual initiative of the thousands of independent farmers. The farmers' associations, membership in which was open to all families receiving 50 percent or more of their income from active farming, provided credit and purchasing, marketing, processing, and agricultural extension services to the farmers. The result was an extremely flexible agricultural system in which farmers were quick to perceive and take advantage of opportunities to increase their income by shifting their energies from one crop to another. For example, in the two years after Japan had lifted restrictions on the import of bananas and the Taiwan government had modified its regulations so that the middlemen got less and growers got more of the proceeds from the sale of bananas, banana production in Taiwan more than doubled, and the yield per hectare increased by over 50 percent.[15] The cultivation of mushrooms for canning and export, begun in 1963 with 38,000 metric tons the first year, increased to 52,000 metric tons by 1968. Asparagus production, first begun in 1954 with 600 metric tons, also increased to 52,000 metric tons by 1968.[16] The export of canned mushrooms and aspargus had a combined value of $82 million by 1971.[17] These dramatic results were made possible by a system that combined government action to provide needed market information, credit, and technical advice to both growers and processors with the freedom by farmers to make individual decisions as to what they would grow.

One additional instrument employed by the government to manage agriculture in Taiwan was the controversial rice-fertilizer barter system, by which the government through the farmers' associations acquired rice and provided fertilizer at a fixed ratio between the two products. The system was controversial because the government in effect sold fertilizer

---

14. In 1955, 96 percent of the 790,000 landowning families owned less than 3 hectares. Kuo-shu Liang and Teng-hui Lee, "Taiwan," in Shinichi Ichimura, ed., *The Economic Development of East and Southeast Asia* (Honolulu: University of Hawaii Press, for Center for Southeast Asian Studies, Kyoto University, 1974), p. 312. See also *TSDB*, p. 54.

15. Banana production in 1963 was 132,000 metric tons, increasing to 460,000 by 1965 and 654,000 by 1967. *TSDB*, p. 59.

16. *TSDB*, p. 61.

17. Walter P. Falcon, "Lessons and Issues in Taiwan's Development," in T. H. Shen, ed., *Agriculture's Place in the Strategy of Development: The Taiwan Experience* (Taipei: Joint Commission on Rural Reconstruction, 1974), p. 275.

to farmers at a high price and obtained rice at a low price, thus giving the farmers a lower income than they would have received if the free market mechanism had been allowed to operate. Yet this arrangement had important advantages. Most important from the viewpoint of Chiang Kai-shek, who on the mainland in the late 1940s had experienced catastrophic inflation which the government was totally unable to control, was the fact that the rice-fertilizer barter system provided the government with ample supplies of rice to take care of the armed forces and civilian government employees and their dependents as well as to dispose of on the open market as a means of influencing prices. The government's control over the price of rice was important in enabling the ROC to hold the average annual price increase between 1953 and 1974 to 7.5 percent, a better record than that of many developing countries.[18]

Another important advantage of the rice-fertilizer barter system was to provide a means of withdrawing resources from agriculture to help finance industry. Moreover, it guaranteed to all farmers, rich and poor, both access to fertilizer and credit and a lessening of price risk.[19] By 1973, however, economic development had advanced to the stage where the government felt it could accomplish the purposes of the rice-fertilizer barter system by other means, so the system was abolished.

Agricultural Contribution to Industrialization

The ROC did not make the early mistake common to many developing countries of devoting all of its attention to industrializing, while neglecting rural development. The efforts devoted to improving agriculture paid off richly in the contribution that agriculture was then able to make to overall economic development. The average annual increase in agricultural production of 5.6 percent from 1953 to 1970 exceeded the rate of population growth by a comfortable margin, providing ample quantity and increased variety of foodstuffs for the island's needs, as well as industrial raw materials and growing amounts of agricultural products for export.[20] Although Taiwan imported increasing

---

18. *TSDB*, pp. 161, 299.
19. Falcon, "Lessons and Issues in Taiwan's Development," p. 277.
20. Liang and Lee, "Taiwan," p. 299. Figure for agricultural increase includes crops. forest and fishery products, and livestock. From 1952 to 1970, per capita daily food consumption increased from 2078 to 2662 calories and protein intake from 49 to 72 grams. Foreign exchange earned by agricultural exports increased from $114 million in 1952 to $626 million in 1972. T. H. Shen, "The Mechanism for Agricultural Planning," in Shen, *Agriculture's Place in the Strategy of Development*, pp. 35, 37.

amounts of wheat, corn, soybeans, and dairy products—amounting to $535 million in 1974—to satisfy the needs of a burgeoning livestock industry and the changing tastes of consumers, the island remained basically self-sufficient in foodstuffs.[21]

In addition to providing for the food needs of the island and a surplus to export, Taiwan's rural economy supplied a substantial share of the resources needed to finance industrialization. The transfer of resources was accomplished in several ways: by government taxation, by payments to landlords and moneylenders, through farmers' savings deposited voluntarily in financial institutions and invested in the non-agricultural sector, and by the terms of trade between farm and factory products, which were unfavorable to the farmer throughout the period 1950–1969. Not only did agriculture play a vital role in providing capital for industry, but exports of agricultural products financed at least one-half of total imports during the early period of industrialization, 1953–1962, when the effective constraint on Taiwan's development was a shortage of foreign exchange.[22]

Despite the heavy squeeze on agriculture, causing substantially more resources to flow out of that sector than to flow in, agricultural production continued to increase at a satisfactory rate, and the farmer's per capita income, although lower than that of the nonagricultural population, increased fairly steadily at a rate commensurate with that of the nonagricultural population until the mid-1960s. With this additional income, the rural population, constituting around one-half of the total population from 1952 to 1962, made another important contribution to industrialization by providing an expanding market for industrial products.

The agricultural sector also contributed to industrialization by providing labor. Underemployment in the countryside together with the attraction of higher wages in industry drew some 824,000 farm laborers into industry from 1953 to 1970, supplying 47 percent of the labor increase in the nonagricultural sector.[23]

By 1975, the place of agriculture in Taiwan's economy was much diminished compared to 1952. The proportion of the total population engaged in agriculture had fallen from 52 percent to 35 percent. The contribution of agriculture to the net domestic product declined from 36 percent to 16 percent.[24] Moreover, the proportion of farm income

---

21. Economic Advisory Office, Ministry of Economic Affairs, *Economic Indicators, Taiwan, Republic of China,* 1975. Foodstuffs valued at $535 million formed a relatively small part of Taiwan's total imports in 1974 of nearly $7 billion.
22. Liang and Lee, "Taiwan," pp. 304–308, 322.
23. Ibid., p. 304.
24. TSDB, pp. 32, 53.

derived from agriculture declined from 82 percent in 1966 to 59 percent in 1973, reflecting both the difficulty of further increasing agricultural income from small fixed plots of land and the opportunities for members of farm families to take jobs in industry.[25]

The Rise of Industry

Stimulated by an inflow of US economic aid averaging $100 million a year between 1951 and 1965 and by the input of resources from the agricultural sector, industrial production in Taiwan increased at an average annual rate of 14.4 percent during the entire period 1953–1974. During the first half of the period, it averaged 12.2 percent, but accelerated to 17.2 percent during the second half. Industrial production as a proportion of net domestic product rose from 11 percent to 31 percent.[26] Industry expanded in ways that changed the structure of the economy, with private enterprise replacing government-owned factories as the dominant form of industrial production, and industrial products outstripping agricultural products to become the principal exports.

The ROC had taken over from the Japanese not only the public utilities supplying electricity, gas, and water to the island but also a number of large industrial plants producing petroleum products, fertilizer, aluminum, and other manufactures. Consequently, in 1952 government-owned corporations were responsible for 57 percent of industrial production, while private enterprise produced only 43 percent. As the result of an early government decision, encouraged by the US aid mission, to rely for industrialization primarily on stimulating private enterprise rather than on expanding publicly owned industry, 77.3 percent of industrial production came from private factories by 1975 and only 22.7 percent from government plants.[27]

One direct measure to expand private industry was the early transfer to private hands of cement, timber, mining, and pulp and paper companies that had been taken over by the government from the Japanese. The transfer was accomplished by turning over stock in the companies to landlords as part of their compensation for lands surrendered to tenants under the land reform program. The decision to emphasize private enterprise was influenced by the dominant view

25. JCRR, *Taiwan Nung Yeh Fa Chan Chih Hui Ku Yü Ch'ien Chan* (*The Past and Future of Taiwan's Agricultural Development*) (Taipei: 1975), p. 16.
26. *TSDB*, p. 32.
27. Ibid., p. 79.

among ROC economic policy makers that at Taiwan's stage of economic development in the 1950s and 1960s light industry should be favored over heavy industry. Private entrepreneurs, who proved highly competent at producing a wide variety of light industrial products, lacked both the capital and the managerial skills to undertake the more complicated task of building and operating heavy industry, such as an integrated steel mill. Essential to a strategy oriented toward private enterprise was improvement of the investment climate, which the government accomplished through various measures such as simplifying government regulations, relaxing controls, increasing the availability of loans, and offering tax incentives for investment.

During the 1950s, the government concentrated primarily on the establishment and expansion of industries to supply the domestic market, especially for the production of fertilizer and other essentials for increasing agricultural output. Inflation, which seriously hampered saving and investment in the early 1950s, was brought under control by 1960, and for twelve years thereafter the annual rise in wholesale prices averaged only 2 percent.[28] Also vital to the growth of industry was the expansion of the economic infrastructure of the island, including electric power, railways, roads, harbors, and telephone and telegraph. Forty-four percent of US aid funds were used for this purpose.[29]

The years 1956 to 1961 marked a critical turning point for the industrialization of Taiwan. The existence of the defense treaty with the United States, the substantial flow of economic and military aid, and the demonstration of US support in the offshore island crisis of 1958 engendered a growing sense of security. The halt in inflation restored public confidence in the currency, and the savings essential to rapid industrialization soared.[30] The domestic market for import substitutes was by this time saturated, and a decision was made to shift the emphasis of economic policy to exports. The government carried out a foreign exchange reform, liberalized imports, adopted a series of measures for directly aiding the establishment and expansion of export industries, and announced a program for the encouragement of foreign investment, including the creation of export processing zones where manufacturers could import their basic materials, process them, and export the finished products free of duty.

The results of the export encouragement program were impressive.

---

28. Ibid., p. 161.
29. Jacoby, *U.S. Aid to Taiwan,* p. 176.
30. From 1952 to 1962, savings as a percent of national income increased only from 5.2 to 7.5. The next year, they almost doubled and, by 1973, had increased to 32.3, exceeding Japan's exceptionally high figure of 30.9. Comparable figures for 1973 were: US 10.1; UK 7.9; Italy 13.6; Netherlands 22.1. *TSDB,* p. 281.

From 1961 to 1973, the annual rate of growth of exports averaged 30 percent, although it dropped sharply under the impact of world recession to 25 percent in 1974 and −6 percent in 1975 but rebounded with an increase of nearly 40 percent in 1976.[31] Imports exceeded exports in most years, the deficit being covered mainly by US economic aid until 1965 and, later, by an inflow of long-term capital from other sources. By 1970, the ROC had accumulated foreign exchange reserves valued at $624 million, equivalent to more than five months of imports, helping to stabilize the exchange rate and establish the creditworthiness of the ROC in the world.[32]

As Taiwan's foreign trade increased, its composition changed. In 1952, agricultural products constituted 22 percent, processed agricultural products (mostly sugar) 70 percent, and industrial products only 8 percent. By 1974, 84 percent of Taiwan's exports were industrial products and 16 percent agricultural or processed agricultural products. Moreover, not only the quantity but also the variety of Taiwan's exports expanded greatly. For example, both the export of canned foods, which in 1952 amounted to only 3 percent of the value of sugar exports, and fisheries products, which were not exported at all at that time, by 1973 surpassed sugar exports, which themselves had more than trebled in value.[33]

The composition of Taiwan's imports likewise changed greatly over this period. In 1952, consumption goods constituted 20 percent of imports, agricultural and industrial raw materials 67 percent, and capital goods 13 percent. By 1975, consumption goods had dropped to 7 percent of total imports, agricultural and industrial raw materials amounted to 61 percent, and capital goods had increased to 32 percent. By becoming more self-sufficient in consumer goods, Taiwan was now able to divert larger amounts of foreign exchange to the purchase of the capital equipment needed for the continued expansion of the industrial plant.[34]

Taiwan has been heavily dependent on the United States and Japan for both imports and exports; in the early 1950s, these two countries accounted for as much as 80 percent of Taiwan's imports and 64 percent of its exports. By 1974, Taiwan had diversified both markets

---

31. Ibid., p. 179; Mei-tsun Wu, *Investment and Trade Climate in the Republic of China,* Apr. 7, 1977 (processed).
32. Liang and Lee, "Taiwan," p. 286. By December 1976, foreign exchange reserves had risen to $3.5 billion, the highest level on record. *The New York Times,* Jan. 30, 1977.
33. *TSDB,* pp. 182, 197; *The New York Times,* Jan. 30, 1977. The next year, 1974, sugar exports more than trebled again because of a temporary world sugar shortage and skyrocketing sugar prices.
34. *TSDB,* p. 183.

and sources of supply, but nearly one-third of its imports continued to come from Japan and over one-third of its exports went to the United States. These two nations together still accounted for over 50 percent of Taiwan's total trade.

Until 1962, the industrialization of Taiwan depended substantially on the inflow of foreign capital, particularly on the availability of US aid to build the economic infrastructure essential to industrialization.[35] From 1952 through 1962, the contribution of US aid and other foreign capital to gross domestic capital formation averaged 40 percent annually. From 1963 to 1970, it dropped to an average of 6 percent and thereafter became negative, as the capital outflow for repayment of loans increased.[36] Although the amount of foreign capital being invested in Taiwan is less important then it was in the 1950s and 1960s in light of the growing amounts of domestically generated capital available, temporary access to foreign loans has been very important to Taiwan's balance of payments, as in 1974, when Taiwan was hard hit by the sudden increase in oil prices and the shrinkage of its overseas markets.[37] Moreover, foreign direct investment has been an effective means of upgrading Taiwan's technology and management skills and marketing its products, and foreign loans have contributed substantially in the 1970s to financing the expansion of capital-intensive industrial projects and further expansion of the economic infrastructure.

Industrial Problems and Policies

Taiwan's solid record of past economic achievement and the present state of its economy encourage cautious optimism as the island faces the unprecedented political problems that loom ahead. An ef-

---

35. The rapid growth of manufacturing was critically dependent on the ability of the power industry to increase its production of electricity rapidly enough to satisfy the demands of both the factories and the growing number of residential consumers. In 1974, industry consumed 77 percent of electric power, commercial establishments 3 percent, and residences 20 percent. US economic aid in the early period and later loans from the World Bank and US Export-Import Bank made possible a 14-fold increase in electricity production from 1.4 million KWH in 1952 to 20.5 million KWH in 1974. *Essentials of the Taiwan Provincial Administration, 1975* (Taichung: Taiwan Provincial Government), pp. 52, 54.
36. *TSDB*, p. 46.
37. The average annual net capital inflow in 1969–1973 was only $42.8 million, a relatively insignificant contribution to gross domestic capital formation, which rose from $1.2 to $1.8 billion during this five-year period. Yet the $883 million net capital inflow in 1974 helped to cover an exceptionally large deficit in payments for goods and services of $1.1 billion. *TSDB*, pp. 45, 172.

ficient agriculture, which makes the island largely self-sufficient in food, and an increasingly diversified light industry, oriented toward the export market, form a sound base on which to build. An ample supply of labor for further industrial expansion is assured from the entry into the labor force of those born during the period of high population growth up to the mid-1960s, as well as through the further transfer of labor from low-paid service jobs and from agriculture, provided that productivity in agriculture can be increased by mechanization. A high savings rate is likely to continue to provide adequate domestic investment resources. The people of Taiwan have become used to increased rewards for hard work in the form of rising living standards. Both management and labor are becoming increasingly skilled, while government leaders and the bureaucracy are experienced in and dedicated to promoting economic growth.

In certain respects, Taiwan today is where Japan was in 1960. Like Japan, Taiwan is a crowded island state, almost totally lacking domestic supplies of raw materials for industry. It is even more dependent than Japan on foreign trade because of its much smaller domestic market. In 1973, exports constituted 44 percent of Taiwan's GNP, but only 10.8 percent of Japan's.[38]

At 1.8 percent, Taiwan's annual rate of population increase, although declining, was higher than Japan's 1.0 percent in 1960.[39] The distribution of Taiwan's labor force in 1975, however, was approaching that of Japan in 1960, with 37 percent in agriculture, forestry, and fisheries, 24 percent in industry, and 40 percent in services and other, compared to Japan's 30 percent, 29 percent, and 41 percent, respectively.[40] The composition of Taiwan's principal exports in 1974 was also similar to that of Japan in 1960. For both, the leading export was textile products, representing 28 percent of total exports in Taiwan and 30 percent in Japan. Next came electrical and other machinery, at 22 percent in Taiwan and 23 percent in Japan, followed by agricultural and fishery products, at 10 percent in Taiwan and 6 percent in Japan, and by primary manufactures, at 9 percent in Taiwan and 4 percent in Japan. Only in the export of basic metals was Taiwan's 1974 level substantially behind Japan in 1960, at 2 percent compared to 10 percent.[41] Taiwan proportionately had almost as many children in secondary school in 1974 as Japan had in 1960, amounting to 9 percent of

38. *TSDB*, p. 177; *Economic Indicators;* Hugh Patrick and Henry Rosovsky, eds., *Asia's New Giant* (Washington, D.C.: Brookings Institution, 1976), p. 939.
39. *TSDB*, p. 4; *UN Statistical Yearbook*, 1961, p. 31.
40. *TSDB*, p. 9; Patrick and Rosovsky, *Asia's New Giant*, p. 591.
41. J. A. Mathieson, "Taiwan's International Trade and Economic Structure," unpub. ms. submitted to Economic Planning Council, Taipei, February 1976, Table 2.

the population compared to 10 percent. But it had a much larger proportion of the population studying in higher educational institutions in 1974 than Japan had in 1960, amounting to 1.7 percent compared to 0.7 percent, although Japan's level rose to 1.7 percent by 1971.[42] Taiwan's savings in 1973 at 32.3 percent were a somewhat higher proportion of national income than Japan's 27.7 percent in 1960.[43]

By the beginning of the 1970s, Taiwan had come to a turning point in its economic development, requiring fundamental decisions as important as those taken during the critical 1959–1961 period when the economy was put on course for the high growth achieved during the subsequent decade. At that time, the ROC's farsighted economic policy makers were able to rely on a continuing flow of US economic aid for a few more years to serve as a cushion and a means of added leverage to enable them to push through needed reforms. Today, they are on their own but can draw on the confidence born of successful accomplishment. Some of the decisions required to bring about extensive structural change in the economy have already been taken; others lie ahead. There are differences within the leadership as to the specifics of policy, but there seems to be a consensus on the main lines that Taiwan's future development should take.

The first important change needed is a drastic upgrading of transportation facilities to support further economic expansion. By 1970, rapid industrialization and the growth of foreign trade had clogged the harbors, highways, railways, and airports of the island. Large investments were needed to ease these bottlenecks if economic growth was not to be seriously hampered. Consequently, decisions were made in the late 1960s and early 1970s to build a new port at Taichung to serve central Taiwan and relieve congestion at Keelung in the north and Kaohsiung in the south; to build a north-south freeway from Keelung to Kaohsiung to increase highway capacity and cut travel time in half; to electrify the west coast mainline railway to reduce running time and oil consumption and increase carrying capacity; to build a new international airport at Taoyuan, 18 miles from Taipei, to increase the capacity for passenger and freight handling; and to expand Suao harbor on the east coast and link it by railway to the principal east coast port of Hualien, thus giving Hualien a railway connection with the west coast. Work on these projects began between 1971 and 1975, all of which are scheduled to be completed by 1981.

A long-range program for greater power expansion is also es-

---

42. *TSDB*, pp. 4, 243; *UN Statistical Yearbook*, 1961, pp. 31, 619; *UN Statistical Yearbook*, 1974, pp. 70, 830.
43. *TSDB*, p. 281.

sential to industrial expansion. Even before the sudden jump in oil prices in 1973–1974, Taiwan had decided to rely primarily on nuclear power plants for increasing its production of electricity. Three plants are to be completed by 1984. Construction of the first was begun in 1970; the first of its two generating units came on line in 1977. Construction of the second plant began in 1975. When all three are completed, they will have an installed capacity of over 5 million kilowatts, exceeding Taiwan's total installed capacity in 1974.

Taiwan's industry, supported by the increased power supply and improved transportation network, will be entering a new phase within the next few years. The government will stress and encourage capital-intensive and technology-intensive industries and de-emphasize the labor-intensive industries that have provided the main stimulus to rapid industrial expansion in the past. The chief symbols of the new emphasis are an integrated steel mill, a petrochemical complex, and a large shipyard, all being built in the Kaohsiung area.

For many years, Taiwan resisted that talisman of industrialization for many developing countries, the integrated steel mill, as not justified economically by the size of Taiwan's market. Now, however, with the annual steel consumption of the island up to 2.7 million tons, the large investment required for an integrated steel mill can be justified. Construction began in 1973 on a mill for the China Steel Corporation, a government corporation, which is to produce 1.5 million tons of steel in 1978 and is to be further expanded to a 6-million-ton capacity by the mid-1980s. Its purpose is not to produce steel bars and plates for export, as South Korea does, but to provide steel to a group of satellite factories, including the new shipyard next door, which will produce finished products for export. With wages only one-third those in Japan, the latest equipment, and a tidewater location, the mill should be able to undersell the Japanese in the Taiwan market.

The petrochemical complex, built around the existing petrochemical facilities operated by the government-owned China Petroleum Corporation, will produce a variety of raw materials now mainly imported from Japan and used by domestic manufacturers of plastics, synthetic fiber, synthetic rubber, and other petroleum-based products. Some of the new plants are being built by the China Petroleum Corporation, others by private investors, domestic and foreign, including Union Carbide. The complex, to be completed by 1978, will not only reduce Taiwan's dependence on imported intermediates but also provide a surplus for export.

The third major heavy industrial enterprise is the Kaohsiung shipyard, started in 1973 and completed in 1975. It is owned by the China Shipbuilding Corporation, a joint venture participated in by the government, Gatx Oswego Corporation of the United States, and several other foreign investors. It has one of the largest dry docks in the world, capable of constructing tankers up to 1 million tons. The first of two 450,000-ton tankers ordered from the yard was launched in 1977. Although the market for large tankers has collapsed and is unlikely to recover for several years, the shipyard probably will be able to survive this period by building other types of ships and doing repairs.

When Chiang Ching-kuo became premier in 1972, he combined these ten projects—some of which were under way, others in the planning stage—into an integrated program entitled the Ten Major Development Projects, the total cost of which was estimated as of early 1975 at $6.5 billion. Of that total, 36 percent was to come from loans from international banking institutions, 28 percent from the national treasury, 27 percent from domestic loans, and 8 percent from companies investing.[44] Initially there was concern among economic policy makers at the heavy burden the program would place on the government budget and the risk of adding to inflationary pressure in the overheated economy of 1972–1973. In fact, however, the program proved an effective counter-recession instrument in 1974 and 1975, and the government was able to meet the costs from reserves accumulated during previous years of conservative fiscal policies. Taiwan, which had a good credit rating abroad, encountered no difficulty in obtaining the necessary loans from foreign financial institutions. Not only did the Ten Major Development Projects provide needed employment, but the government was also able to use the program effectively to symbolize Taiwan's progress to the public. Continuous press and TV coverage of the program, including frequent visits by the premier to check on the progress of one or another project, has projected an image of economic dynamism in Taiwan.[45]

The planned shift from labor-intensive to more sophisticated technology-intensive industries is necessary for several reasons. First, rising wages in Taiwan will make the island's labor-intensive export products less competitive with those of lower-wage countries such as South Korea, Thailand, Malaysia, and the Philippines.[46] Although Taiwan's leading export product, textiles, probably can continue to

---

44. *Ten Major Construction Projects* (Taipei: China Publishing, July 1975), p. 1.
45. Based on interviews with economic officials, US embassy officers, journalists, and others in Taiwan, October 1975, May–June 1976, April 1977. Typical of the impression made by the program on the common man was that of a taxi driver and former military officer who, on his own initiative, launched into an enthusiastic recital of the Ten Major Projects.
46. South Korea is today Taiwan's most aggressive competitor, especially in textiles, the leading export for each country. As of August 1975, comparative monthly wages for textile workers were $86 in Taiwan and $66 in South Korea. Mathieson, "Taiwan's International Trade and Economic Structure," p. 14. A survey by Japan's Sanwa Bank shows comparative general wage levels as: Japan 100; Hong Kong 40; Taiwan 25; South Korea 20.4. *Japan Times*, Aug. 6, 1977, p. 9.

expand its markets for a number of years, especially if manufacturers concentrate on higher value products, it must eventually lose ground because of rising wages, just as Japan's textile industry has. Second, Taiwan will gain a larger proportion of the value added to an export product to the extent that it becomes able to provide itself with the basic steel and chemical products needed by its industry. Third, by expanding heavy industry and increasing the sophistication and variety of its electronic and machine-building industries, Taiwan can become more self-reliant, especially in its ability to produce modern military equipment. Finally, a continuing transfer of labor from relatively low productivity jobs to higher productivity jobs will be needed to ensure continued economic growth and rising living standards.

The structural transformation of Taiwan's industry will take a decade or more. The government has begun to modify its policies to favor investment in capital-intensive over labor-intensive industries. A continued inflow of foreign capital will be needed to ease the burden on the balance of payments, facilitate the introduction of new technology, and help finance large projects too big for local private capital. The government no doubt also sees foreign investment as a means of strengthening Taiwan's political position. For all these reasons, the government will seek to maintain a favorable investment climate.

Structural change will also require policies to encourage the creation of some large-scale diversified companies. The typical family-owned, small-scale Taiwan enterprise has proved adequate for the relatively simple industries of today, but it will not suffice for the more complex and sophisticated industries of the future. Bigger companies will be better able to raise the large amounts of capital needed for more costly machinery, as well as to engage in market research, product development, and aggressive marketing. Some government officials advocate an increasing reliance on government corporations for these purposes, citing as precedents government investment in the integrated steel mill, the shipyard, and the petrochemical complex. But a reversal of the past policy of relying primarily on the expansion of private industry as the engine of economic growth could make the economy less flexible and less responsive to changes in international economic conditions and thus retard economic growth in this heavily export-dependent economy.

One conceivable way for Taiwan to reduce its dependence on others is to discover sizable quantities of oil or gas on the island or offshore. The production of natural gas, which has been slowly increasing over the years, was equivalent in energy terms in 1974 to 14 percent of Taiwan's import of crude oil and petroleum products. Its production of crude oil was negligible, amounting to less than 2 percent of its imported crude oil and petroleum products. Nevertheless, geologic and seismic studies of Taiwan and offshore areas indicate the likely presence of more oil and gas. Consequently, the China Petroleum Corporation entered into joint ventures with Gulf Oil for undersea exploration north of Taiwan and with Amoco and Conoco for exploration southwest of Taiwan, but results so far have been discouraging. One well drilled in the southwest area in 1974 showed promising amounts of gas and condensate, but further drilling has failed to confirm the existence of a commercially exploitable field. Although the discovery of sizable amounts of oil in the Taiwan Strait would be of great economic significance for Taiwan and a tremendous psychological boost, it's development would require massive investment. Moreover, the PRC also claims the undersea resources in the Taiwan Strait and might not tolerate the undisturbed exploitation of oil there by the ROC.

The skills of both management and labor will have to improve to meet the demands of the rising level of industrial technology in Taiwan. The government has been aware of this need for some time and has begun to reshape educational programs to cope with it. The number of persons in school, amounting to 27 percent of the total population, has reached its peak and will decline in the future. In the spring of 1976, for the first time the number of students registering for college entrance examinations fell. The need now is not to increase the quantity of students being educated but to improve their quality. The educational system has expanded so rapidly in recent years that in many schools the quality of teaching is low. To improve the teaching and to reshape the educational system so that graduates at all levels are better able to meet the requirements of a changing society will be slow and difficult.

One area in which exceptional progress has occurred is in vocational training. In 1972, the ratio of students in academic or college-preparatory high schools to those in vocational schools was 6 to 4. Parents had a strong bias in favor of training their children for college rather than for a vocation. But the realization that more jobs were available for vocational school graduates, the limitation of the number admitted to college, and the government efforts to educate parents on the merits of vocational education have turned the situation around. As of 1976, the ratio of those in academic high schools to those in vocational schools had fallen to 3.2 to 6.8.[47]

47. Interview with Education Minister Y. S. Tsiang, June 1976. There are six categories of vocational schools: agriculture, industry, commerce, marine products, nursing and midwifery, and home economics. The changing structure of Taiwan's economy is shown by the percentage distribution of students in vocational schools, which in 1950–1951 was agricultural 35, industrial 26, commercial 32, others 10, and in

Advanced training for those who choose technical vocational schools and technical junior colleges in preference to college or university education is provided by the National Taiwan Institute of Technology, established in 1974. It accepts graduates of vocational schools or technical colleges who have completed their military service and have at least one year of practical work experience. Graduates of junior colleges receive their engineering degree in two years, graduates of vocational schools in four. The institute is designed to provide more practical training than the engineering colleges of universities and offers courses tailored to the needs of Taiwan's industries. It enrolled 178 students in the first year and expects to have 2000 by 1980.[48]

Agricultural Problems and Policies

By 1970, Taiwan had reached a turning point not only in the development of industry but also in the development of agriculture. It was becoming increasingly clear that the agricultural policies that for two decades had been so successful in increasing agricultural production, providing resources for industrialization, and raising the farmers' standard of living were becoming less effective. In 1968, the absolute number of farm workers began to decline.[49] The cost of farm labor rose, as did the other expenses of operating a farm. For some time, farm income had been declining relative to nonfarm income. Although the real income of farm families increased 94 percent from 1952 to 1967, the per capita income of farm families from all sources, which had been 75 percent of that of nonfarm families in 1954, dropped to 58 percent by 1968.[50] Clearly, new policies were needed to halt this slide in order to increase agricultural production further and to allay dissatisfaction on the part of farmers.

1974–1975 was agricultural 5, industrial 46, commercial 42, others 8. Ministry of Education, *Educational Strategies of the Republic of China*, 1975, p. 16.

48. The Institute of Technology is headed by Ch'en Li-an, son of the late vice-president, Ch'en Ch'eng, an engineer trained at MIT and New York University who worked for Honeywell in New York City before returning to Taiwan to become director of the institute. The institute has departments of industrial management, electronic engineering, mechanical engineering, textile engineering, construction engineering, chemical engineering, and electrical engineering.

49. The United States reached this point in the 1930s, Japan in 1955. Falcon, "Lessons and Issues in Taiwan's Development," p. 279; Patrick and Rosovsky, *Asia's New Giant*, p. 130.

50. T. H. Shen, "A New Agricultural Policy," and Terry Y. H. Yu and C. S. Lee, "Agricultural Technology and Income Distribution in Taiwan," in Shen, *Agriculture's Place in the Strategy of Development*, pp. 39, 229.

The five basic objectives of the government's agricultural policy had not changed. They were to increase production at least at the rate of population growth and thereby maintain self-sufficiency in food for security reasons, to keep the price of rice relatively low and stable and thereby hold down other prices and prevent popular dissatisfaction, to maintain the small farm economy established by the land reform and thereby prevent the concentration of landed wealth in a few hands, to continue the rapid expansion of industry by shifting labor from agriculture to industry; and to reduce the gap between rural and urban incomes. But as the expansion of industry drained labor from agriculture, conflicts between these objectives became sharper, forcing difficult choices on the government. How could agricultural production be maintained if the rewards to those remaining on the farms continued to decline relative to those received by factory workers? If labor continued to leave the farms, could the productivity of the remaining workers be so improved that production continued to increase or even maintained its present level? But how could labor-saving machinery be introduced when farm units were too small to afford the capital investment? Could farm income be increased by raising the prices of farm products? Or would this create an unacceptable risk of inflation? How much could the gap between farm and urban income be narrowed without slowing the flow of labor from farms and creating a labor shortage in the factories?

By 1969, the government recognized that new measures were needed. It took steps to promote farm mechanization, alter the rice-fertilizer barter ratio in favor of the farmers, and reduce the taxes and interest rates paid by farmers. But the rise in farm wages to some extent offset these gains. Thus, although the incomes of farm families had improved by 1972 to 66 percent of those of nonfarm families, the increase came in considerable measure from a rise in the nonfarm income of farm families.[51]

In 1972, Premier Chiang Ching-kuo embarked on a more far-reaching program to improve the lot of the rural population. The rice-fertilizer barter system was abolished, making the prices of these products more subject to market forces, although the government continued to maintain large rice stocks and intervened in the market to influence prices. Agricultural taxes were further reduced and the terms of agricultural loans eased. An appropriation of $62.5 million was made for a two and one-half year program of constructing dikes, roads, and irrigation facilities; accelerating the introduction of new technology, including the mechanization of farming; establishing spe-

---

51. Shen, "A New Agricultural Policy," p. 39.

cialized crop areas; strengthening research and extension work; and in other ways seeking to improve conditions for agriculture. An additional $50 million was appropriated for the program in fiscal 1976. But agricultural specialists doubt that these measures go far enough to provide the needed stimulus to agriculture.[52]

A basic obstacle to improving the productivity of Taiwan's farmers is the small size of the farm. In 1972, the average farm was only 0.84 hectares, and more than 40 percent of the farmers had less than 0.5 hectares.[53] A power tiller, the most important labor-saving device usable on Taiwan's small farms, is too costly for the average farmer. Moreover, the average farmer lacks the skills to keep the machine in good working order. The government has taken a number of steps to overcome these problems: it has offered long-term low-interest loans for purchasing power tillers and other farm machinery, improved the quality and lowered the price of Taiwan-produced machines, established mechanization promotion centers to help farmers maintain machines, and encouraged the formation of farm machine teams to do plowing, transplanting, spraying, and harvesting for neighboring farmers for a fee.

Whether or not such measures alone can successfully mechanize Taiwan's farms is questionable. Larger farm units are needed to take advantage of economies of scale, in regard not only to mechanization but also to modernized marketing, accounting, and other agricultural techniques. The government has been experimenting since 1964 with a program of joint farming operations, extending special assistance to families who combine their efforts in groups as large as 30–40 families to farm together 20-hectare units. The system differs from that on the China mainland, in that each family retains title to land, tools, and produce from its own fields. But members of all families work as a team and receive wages agreed upon by the group. Studies by the JCRR indicate that joint operations increase both labor productivity and yield

---

52. The $50 million appropriation for accelerating agricultural production and rural development in FY76 is small compared to the $750 million annually which the Ministry of Economic Affairs proposes to invest in the 13 government corporations from 1978 to 1981. Of this amount, some $340 million annually is to go to the Taiwan Power Corporation alone. *China News,* June 15, 1976. Nevertheless, the ratio of total investment in agriculture to investment in the nonagricultural sector, which declined steadily for many years and reached a low of 5.88 percent in 1970, turned around the next year and rose to 9.79 percent by 1973. JCRR, *Taiwan Nung Yeh Fa Chan,* p. 12. See also Falcon, "Lessons and Issues in Taiwan's Development," pp. 268–284; *Far Eastern Economic Review,* Dec. 5, 1975, pp. 41–45; Sung-hsing Wang and Raymond Apthorpe, *Rice Farming in Taiwan: Three Village Studies* (Taipei: Academia Sinica, 1974), pp. 194–212.

53. Yu and Lee, "Agricultural Technology and Income Distribution in Taiwan," p. 227.

per hectare. By 1971, 3561 farmers had been organized into 490 joint farming groups, but this is a negligible proportion of Taiwan's 879,000 farm families.[54] The use of farm machinery, which has been increasing slowly, is still beyond reach of the great majority of farmers. By 1974, 43,000 power tillers were in use, 120,000 pumps, 45,000 power sprayers, and 204,000 hand sprayers.[55]

A few officials advocate making greater use of the agrobusiness concept pioneered in Taiwan by the government-owned Taiwan Sugar Corporation as a possible solution to the problem of mechanization. Although 70 percent of the sugar processed by the corporation is produced by private growers, the corporation owns the machines that do the harvesting. However, the agricultural experts in the JCRR do not favor extension of the agrobusiness concept to other crops. The majority view within the government appears to favor a pattern similar to that followed by Japan, where farm units are also small, although somewhat larger than those in Taiwan. In Japan, the income of farm families is on a par with that of nonfarm families, and farm families earn most of their income from nonfarm employment. Japan has thus become a nation of part-time farmers, and Taiwan is moving in the same direction.[56]

Japan has maintained a high level of rice production while releasing labor for industry largely through extensive mechanization of agriculture, especially by bringing the power tiller into general use. During the 1950s, these tillers were used mainly on the larger farms, but in the 1960s, they also came to be used widely on smaller farms of less than one hectare.[57] Power tillers were somewhat less expensive in Japan than in Taiwan, but the main reason that Japanese farmers have been better able to afford them has probably been the Japanese policy of heavily subsidizing agriculture. Japanese domestic price supports for major crops, principally rice, have been among the highest in the world.[58] But for Taiwan to adopt the Japanese policy of heavily subsidizing farmers and

---

54. T. H. Shen and Y. T. Wang, "Technological Adjustments," in Shen, *Agriculture's Place in the Strategy of Development,* pp. 382–88; *TSDB,* p. 54.

55. Taiwan Provincial Information Office, *T'ai Wan Kuang Fu San Shih Nien (Thirty Years After Taiwan's Restoration),* 1975, ch. 3, sec. 2, p. 18.

56. In Japan, only 40 percent of farm family income is from agriculture, compared to 59 percent in Taiwan. Patrick and Rosovsky, *Asia's New Giant,* p. 40. Both Taiwan and Japan, as a result of land reforms, have statutory limitations on the size of farms. In Japan, it is 3 hectares, except in Hokkaido where it is 12; in Taiwan, it is 3 hectares for paddy fields, 6 hectares for upland fields.

57. In 1970, 20 percent of Japan's labor force was in agriculture, forestry, and fisheries, compared to 37 percent in Taiwan in 1974. Kazushi Ohkawa and Henry Rosovsky, *Japanese Economic Growth: Trend Acceleration in the Twentieth Century* (Stanford: Stanford University Press, 1973), pp. 107, 311; *TSDB,* p. 16.

58. Japan spent $2.3 billion on farm price supports in FY74, compared to $3.5 billion for national defense. Patrick and Rosovsky, *Asia's New Giant,* p. 773.

allowing food prices to rise more rapidly than other prices in order to raise farm incomes and facilitate farm mechanization would go directly counter to the government's traditional policy of keeping the price of rice low to benefit the consumer. It could not go far in this direction without encountering anguished consumer protests.

Since abolishing the rice-fertilizer barter system, the government has raised the price paid to the farmer, while at the same time keeping the price low for the consumer. But this practice, if continued, promises to be an increasing burden on the treasury, which already worries some senior finance officials. Nevertheless, if agricultural production is to be increased, the gap between rural and urban incomes to be narrowed, and agriculture to continue to furnish the labor needed by expanding industry, the need to increase the proportion of resources invested in agriculture by one means or another is inescapable. The most feasible way may be to combine modest subsidization of the price of rice with subsidies for fertilizer, farm machinery, and other farm costs. In any case, the declining farm population can no longer provide the same flow of resources into the industrial sector as in the past, and there will have to be an increase in the reverse flow if the government's goals regarding agriculture and rural development are to be achieved.

The mechanization of agriculture to free labor for industry will simultaneously increase the incomes of those farm families some of whose members can be released from farm work for full-time or part-time industrial jobs. This trend will also make an important contribution to industrial growth, for the history of development in Japan and Taiwan demonstrates that even though the productivity of agricultural workers rises with mechanization, the productivity of industrial workers rises more rapidly. But in order to provide part-time industrial jobs for farmers, factories must be located near the farmers' homes. In this respect, Taiwan is better off than many developing countries, for most of its factories are small, and many are located in small towns and cities outside the five principal industrial cities.[59] The 1972 program for accelerated agricultural and rural development in Taiwan calls for encouraging the establishment of industrial plants in rural areas, but it is unlikely to be very effective unless the token amount of $780,000 allocated for this purpose in the initial two-year program is increased substantially in future years.

---

59. In the early 1960s, three-fourths of industrial jobs in Colombia were concentrated in the three largest cities, while in Taiwan only one-third of industrial jobs were located in the five largest cities. Edgar Owens, "The New Look in Development: Investing in People Is the Best Economics," paper presented in 1973 before Committee on Foreign Affairs of House of Representatives in a hearing on the Mutual Development and Cooperation Bill (H.R.8528), processed.

Planning and Prospects

A strong and stable government, capable of making and carrying out decisions affecting the economy, and a practice of planning ahead have been essential to Taiwan's economic progress. Beginning in 1953, the government developed a series of four-year plans. Taiwan does not have a "planned economy" like that of Communist countries, for the government has far less control over the largely free enterprise economy of Taiwan than Communist states have over their economies. Taiwan's four-year plans were intended as desirable goals for the island's economy and served as guides for economic policy makers. They were revised annually to conform to changing domestic and international conditions. The targets were conservative, and the economy usually exceeded them, especially during the period of rapid growth of industry and exports from 1965 to 1973. Since 1969, however, despite the program for accelerated agricultural development launched in that year, agricultural production has fallen short of the target.[60]

The surge in oil prices and the onset of world recession made the sixth four-year plan of 1973–1976 meaningless. It was scrapped and replaced by a six-year plan of 1976–1981, which is better able to accommodate the relatively long-term projects now under way. As of mid-1976, this plan envisaged a real annual growth rate of 7.5 percent during the plan period and an annual increase in per capita income of 5.8 percent. Agricultural growth is expected to average 2.5 percent a year, with the share of agricultural production in the gross domestic product dropping from 14 percent in 1975 to 10.5 percent in 1981 and the proportion of the labor force in agriculture declining from 31 percent in 1974 to 24 percent in 1981. Average annual growth in manufacturing is projected at 9.5 percent, with the proportion of capital-intensive industry increasing from 37 percent to 45 percent and that of light industry dropping from 63 percent to 55 percent. Exports are expected to increase at 12 percent annually, and an annual deficit of some $330 million is anticipated, owing to the large imports of capital goods needed during the plan period. Inflation will be held below 5 percent annually unless a rapid rise in world prices makes this impossible.[61]

The goals of the six-year plan are typically conservative and will probably be exceeded, as past plan targets were, unless political moves by Taiwan's principal trading partners seriously disrupt its economy.

---

60. Wanyong Kuo, "Economic Planning in Taiwan," in Shen, *Agriculture's Place in the Strategy of Development*, p. 258.
61. Economic Planning Council, Taipei, *The Six-Year Plan for Economic Development: An Outline*, preliminary, June 1976, processed.

Government leaders have some difficult choices to make in both industry and agriculture, but their past successes in handling tough problems provide grounds for confidence that they will manage reasonably well. The outlook, then, is for continued, fairly rapid growth, although slower than in the high growth years of the late 1960s and early 1970s and lower than Japan's high growth rate of the 1960s.

Although Taiwan in the mid-1970s had in important respects reached the position attained by Japan in 1960 and will probably be able to draw on some of the factors that contributed to Japan's extraordinary growth in the 1960s, it cannot expect to duplicate all of them. Its principal deficiency is its small domestic market, denying Taiwan the economies of scale that are believed to have accounted for as much as 20 percent of Japan's growth. In Japan, the largest contribution to growth, accounting for 27 percent of it, was made by capital investment. The doubling of Taiwan's savings from 16 percent to 32 percent of national income from the years 1965 to 1973 suggests that substantial amounts of domestic capital will be available for investment in the future, provided a high growth rate can be maintained. A decline in the growth rate brings savings down quickly, as shown by the drop to 23 percent of national income in 1975, the second year of recession.[62] The second largest contribution to Japan's growth, accounting for 25 percent, was made by advances in knowledge. Since Taiwan's present state of technology, business organization, and managerial practice is far behind that of Japan and the industrialized West, it has much to gain from acquiring such knowledge. A source important to Japan but not yet adequately tapped by Taiwan is the purchase of technology through licensing arrangements and payment of royalties. Taiwan has relied mainly on foreign direct investment to obtain foreign technology. Although foreign technology is more costly and less readily available for licensing than it was fifteen years ago, Taiwan would benefit from devoting more of its carefully husbanded foreign exchange to this end. Although the third most important growth source in Japan, economies of scale, can be drawn on far less in Taiwan, the fourth and fifth growth sources in Japan, additional hours worked and the shift of labor from less productive to more productive employment, accounting for 15 percent and 8.5 percent respectively, probably can make at least as great a proportional contribution to Taiwan's growth as they did to Japan's.[63]

Taiwan will probably grow more slowly than South Korea too, but not so much because South Korea's population is twice that of Taiwan as

---

62. *TSDB*, p. 47.
63. All estimates of factors accounting for Japan's growth rate are from Edward F. Denison and William K. Chung, *How Japan's Economy Grew So Fast* (Washington, D.C.: Brookings Institution, 1976), p. 48.

because the economic policy makers in Seoul are willing to risk a larger foreign debt and a higher rate of inflation in order to accelerate growth. Taiwan's conservative government holds to a balanced budget, a relatively low level of foreign indebtedness, and a stable exchange rate. Some leading economic officials favor devaluing the currency, as South Korea, Taiwan's chief competitor, has done frequently in recent years in order to improve the competitiveness of its exports. But such is the concern in Taiwan about inflation, probably growing in part out of the ROC's disastrous experience with galloping inflation during the late 1940s and more recently in 1974, when the consumer price index shot up 48 percent in a year, that Chiang Ching-kuo and some of his other economic advisers do not wish to risk the increased inflationary pressure that would result from devaluation.[64]

An even more important reason than past experience with inflation for following cautious economic policies is uncertainty about the future of Taiwan's international position. Consequently, Chiang Ching-kuo and other ROC leaders want to make the economy of the island as strong, stable, and self-sufficient as possible. Obviously, an island as dependent on foreign trade for its economic health as Taiwan is can never be self-sufficient without a catastrophic decline in living standards. But the government can reduce its vulnerability to outside shocks by following policies that hold down inflation, distribute income widely, and minimize dependence on outside capital.

The Taiwan of the future, as envisioned by the economic policy makers who are largely responsible for fashioning Taiwan's modernizing economic system, will be a medium-sized, industrialized, increasingly affluent society. These policy makers see Taiwan as ultimately fulfilling the role of a Sweden or Switzerland, relying heavily on the export of high technology items. Taiwan has a long way to go, but it is making substantial progress. There are no inherent economic obstacles that would make attaining such a goal impossible. Taiwan's fundamental problems are not economic, but political. And the most worrisome political problem for the government of the ROC is whether or not Taiwan can survive and prosper without formal diplomatic relations, particularly with its most important trading partner, the United States.

---

64. *TSDB,* p. 157. Chiang Ching-kuo may be influenced by the memory of his own short-lived, unsuccessful attempt to stem inflation in Shanghai in 1948 by stringent police measures.

The Unfinished Civil War

4

During the more than twenty-five years since the founding of the PRC on October 1, 1949, the Nationalist and Communist governments have continued to think of themselves as participants in an unfinished civil war, but there has been no large-scale fighting since the offshore island clash of 1958. The commitment by the United States to the defense of Taiwan, made at the outbreak of the Korean war and subsequently formalized in the mutual security treaty of 1954, forced the PRC to postpone indefinitely its plans to invade Taiwan, and a military assault against the PRC was ruled out by the refusal of the United States to support it.

Peking has demanded as a condition for normalization of relations with Washington that the United States terminate its intervention in the Chinese civil war by ending the security treaty with the ROC and withdrawing all its military personnel and facilities from Taiwan. Should the United States agree to refrain from intervening militarily in the event that large-scale warfare resumed, the principal—although by no means the only—impediment to the use of force by the PRC against Taiwan would be removed. The PRC firmly rejected US proposals during the Warsaw talks that it renounce the use of force in the Taiwan area. In September 1977, shortly after Secretary of State Cyrus R. Vance's visit to Peking, Deputy Premier Teng Hsiao-p'ing, in an interview with executives and directors of the Associated Press, reiterated the PRC's position that the Taiwan problem was an internal matter to be settled among the Chinese themselves. Asked what would happen if the people of Taiwan resisted an attempt by the PRC to take them over, Teng replied that this would lead to conflict, although he added that he would not rule out a peaceful settlement if the United States did not intervene.[1] Even if the United States should decline to intervene with its own forces against a PRC attack, however, the ROC is not defenseless.

Aside from the important political constraints on the use of force against Taiwan by the PRC, significant military constraints are also implicit in the balance of forces between the contending governments. Although some allege that Taiwan would soon be overwhelmed militarily if US protection were withdrawn, others assert that the PRC lacks the military capability to cross the strait and defeat Taiwan's defenders. These purely military considerations, while not necessarily decisive, must be taken into account by American, PRC, and ROC leaders in their overall evaluations of the costs and benefits of various possible courses of action.

Suspension of Military Conflict

When the Korean war broke out, preparations for invading Taiwan had been under way in the PRC since early 1950 under Su Yu, deputy commander of the Third Field Army. The invasion of Taiwan had been designated the principal task for the year. Assault forces variously estimated at 150,000 to 300,000 men, many of them trained in amphibious operations, had been assembled on the Fukien coast. New airfields had been built, some 400 aircraft rounded up, a fleet of invasion barges constructed, and 5000 to 6000 junks and sampans mobilized.[2] The People's Liberation Army (PLA) had already had some experience in amphibious operations, including the crossing of the Yangtze River in April 1949 and the invasion of Hainan Island in April 1950. A large invasion force supplied with thousands of junks had also been assembled opposite the Choushan Islands, some 75 miles southeast of Shanghai in May 1950, where upon the ROC withdrew its defensive force of 125,000 men to Taiwan, and the islands were taken without a battle.

The Hainan Island landings bore some resemblance to the amphibious operation that the PLA expected to carry out against Taiwan, but on a much smaller scale and without the formidable obstacles that an invasion of Taiwan presented. Hainan, at its closest point, was only

1. *The New York Times,* Sept. 7, 1977.
2. John Gittings, *The Role of the Chinese Army* (London: Oxford University Press, 1967), pp. 41–42; Hollington K. Tong, *Chiang Kai-shek* (Taipei: China Publishing, 1953), pp. 500, 505.

15 miles from the mainland, not 90 miles. A large Communist guerrilla force had controlled the interior of the island for many years and was available to harass the defending forces from the rear. Moreover, Hainan was not, like Taiwan, the last redoubt of Chiang Kai-shek, which he could be expected to defend tenaciously. Consequently, although the invading troops, inexperienced in amphibious operations, suffered heavy casualties in landing on Hainan from some 400 motorized junks, resistance soon crumbled, and the bulk of the 40,000 defending forces were withdrawn to Taiwan.[3] A better precedent than Hainan Island for the kind of resistance that the PLA was likely to encounter in Taiwan was the attempted invasion of Quemoy in October 1949, when the invading force was thrown back with losses of 7000 captured and 2000 killed.[4]

In 1950, Taiwan's defenses were far stronger than those of Hainan Island. Of the 800,000 troops withdrawn to Taiwan from the mainland, perhaps 300,000 were first-line combat troops, including a nucleus of men trained and equipped by the United States. An armored force under Chiang Kai-shek's younger son, Major General Chiang Wei-kuo, had between 750 and 1000 tanks, as well as armored cars and other motorized equipment. Some 300 to 600 fighter aircraft and transports had escaped to Taiwan, as well as about 70 sizable naval ships, including 7 destroyer escorts, minesweepers, and LSTs. The only larger ship in the ROC navy, the cruiser *Chungking* (formerly the British *Aurora*), had defected to the PRC but had been disabled by ROC bombing. The ROC forces on Taiwan were less effective, however, than these numbers suggest. They were crippled by severe shortages of arms and ammunition. The air force was so short of aviation gasoline and spare parts that only a small portion of the force could operate at one time. Moreover, the PLA doubtless counted on low morale and agents planted in strategic positions to diminish the combat effectiveness of the Nationalist armed forces.[5]

While the PLA was gathering its forces for an assault on Taiwan, the ROC sought to make effective the closure of mainland ports to for-

---

3. William W. Whitson, *The Chinese High Command* (New York: Praeger, 1973), p. 323; Tong, *Chiang Kai-shek*, pp. 484–485.
4. Whitson, *The Chinese High Command*, p. 244. A. Doak Barnett, writing from Taipei in November 1949, reported the attacking force as 17,000, of whom 8000 were captured and 9000 killed or drowned. Barnett, *China on the Eve of Communist Takeover* (New York: Praeger, 1963), p. 310. A still higher figure of 15,000 to 19,000 killed or wounded appears in Angus M. Fraser, "The Military Posture and Strategic Policy in the Republic of China," *Asian Affairs*, no. 5 (May/June 1974): 313.
5. Barnett, *China on the Eve of Communist Takeover*, pp. 310–311; Tong, *Chiang Kai-shek*, pp. 478–80, 483, 492–493; Fred W. Riggs, *Formosa under Nationalist Rule* (New York: Octagon Books, 1972; 1st ed. 1952), pp. 20–24.

eign ships that had been announced in June 1949 and also carried on nuisance bombings of Nanking and Shanghai. The ROC navy claimed to have prevented some forty vessels from entering Shanghai during the first six months of port closure operations, but the blockade was far from effective, and efforts to enforce it were discontinued after the withdrawal of Nationalist forces from the Choushan Islands, except for the ports of Amoy and Foochow, which could be blocked from Quemoy and Matsu. More effective in readying Taiwan for the expected attack were the reorganization of the armed forces by Ch'en Ch'eng and the rooting out of Communist agents, including Lieutenant General Wu Shih, the deputy chief of the general staff, and his wife.[6]

If the PLA had invaded Taiwan in 1950 with its primitive amphibious equipment, the success of the first waves in securing and consolidating beachheads would have depended heavily on the weather and the relative morale of attackers and defenders. Neither side had enough usable aircraft to make much difference, and the PRC lacked the heavy naval guns needed for a landing against determined opposition. Although the PRC had no guerrilla forces in the interior to support an expeditionary force landing on the coast, it probably could have airdropped a small number of parachutists to spread fear and confusion. If the PLA had persisted, the defenders would have exhausted their ammunition, and if there was no offer of replenishment and defeatism infected their ranks, as it did on the mainland, the PLA would have eventually prevailed, although losses on both sides would probably have been heavy.

President Truman's decision to interpose an American armed force between Taiwan and the mainland changed the ground rules for conducting the unfinished civil war. An invasion of Taiwan from the mainland was no longer practicable. The PRC therefore halted its preparations for a large-scale invasion and began strengthening its coastal defenses, particularly after its assault on the US forces in Korea increased the possibility that the United States might support ROC military operations against the mainland.

After the Korean war ended, however, the PRC did not remain exclusively on the defensive. It built numerous additional airfields in the coastal area usable either defensively or offensively. In September 1954, PRC forces heavily bombarded Quemoy. The ROC retaliated by bombing artillery positions on the mainland. In November, PRC aircraft bombed the Ta Chen Islands and other small islands off the coast of Chekiang and Fukien provinces. In January 1955, they again bombed

---

6. Tong, *Chiang Kai-shek,* pp. 483, 492–493.

the Ta Chens, this time with one hundred aircraft; a week later, they followed up with a well-executed amphibious assault against Ichiang Shan, a small island seven miles north of the principal group, and overwhelmed its one thousand defenders. Although the force defending Ichiang Shan was small and equipped only with small arms and mortars, the PRC, with its new Soviet equipment and Korean war experience, demonstrated a capacity for coordinated sea and air attack that it had not possessed in 1950. The ROC withdrew its remaining forces from the Ta Chens with the help of the US Seventh Fleet because the islands were too far from Taiwan to be given air support; however, it did retaliate by bombing shipping in several mainland ports.

From that time, the only large-scale military clash between the adversaries was the PRC attempt in 1958 to isolate Quemoy and Matsu with artillery fire. Since 1958, the ROC has conducted a number of raids against the mainland, the largest of company size, but most much smaller, and the last in 1969. Specially equipped reconnaissance aircraft from Taiwan have occasionally flown over the mainland to gather intelligence; ROC planes have regularly patrolled the Taiwan Strait, paced a short distance inland by PRC fighter aircraft scrambled from nearby airfields; ROC ships have landed supplies regularly on Quemoy, Matsu, and the smaller Nationalist-held offshore islands and have rotated their garrisons without PRC interference; and ROC planes, flying low to avoid PRC radar, have frequently taken dignitaries to Quemoy on the even-numbered days, when there is no shelling, to gaze through powerful binoculars at PLA soldiers on PRC-held islands 2000 yards away. In recent years, the chief reminder of the suspended civil war has been the propaganda shells that whistle in over Quemoy on odd-numbered days scattering leaflets. Indeed, the quiet life led by the opposing forces suggests the existence of a tacit agreement between them.

The Taiwan Strait has been dominated for the most part by the ROC air force and navy, although ROC naval ships have been sunk by the PRC navy when they ventured too close to the mainland. The PRC air force and navy have stayed near the coast. Tacit understandings, growing out of years of experience, have defined with some precision the lines beyond which neither side will interfere with the other's transit of sea and sky. For many years, the US Seventh Fleet maintained a Taiwan Strait patrol, which served to remind Peking of the US commitment to defend Taiwan, but the patrol was discontinued in 1970. If, in normalizing relations with Peking, the United States should end the security treaty and the PRC should exert military pressure on Taiwan, the first move is likely to be a challenge to the domination of the Taiwan Strait by the ROC navy and air force.

Modernization of PRC Armed Forces

In 1950, the PLA numbered 5 million men, many of them Nationalist soldiers who had surrendered or defected to the PLA. These forces were armed with a hodgepodge of American, Japanese, German, and Russian equipment of varying ages and conditions. By June 1949, the PLA claimed to have captured from Nationalist forces 60,000 heavy and light artillery pieces, 250,000 machine guns, over 2 million rifles and other small arms, 582 tanks, 134 aircraft, and 123 naval vessels.[7] But there was a severe shortage of ammunition, and many of the tanks and aircraft were unserviceable. During the first year of combat by Chinese forces in Korea, it became clear that they lacked the equipment needed for modern warfare. The shortages of trucks, communications equipment, artillery, rifle and artillery ammunition, and tanks and aircraft, which severely hampered their operations, were compensated for by costly human wave tactics.

By the autumn of 1951, however, the Chinese forces in Korea began receiving quantities of Soviet equipment, including T-34 tanks, self-propelled armored artillery, 105mm and 125mm guns, antiaircraft guns, and infantry weapons. Ammunition, although still rationed as of 1952, was becoming more plentiful. With Soviet assistance, the PLA air force, which in 1950 had consisted of only a few hundred, mostly commercial-type transports, grew to 2000 aircraft by the end of the Korean war, nearly half of them jets, including 700 to 850 MIG-15 fighters and up to 100 IL-28 light bombers.[8]

When the Korean conflict ended, the PLA was reorganized along more modern lines, initially following the Soviet pattern. Millions of old or unfit soldiers were demobilized; a conscription system was established to bring in younger, better educated men; the PLA was trimmed to under 3 million men; and a professional officer corps with a system of ranks was created. New emphasis was placed on discipline, professional military training, and technical proficiency.

The PLA continued to receive Soviet equipment until the deepening of the rift between Moscow and Peking caused the withdrawal of Soviet advisers in 1960. During this period, the PLA received substantial numbers of T-34 and T-54 medium tanks, some JS-2 heavy tanks, self-propelled assault guns, truck- or tractor-drawn guns and howitzers, anti-

---

7. Gittings, *The Role of the Chinese Army*, p. 133. Samuel B. Griffith gave different figures: 54,000 artillery pieces, 319,000 machine guns, 1000 tanks and armored cars, and 189 aircraft. Griffith, *The Chinese People's Liberation Army* (New York: McGraw-Hill, 1967), p. 103.
8. Gittings, *The Role of the Chinese Army*, pp. 137–138.

aircraft artillery, surface-to-air (SAM) missiles, radar, submarines, missile-firing patrol boats, MIG-17s, MIG-19s, IL-28s, a few MIG-21s, TU-4 heavy bombers, and TU-16 medium bombers. More important in the long run than the actual military equipment was the Soviet assistance in developing military production facilities. China can now produce all types of infantry weapons, light and medium artillery, small arms and artillery ammunition, armored personnel carriers, T-59 medium tanks (the Chinese version of the Soviet T-54), destroyers, submarines, missile-armed patrol craft, MIG-19 and TU-16 aircraft, and the F-9 fighter-bomber, a Chinese design based on the MIG-19. In addition, Soviet training in nuclear technology enabled PRC scientists and engineers to explode a nuclear device in 1964 and since then to produce and deploy medium- and intermediate-range nuclear-tipped ballistic missiles.

With the exception of a few TU-4s and TU-16s, the Soviet Union did not provide the PRC with aircraft or ships that could project military power much beyond the borders of China. The TU-4s were Soviet copies of the propeller-driven B-29, far too slow and vulnerable to be of much value in the jet age. The TU-16 medium jet bomber, which the Chinese began to produce about 1970, has become, ironically, one of the principal delivery systems for nuclear weapons potentially usable against the Soviet Union. The short-range submarines and other types of naval craft furnished were useful mainly for defending China's coast, although they could be used offensively against nearby Taiwan.

The initial enthusiasm for closely modeling the PLA after the Soviet armed forces soon faded. Chinese Communist party leaders and many PLA veterans believed that the excessive emphasis on professionalism in the military alienated officers from enlisted men and the army from the people. The split with the Soviet Union accelerated the return of emphasis to the traditional "people's war" doctrine and practices of the PLA. In 1965, the system of ranks and insignia modeled on that of the Soviet Union was abolished.

Mao Tse-tung, in particular, stressed the need for political training in the armed forces, not only because he was convinced that a "people's war" was the only way to compensate for China's comparative weakness in modern weapons, but also because the PLA was needed to perform other duties no less important than the defense of the country. Troops participated in food production and played an indispensable role in maintaining domestic political stability during and after the cultural revolution.[9] The continuing debate between those who stressed military

---

9. The PLA is thought to produce as much as half of its own food supply, besides assisting civilians in planting, harvesting, and building roads, canals, railroads, and water conservation projects. Sydney H. Jammes, "The Chinese Defense Burden,

training and techniques and those who stressed politics tended to favor the latter during most of the period from the late 1950s until the death of Mao in 1976, but Mao's death and the ousting of the "gang of four" in October 1976 have resulted in a reduction of the past emphasis on political training and other nonmilitary activities by the PLA and a marked increase in the emphasis on professional military training.[10] In a large-scale military action against Taiwan, the PLA would be significantly handicapped by the extent to which it has been diverted from military training by other demands on its time.

With the exception of its nuclear missiles, the PLA's major weapons are obsolescent, having been either delivered to China by the Soviet Union in the 1950s or produced in China since then, but representing little if any technological improvement over the Soviet weapons of the 1950s. Whether the Chinese have been able to produce high-quality spare parts for their aging weapons is not known, but the condition of those in service for twenty years has probably deteriorated somewhat. In a major effort to modernize its air force, the PRC contracted with Rolls-Royce in December 1975 to provide the technology for Chinese production of Spey jet engines. But it will take years to produce these engines in quantity, or to design and build a new fighter aircraft to use them. American visitors to China in late 1976 noted the PLA's lack of modern weapons and the absence of any Chinese industry capable of producing major new weapons systems effective against modern Soviet weapons.[11]

Modernization of ROC Armed Forces

In 1950, ROC forces not only were much smaller than the PLA but also had lost much of their military equipment to the PLA. Chiang Kai-shek and his principal lieutenants did their best to reorganize and revive the flagging spirits of the demoralized troops but could do little to increase the quantity or improve the quality of their arms and ammunition until the Korean war broke out and the United States resumed its military aid to the ROC. Even after American equipment began to arrive in Taiwan, many serious problems remained. The troops evacuated to Taiwan from the mainland contained an unusually large propor-

1965–74," in *China: A Reassessment of the Economy* (Washington, D.C.: Joint Economic Committee, US Congress, 1975), p. 460.
10. The "gang of four" included Mao's wife, Chiang Ching, and three party officials from Shanghai who rose to high positions during the cultural revolution: Chang Chun-chiao, Wang Hung-wen, and Yao Wen-yuan.
11. *Washington Post,* Sept. 29, 1976; *The New York Times,* Dec. 1–3, 1976.

tion of older men, who had been in rear service units near the ports and could be more readily evacuated than the younger combatants in the front lines. There was a high incidence of tuberculosis and other diseases among them, and they were undernourished. There was no retirement system to remove enlisted men no longer fit for combat or surplus officers.[12]

The modernization of the ROC forces under the guidance of US military advisers in the early and mid-1950s was the counterpart of the modernization of the PLA along Soviet lines during the same period. Organization and training tended to follow the US pattern. Military academies were established for each of the services, and thousands of officers and men were sent to the United States for training. As US equipment and advice flowed in, the ROC military began to resemble outwardly the US military, even to the establishment of officers' clubs. One important difference, however, was the assignment throughout the armed forces of political officers, under the control of Chiang Ching-kuo, to educate the troops politically and to guard against subversion and treason. Chiang Kai-shek was convinced that the defeat of his forces on the mainland resulted largely from the lack of such an apparatus of indoctrination and control.

The most fundamental change was in the recruitment and management of personnel. A modern centralized finance system eliminated the traditional practice of commanding officers skimming off for their own use part of the salary intended for the troops. The diet of the soldiers was improved, new standardized uniforms were issued, hospitals were built, and medical services were expanded. Universal military service was instituted, requiring each able-bodied male at age eighteen to serve two years in the army or three years in the navy or air force. The average age of enlisted men dropped rapidly as the older men were retired under a newly established retirement system. Large numbers of excess officers were also retired. A Vocational Assistance Commission for Retired Servicemen, financed initially by US aid funds, helped to find jobs for those able to work. On completing their military service, conscripts who did not wish to reenlist were assigned to one of nine reserve divisions, to which they were called up from time to time for short refresher training courses. Chiefs of the general staff and commanders of the services were replaced every two years, creating openings at the top for able and ambitious officers. The traditional problem of unit loyalty to the commander rather than to the service was eased as mainlander enlisted men were replaced by short term Taiwanese conscripts. By the early

12. Ravenholt, "Formosa Today," pp. 612–614. He reported 125 admirals and 1600 generals in Taiwan in 1952.

1960s, the ROC military had been transformed into a young, well-trained regular force of 600,000 men with several hundred thousand reserves.

At first, ROC forces were reequipped with weapons and other material similar to that used by US forces in World War II and the Korean war. The infantry received M-14 rifles, replacing its heterogeneous mixture of older rifles, machine guns, recoilless rifles, jeeps, trucks, and armored personnel carriers increased its firepower and mobility. Artillery battalions acquired 75mm and 105mm guns and howitzers, later supplemented by the longer-range 155mm guns and, at the time of the 1958 offshore island conflict, the nuclear-capable 8-inch howitzers, although there was never any suggestion that the ROC would be provided with nuclear warheads. The ground forces were also supplied with substantial numbers of air defense weapons, first with batteries of antiaircraft guns and then, by the 1960s, with Nike-Hercules and Hawk missiles. The armored divisions obtained M-41 light tanks and the M-47 and M-48 medium tanks that became their standard equipment. By the early 1970s, helicopters coproduced in Taiwan were being incorporated into combat exercises.

The few obsolete P-51 propeller aircraft which remained in the hands of the ROC air force were soon succeeded by substantial numbers of the F-86 jet fighters that had performed so effectively against MIG-15s in Korea. Additional C-46 and C-47 transports made it possible for the ROC to begin training parachutists and organizing airborne brigades. Later, the ROC received F-100 fighter-bombers, which are still used by the air force. The F-86 fighters have now been replaced by F-104s and F-5s. Since the off shore island conflict of 1958, ROC fighters have been equipped with Sidewinder air-to-air missiles. The C-46s and most of the C-47s have been phased out and replaced by C-119 and C-123 transports. The ROC also has one squadron of S-2 Tracker planes for antisubmarine warfare. The radar air defense system originally set up on Taiwan is being modernized by a sophisticated new system purchased in 1976 from the Hughes Aircraft Corporation, which will coordinate the command and control of both interceptors and missiles. The ROC navy was strengthened with destroyers, destroyer escorts, minesweepers, torpedo boats, additional LSTs, and small craft, besides receiving two disarmed submarines so that it would not have to depend on US submarines as simulated enemy vessels in antisubmarine warfare training. The marine corps was expanded to two divisions, equipped with tracked vehicles for amphibious landings, and trained in amphibious warfare.

Support for the combat forces was provided by a combined service force, which handled salaries and pensions, managed arsenals, and took charge of procurement. The ROC forces were far more dependent on the United States for military supplies and equipment in the 1950s than the PLA was on the Soviet Union. Factories on Taiwan were unable to refit the military forces with material up to US military standards, and the US Military Assistance Advisory Group ordered not only weapons from the United States but even shoes, truck tires, and flashlight batteries. Gradually, however, as Taiwan's industry grew, many military needs were supplied from local production. Arsenals equipped with the most sophisticated machine tools on the island, which initially produced 30-caliber ammunition for small arms, artillery shells, mortars, machine guns, and clothing, increased their capability until by 1976, they were producing M-14 rifles and light and medium artillery. Bell helicopters and F5-E fighters were coproduced on the island, mainly from imported parts, although the proportion of locally produced components was steadily rising. The ROC was capable of maintaining and overhauling its military aircraft, tanks, and submarines with little assistance from the United States.

The ROC is far less self-reliant in weapons production, however, than the PRC. Unassisted, it cannot produce tanks, aircraft, missile-armed patrol craft, destroyers, or submarines. And it entirely lacks a nuclear missile program. Even to keep the tanks, aircraft, warships, and missiles that it has in operation, it must have access to spare parts from the United States. The ROC, which is working hard to increase its self-reliance in military production, will probably make substantial progress over the next ten years as its industry becomes more advanced and diversified. Nevertheless, Taiwan will probably be dependent even beyond that time for certain critical spare parts for military equipment manufactured in the United States, particularly such advanced and sophisticated items as the improved Hawk missiles and the radar air defense system purchased in 1976.[13]

Over the twenty-five-year period during which the ROC armed forces have been modernized with US assistance, the emphasis in the modernization program has gradually shifted from ground forces to the air force and navy. In the 1950s, a larger army than necessary for the defense simply of Taiwan and the Pescadores was equipped with American weapons, for a number of reasons. First, the army existed. It was thus easier to keep the men and officers in military units than to find places for them in the civilian economy. Second, the army was the senior service. It therefore had more political clout than the other services and pressed hard to have all its units provided with modern weapons. Third, the commitment of Chiang Kai-shek and other influential political and military leaders in Taiwan to the goal of mainland recovery caused them to plan and argue for an even larger army than the United States

---

13. *The New York Times*, Aug. 4, 1976.

was otherwise willing to equip. Fourth, it was US policy in the 1950s to provide the ROC with "limited offensive capabilities" so that it could be of assistance outside Taiwan in the event that the United States became involved in a general war in East Asia.[14] And last, the determination that Quemoy and Matsu were territories that must be defended at all costs required considerably larger ground forces than would be needed for the defense of Taiwan and the Pescadores alone.

Since 1950, US air and naval forces have been the principal military deterrent to a PRC attack on Taiwan and the Pescadores. Providing the ROC with naval and air forces that could perform this function would have been extremely costly, but it was also politically impracticable for the US Seventh Fleet to assume sole responsibility for the air and sea defense of ROC-held territory, particularly the offshore islands. Consequently, the ROC air force and navy were equipped with enough modern weapons to take a substantial part in the defense of Taiwan and the Pescadores and, as in 1958, to defend and resupply Quemoy and Matsu without the combat participation of US forces.[15] Since the early 1960s, the bulk of US military aid and military procurement by the ROC has consisted of items that further strengthen ROC air and sea defenses, although in the late 1960s the army did receive additional trucks, tanks, and howitzers when large numbers of these items were declared surplus to the needs of US forces in Vietnam.

In supplying equipment to the ROC air force and navy, the United States exercised greater restraint than the Soviet Union did with respect to supplying the PRC with weapons suited for offensive use. The ROC has a small number of short-range F-100 fighter-bombers, but it has no bombers and none of the modern F-4 long-range fighter-bombers.[16] It has a small sealift and airlift capability and troops trained in amphibious operations, all of which are useful in supplying and defending the offshore islands but fall far short of what would be needed to seize and expand a beachhead on the mainland.

During the 1970s, ROC forces have been trimmed back from the 600,000 level, where they stood throughout the 1960s, to about 500,000. Since personnel costs form a high proportion of the defense budget and eat into resources that could be used to beef up sea and air defenses, some US and ROC officials believe that the army could be cut back even further, especially if offshore island garrisons were reduced. It might

14. Rankin, *China Assignment*, p. 268.
15. US ships and aircraft did, however, convey ROC resupply vessels as far as the three-mile limit from the offshore islands.
16. ROC supporters in the US Congress proposed unsuccessfully in 1969 that a squadron of F-4s be provided to the ROC. *United States Security Agreements and Commitments Abroad*, pp. 1062–1063.

also make sense to reduce the tank forces, which have high maintenance costs, and to put more resources into preventing PLA men and tanks from getting across the strait so that there would be fewer to cope with after they land. But overcoming the resistance of senior army generals, who have a vested interest in established defense strategy and in maintaining the army at its present level, is likely to be difficult.

The military equipment provided to the ROC by the United States and to the PRC by the Soviet Union was roughly comparable in quality, although not in quantity. Some of the weapons sold to the PRC by the Soviet Union in the 1950s, however, such as the TU-16 and IL-28 bombers, the missile-firing patrol boats, and the submarines, had no counterpart in the ROC inventory. From 1960 on, the ROC has had the advantage of access to more advanced models of certain US items, notably aircraft, while the PRC has been denied later models of Soviet weapons. The ROC has benefited significantly from this unequal access to advanced military technology, at least in the short run, but the PRC, forced by circumstances to rely on its own design and production facilities, may benefit more in the long run.

The ROC leaders recognize that they can never overcome PRC advantages in numbers of men and weapons. If US protection should be withdrawn from Taiwan, they would have to rely on the defensive advantages of their geographical position, superior weapons, and superior training and tactics. Consequently, they would like to obtain recently developed US weapons, such as laser-guided bombs, TOW antitank missiles, and Vulcan antiaircraft guns. They are also investigating European sources of supply, although these might be denied them for political reasons.[17] Looking ahead to the time when Taiwan might be thrown entirely on its own resources, the ROC is training technicians in radar, sonar, nuclear, and missile technology, as well as conducting its own military research and development program.

Resumption of Military Conflict

When the total numbers of men and weapons possessed by the PRC and the ROC are compared, the PRC appears to have the overwhelming military advantage. The PRC regular armed forces consist of over 3 million men; the ROC has only 500,000. The PRC has medium- and

---

17. E.g. the British government turned down an ROC request to buy a substantial number of Rapier surface-to-air missiles from the British Aircraft Corporation. *New York Times,* Jan. 15, 1977.

intermediate-range nuclear missiles; the ROC has none. The PRC air force has about 60 TU-16 medium bombers and 300 IL-28 light bombers; the ROC has none. The PRC has over 3000 fighter aircraft, mostly MIG-17s and MIG-19s; the ROC has fewer than 300 F-100s, F-104s, and F-5s. In naval forces, the PRC has about 50 submarines to the ROC's 2 and far larger numbers of small gunboats than the ROC, including about 60 missile-armed fast patrol boats for which the ROC has no counterpart. Only in destroyers can the ROC match the PRC, with 18 destroyers to the PRC's six detroyers and ten destroyer escorts. The PRC ground forces possess 8500 tanks to the ROC's 2200, and 15,000 artillery pieces to the ROC's 1600. These figures, although only approximate, give an idea of the disparity in numbers and equipment between the two sides.[18]

A gross comparison of the numbers of men and weapons on each side is, however, misleading. Leaving aside the political constraints on PRC military operations against Taiwan, the military contraints are substantial. The water barrier limits the ground forces that could be brought to bear against Taiwan at any one time to a small fraction of the PRC's total forces, even if the PRC had control of the sea and air. Moreover, defense generally requires smaller numbers than offense. In the air battle, the quality of aircraft, pilots, and tactics might be more important than the quantity of aircraft, as demonstrated in 1958 when the kill ratio of F-86s against MIG-15s was 8 to 1.

Most of the troops on both sides lack battle experience. A relatively small number still in the armed forces may have taken part in the 1958 offshore island conflict, now nearly twenty years in the past. Raids against the mainland and small-scale naval engagements have involved insignificant numbers on each side. Very small numbers of PRC forces were engaged in the clashes with Soviet forces on the Ussuri River in 1969 or in the occupation of the Paracel Islands in 1974. The latter event was primarily a naval battle which, according to South Vietnamese accounts, was participated in by eleven small PRC vessels and a battalion of ground forces. The largest operation involving PRC forces was the attack in the eastern sector of the China-India border in 1962, in which about three divisions took part.

There has been no evidence in recent years of PRC preparations for large-scale operations against Taiwan. The PLA does not appear to be enlarging or improving to any significant extent its aging fleet of amphibious craft and motorized junks. Nor have significant numbers of troops been engaged in training for amphibious operations. Naval gun-

---

18. International Institute for Strategic Studies, *The Military Balance, 1975–76* (London, 1975), pp. 49–50, 53–54.

fire and tactical air support have rarely been included in PLA training programs.[19] The military exercises carried out by the PRC have been related almost entirely to the defense of national territory rather than to offensive operations. Meanwhile, the ROC forces have been concentrating their training on the defense of Taiwan, the Pescadores, and the offshore islands. Although the PRC could someday decide to train and equip its forces to invade Taiwan, the undertaking would probably take several years. Any use of force against Taiwan by the PRC would also entail heavy political costs in terms of its relations with the United States and Japan, but such considerations should be kept apart from actual military possibilities.

There are a variety of military options available to the PRC besides the invasion of Taiwan. These range from low-level harassment at one extreme, through blockade, to an all-out attack including nuclear bombing at the other extreme. Harassment is the least costly, the most easily intensified or diminished, and therefore the most likely to be tried. It coud be part of a concerted effort to bring about negotiations between Taipei and Peking. Military pressures would be accompanied by the announcement of conditions under which Taiwan might be reassociated with the mainland—conditions more concrete and attractive than those offered in the past and designed to appeal to a populace whose confidence in Taiwan's future had been shaken by the resumption of military conflict.

Harassment could begin on a small scale with PRC aircraft and ships operating farther out into the Taiwan Strait and in larger numbers than in the past, challenging the ROC navy and air force to interfere with them. The PRC might then mount small raids against Taiwan, similar to those that the ROC has carried out against the mainland. It could airdrop a few saboteurs or intelligence agents in Taiwan's mountainous regions. The purpose of such activities would be more political than military, producing fear and uncertainty. At a later stage, harassment might be expanded to include artillery bombardment of the offshore islands, a determined effort to gain air and naval dominance over the Taiwan Strait, submarine attacks on the ROC navy, and even selective bombing of strategic targets on Taiwan.

Harassment would not be without cost to the PRC, which would lose ships and planes to ROC attack. How many would depend on how determined the PRC was to gain dominance over the Taiwan Strait and how determined the ROC was to prevent it. If the ROC was determined

---

19. Whitson, *The Chinese High Command,* p. 480.

and if the ROC was superior, plane for plane, to the PRC air force, the PRC would have to decide whether to persist with an air war of attrition against the ROC. Much would depend on whether the ROC was able to obtain replacements for lost aircraft. Whether the PRC decided to keep harassment at a low level over a long period of time or raise it to a high level, perhaps as a prelude to blockade or invasion, would depend on the judgment of PRC leaders concerning the political effect on Taiwan of PRC military operations, as well as the international impact of the alternative policies. Militarily, the ROC could withstand low-level harassment indefinitely, but not without damaging effects on both the economy and, at least initially, the morale. Whether the damage to morale would be lasting is uncertain. Sometimes, as in the Battle of Britain or the bombing of North Vietnam, successful resistance against heavy odds can be dramatized by skillful leadership as a means to strengthen morale.

High-level harassment, if it developed into a contest for sea and air dominance of the Taiwan Strait, could ultimately result in the loss of the bulk of the ROC air force and navy, unless the ROC abandoned the contest in order to reserve some ships and planes to resist invasion or unless the United States became deeply involved in providing replacements for lost ships and planes and in training crews. Although the cost to the PRC in lost aircraft would also be high, the loss of air and sea dominance over the Taiwan Strait would severely shake morale in Taiwan, imperil the offshore islands, and decrease Taiwan's ability to resist invasion.

The blockade of Taiwan, which is a step above harassment on an ascending scale of military actions, would severely damage the economy of the island by interfering with the foreign trade and investment on which Taiwan's prosperity so heavily depends. But because it would damage the interests of all countries trading with Taiwan, especially the United States and Japan, the political costs to the PRC would be high. The PRC has the military capacity to make a blockade effective, although it would probably require a costly battle of attrition with the ROC air force and navy.

The ROC lacks the navy necessary to convoy ships for more than short distances to and from Taiwan. It could seek out and attack PRC surface ships, submarines, or planes interfering with shipping, but it could not prevent a drastic decline in the number of ships servicing Taiwan's ports. If the PRC imposed a full-scale blockade, Taiwan would become an island under siege; rationing and other wartime control measures would be required. But by mobilizing the entire ROC-owned merchant fleet, buying additional ships, utilizing only the sea-lanes approaching Taiwan from the east, and convoying ships for relatively short distances as they drew near the island, the ROC could probably endure a blockade for a long time.[20]   If the Philippine government looked the other way, small, fast blockade-runners might bring in urgently needed small items transshipped from depots on islands just south of the Bashi Channel, which separates Taiwan from the Philippines, the same as when enterprising British merchants used the Bahamas to smuggle goods through the Northern blockade during the American Civil War.   How long Taiwan could hold out would depend on a variety of factors difficult to foresee, including the international reaction to the blockade, the morale of the population, the conditions laid down by the PRC for ending the blockade, and the stockpiles of essential materials on hand when the blockade began, especially military supplies and the raw materials for manufacturing the chemical fertilizers needed to maintain food production.

Thus, the PRC could exert heavy pressures on Taiwan by imposing a blockade, although the military costs to the PRC itself would be substantial.   Moreover, the international complications arising from a blockade would be much greater than those resulting from the policy of military harassment.   Not only would foreign economic interests be directly affected, but foreign governments would be compelled to decide how to react to the PRC's attempt to throttle Taiwan's international trade in terms of international law.   A blockade would probably increase the international sympathy for Taiwan, make the ROC's declaration of independence more likely, and improve its prospects for recognition as an independent state.

Invasion would be the most decisive means of bringing Taiwan under the PRC's control, but also the most risky and costly.   The first requirement would be a willingness to pay the price of gaining control of the sea and air over the Taiwan Strait.   The second requirement would be the determination to train large numbers of troops in amphibious and airborne operations and to build the specialized landing craft that would be needed to land men, tanks, and artillery on hotly contested beaches.

A large-scale attack on Taiwan is improbable so long as the PRC feels seriously threatened militarily by the Soviet Union.   Such an attack would require the diversion of a substantial proportion of the PRC's military power, especially air units, now deployed to defend against a

---

20. The ROC had 167 merchant vessels of about 2 million deadweight tons at the end of 1976, but less than 20 percent of Taiwan's trade was carried in ROC-flag carriers.   *Far Eastern Economic Review*, Feb. 11, 1977, p. 60.   The total volume of imports and exports unloaded at Taiwan's three principal harbors in 1975 was 29 million tons.   *China Yearbook, 1976*, p. 225.

possible Soviet attack. Losses suffered by the PLA in an invasion of
Taiwan would add to the already great superiority of the Soviet military
forces facing China.

The battle for control of the air over the Taiwan Strait could begin
with a surprise attack on Taiwan's airfields by hundreds of planes, in
cluding TU-16 and IL-28 bombers escorted by fighter aircraft, in order
to destroy as many as possible of the ROC's aircraft on the ground. The
small number of airfields on Taiwan and the lack of any protection for
the aircraft other than revetments almost invites this form of attack. The
warning time would be short, as the attacking planes would come from
airfields less than three hundred miles away. Assuming, however, that
the ROC had strategic warning of an impending attack, as a result of the
buildup of aircraft on mainland bases near Taiwan and other indicators,
some attacking aircraft would be lost to ROC interceptors on high-alert
status that had been scrambled upon warning of the attack. Other PRC
aircraft would be knocked down by Nike-Hercules or Hawk missiles or
by antiaircraft guns. The ROC losses to surprise attack could be greatly
reduced by building reinforced concrete shelters for military aircraft, as
has been done in South Korea. Since the PRC's obsolescent planes are
ill-suited to attacking concrete shelters, the advantages to the PRC of a
surprise attack under these circumstances would be questionable. It
would probably lose many more planes than it could destroy. Building
concrete shelters would be an inexpensive way for the ROC to improve
its military position relative to the PRC.

The result of a prolonged air battle for supremacy over the Taiwan
Strait would depend considerably on where it was fought. If, for example,
it was a battle over resupply of the offshore islands and the ROC was
using its small number of fighter-bombers against PRC air bases, the PRC
would be at a disadvantage. Not only would PRC fighters be operating
closer to their bases, but ROC aircraft flying over the mainland would
come under fire from the PRC's SA-2 ground-to-air missiles and antiaircraft guns. On the other hand, if the battle took place near and over
Taiwan, ROC fighters would be close to their bases, and PRC aircraft
would have to run the gauntlet of the ROC's ground-to-air defenses.

The result of the battle would also depend on the relative quality of
the aircraft used, the tactical situation, and the skill of the pilots, all of
which are difficult to judge in advance. The F-5E, some 180 of which
will become the mainstay of the ROC air force within a few years, has
been little tested in battle, but it is generally regarded as comparable to
the MIG-21, of which the PRC has only about 50.[21] The bulk of the

---

21. International Institute for Strategic Studies. *The Military Balance, 1975–76*, p. 50.

PRC's air force is composed of 3000 MIG-17s and MIG-19s, which are probably inferior, plane for plane, to the F-5E and the F-104. If the ROC air force, fighting in a favorable tactical position and aided by ground-to-air defenses, were to achieve a kill-ratio of 5 to 1, less than the 8 to 1 recorded in 1958, it would destroy nearly half of the PRC's air force before it was itself wiped out. The PRC would have gained air supremacy, but at a high cost. And if the United States were to replace aircraft lost by the ROC and a large number of trained ROC pilots were available in reserve, the cost to the PRC in lost aircraft could become much higher, although it could resume manufacturing MIG-19s and replace some of its losses. In any case, the cost to the PRC in aircraft and trained pilots of securing air supremacy over the Taiwan Strait would be heavy.

Gaining naval supremacy in the Taiwan Strait would be far easier for the PRC. It is difficult to believe that the ROC navy could last very long against the PRC's overwhelming superiority in submarines and missile patrol craft. Moreover, the PRC could greatly complicate the task of the ROC navy by mining the entrances to Taiwan's harbors. The ROC navy could probably be neutralized within a few weeks if the PRC used its maximum capability against it. Still, the PRC would suffer significant losses.

If air and sea supremacy were secured, the PRC would be in a position to launch an invasion force. Such a force could number as many as several hundred thousand men or more if the PRC were willing to invest the necessary resources in providing the appropriate craft to transport them and their heavy equipment. But even with control of the sea and air and an ability to attack several beaches at the same time, seizing and consolidating the beachheads would be costly. The PRC lacks the heavy naval guns used by US forces in the Pacific during World War II to soften up beaches before landing. It could use its bombers, but these are relatively slow and vulnerable to ROC antiaircraft guns and to Nike-Hercules and Hawk missiles, provided that the ROC still had missiles left after the air battle over the Taiwan Strait. The landing forces would have to come ashore in small incremental waves at places where they would be outnumbered by the defenders. The PRC would probably support its amphibious forces by dropping parachutists in an attempt to seize airfields that could then be used for a rapid buildup of airborne forces. Whether they would succeed or would be surrounded and captured like the Allied forces at Arnhem is difficult to predict.

The Taiwan Strait itself could be a significant barrier to effecting a landing on schedule and maintaining continuous reinforcement and resupply, even though the PRC had wiped out most of the ROC's navy and air force. The sea is often rough, especially during the winter monsoon

113

from late October through March. Moreover, typhoons can strike during any month of the year, although they are most frequent between June and October. Their unpredictability complicates military planning.

To resist the invaders, the ROC would have a regular army of 260,000 to 320,000, depending on how many remained on the offshore islands, plus 35,000 marines. The ROC could also call up several hundred thousand reserves, although how well equipped and trained these would be is uncertain. Taiwan has the necessary roads and railroads to permit reinforcements to be moved quickly to points where they might be needed, but the PRC, having control of the air, could interfere with such movements by bombing and strafing. Intangible factors such as the morale of the defenders and unpredictable factors such as the weather would affect the outcome. It seems probable that if the PRC were willing to persist long enough, it could overpower the defenders, but it also seems probable that PRC losses in men and material would be very high.

In addition to these military measures against Taiwan, the PRC could use, or threaten to use, nuclear weapons. Peking might calculate that the mere threat to use nuclear weapons would so intimidate people on Taiwan that the authorities would have no choice but to open negotiations to place the island under mainland control. Or if the threat alone were not effective, the PRC could drop a small nuclear weapon on one of Taiwan's smaller cities as a demonstration of what was in store if resistance continued. But neither the threat to use nuclear weapons nor their actual use seems a remote possibility. Ever since the PRC exploded its first nuclear device in 1964, it has stressed that it will never be the first to use nuclear weapons. Should it resort to nuclear blackmail or, much worse, become the first nation in over thirty years to use a nuclear weapon, the PRC's position in the world would be profoundly affected. The Soviet Union, the United States, Japan, and China's smaller neighbors all would view the leaders of the PRC as far more of a threat to peace than they do today and would take measures to improve their own security. The resulting military buildup and strengthening of political ties among nations that felt threatened by China would place the PRC in an isolated and weakened position. For these reasons, as well as because of the political disadvantages of using or threatening to use nuclear weapons against fellow Chinese, there is little likelihood that PRC leaders would resort to such action.

The Offshore Islands

Occupation of the offshore island groups of Quemoy and Matsu by the ROC has advantages and disadvantages for both sides in the civil war. For both Peking and Taipei, the islands constitute a link between Taiwan and the mainland, symbolizing the "one China" position maintained by both governments. For Taipei, they also serve to bottle up the ports of Amoy and Foochow, preventing their use as assembly points for forces preparing to invade Taiwan. For the PRC, the islands offer a convenient place to exert controlled military pressure on the ROC at an acceptable cost. They can be bombarded, or their resupply interdicted, without the awkward international repercussions that would result from blockading or attacking Taiwan.

An invasion of the islands, however, would be extremely costly for the PRC. The ROC stations nearly one-third of its army on the two principal islands, with about three-fourths of that contingent on Quemoy. The defending troops are so well protected in deep fortifications that an attacking force would be at a great disadvantage.[22] The PRC is deterred from invasion not only by the high military costs but also by the political disadvantage of severing the link between Taiwan and the mainland. To resume bombardment with high explosive shells would be a relatively inexpensive way of heating up the civil war and causing alarm in Taiwan, but bombardment alone would do little damage to the entrenched forces. The most productive military action against the islands would be to interdict their resupply.

By keeping one-third of its army on Quemoy and Matsu, the ROC may reduce the risk that the PRC would attempt to invade the islands, but at the same time it may increase the risk that the PRC will interdict their resupply. No doubt there are enough supplies on the islands to enable them to hold out for a long time, but sooner or later the ROC would be compelled, as a political necessity, to try to break the blockade. In order to breach the blockade, the ROC navy and air force would be forced to join battle with PRC forces at locations relatively favorable to the PRC, which would result in a gradual attrition of the ROC's air force and navy at minimal cost to the PRC. And American political leaders would find it difficult to justify the replacement of ROC ships and planes lost in defending the offshore islands.

The ROC could strengthen its military position by drastically reducing its garrisons on Quemoy and Matsu. Converting these islands into relatively lightly defended forward outposts would eliminate the ROC's risk of losing one third of its army as well as a large part of its air force and navy in a vain effort to break the blockade. All of these forces are needed for the defense of Taiwan itself. Paradoxically, the thinning out of ROC forces on the offshore islands might reduce the chances that the PRC would invade them, for the withdrawal would

---

22. *Far Eastern Economic Review,* Oct. 1, 1976, pp. 62–63.

stress to Peking that the leaders on Taiwan had the option of declaring independence of the mainland and that they were more likely to do so if the PRC itself severed the mainland link by military force.

Some ROC officials accept the logic of this argument and agree that too large a portion of the ground forces is stationed on the offshore islands. But the political opposition to large reductions in these deployments would be formidable. Many senior military officers would oppose the move because they have a vested interest in preserving the large force structure designed to defend the offshore islands. Powerful critics in the party and the armed forces would denounce proposals for reductions as tantamount to yielding to Communist pressure and as a step toward abandoning the fundamental national goal of mainland recovery. The symbolic importance of the offshore islands, created over many years by the heavy publicity given these "front-line" positions, makes suspect any proposal to defend them less strongly than in the past. Consequently, despite the military disadvantage of leaving too large a part of the army in exposed positions, no substantial change in deployments seems likely in the near future.

Nuclear Weapons for the ROC

Faced with the possibility of a PRC attempt to invade Taiwan should the United States withdraw its military protection, ROC leaders have considered manufacturing nuclear weapons.[23] Possession of even a few nuclear bombs would constitute a quantum jump in firepower for the ROC. Nuclear bombs dropped on areas where mainland invasion forces were assembling for embarkation or on beachheads in Taiwan where invaders were trying to consolidate would gravely jeopardize the attempted invasion. The PRC could threaten catastrophic retaliation against Taiwan if the ROC were to use a single nuclear weapon. Half of Taiwan's population and most of its industry could be wiped out by a few nuclear weapons, while the ROC could inflict only peripheral, although locally serious, damage on continental China. While the logic of this unequal situation argues strongly against the use of nuclear weapons by the ROC, the decision makers in Peking

---

23. Premier Chiang Ching-kuo was quoted as reporting to the Legislative Yuan on Sept. 23, 1975: "We have both the facilities and the capability to make nuclear weapons and actually considered to build up a nuclear arsenal last year; but when I broached the idea to the late president, he rejected it flatly on the ground that we cannot use nuclear weapons to hurt our own countrymen." *Daily Report, East Asia and Pacific,* Sept. 24, 1975, p. B1.

could not rule out the possibility that someone on Taiwan might order their use as an act of desperation during an invasion of the island. Nuclear retaliation would gain the PRC a devastated and radioactive Taiwan, perhaps at the price of a blasted Shanghai. The potential effectiveness of nuclear weapons as a deterrent to invasion will doubtless continue to attract the attention of ROC leaders, particularly if they come to believe that Taiwan will be abandoned by the United States.

Taiwan's possession of nuclear weapons would also have an international political impact. If, for example, ROC leaders, confronted by the threat of invasion and feeling abandoned by the United States, were to declare Taiwan an independent state and announce their determination to defend its independence with nuclear weapons, the importance of their declaration of independence would be magnified. If Taiwan became the world's seventh nuclear power, the nations of the world, particularly those nearby such as Japan, would be much more deeply concerned with preventing a nuclear exchange between the PRC and Taiwan than they are now in preventing a resumption of hostilities with conventional arms.

The ROC could, within a few years, develop the capability to produce simple nuclear weapons made of plutonium. The technology for assembling such weapons is publicly available, and the F-5E fighter aircraft can be modified to carry a small nuclear bomb. The plutonium could be produced in Taiwan either by the 40-megawatt heavy water research reactor bought from Canada, which has been operational since 1973, or by the two 636-megawatt boiling water reactors bought from the United States and being installed in Taiwan's first nuclear power plant, the first unit of which came on line in 1977. The Canadian reactor is similar to India's Trombay reactor, which produced the plutonium for India's nuclear explosion. The ROC has on hand a supply of natural uranium bought from South Africa, and in 1973, it completed a fuel fabrication plant to process the natural uranium into fuel for the heavy water reactor.[24]

The ROC has a substantial number of nuclear physicists, engineers, and other technicians trained in various aspects of nuclear technology. Since 1961, a small research reactor supplied by the United States has been operating at the Institute of Nuclear Science at National Tsinghua University. It was supplemented in 1973 by an Argonaut research reactor, lent by the US Argonne National Laboratory and used primarily to train personnel for the nuclear power program. Additional

---

24. The ROC's decision to raise its representation in South Africa from a consulate general to an embassy in 1976 may have been influenced in part by a desire to assure access to its source of uranium.

nuclear research is under way both at the Institute of Nuclear Energy Research, which operates the Canadian reactor and is responsible for studying the entire nuclear fuel cycle, and at the Chung Shan Institute of Science, operated by the ROC military. There are 713 Taiwanese who have studied nuclear technology in US governmental laboratories or universities under US government sponsorship.[25] During 1975 and 1976, 15 engineers from the Chung Shan Institute received eighteen months of training at MIT in the technology of inertial navigation systems, which could be applied to the construction of nuclear-tipped missiles.[26]

In order to produce weapons-grade plutonium, the ROC needs only a plant to reprocess the spent fuel from its nuclear reactors. Such a plant can be used either to produce recycled fuel for reuse in power reactors or to produce plutonium for weapons, although the recycling of fuel is not economic except for countries with very large nuclear programs. Reprocessing is a well-known chemical engineering procedure, and the Indians were able to build their own plant for this purpose. The ROC has long been interested in the possibility of acquiring a reprocessing plant to recycle fuel for the three large nuclear power plants that it expects to be operating in the 1980s, as well as for the Canadian heavy water research reactor. In the early 1970s, using parts procured from various countries, it began construction at the Institute of Nuclear Energy Research of a pilot plant that would be capable of re-processing spent fuel from the small research reactor at Tsinghua University. In 1975–1976, a nuclear scientist was sent to the Argonne Laboratory for a year's training in reprocessing.

In the summer of 1976, it was reported in the American press that the ROC had been secretly reprocessing nuclear fuel, although neither the source of the fuel nor the location of the plant were given.[27] ROC officials denied the report. Referring to the construction of the pilot plant and to a request made to the US government for permission to reprocess in that plant the spent fuel from the Tsinghua University reactor, they pointed out that this tiny experimental facility would produce only .03 pounds of plutonium per year, or far too little for an atomic bomb.[28] Shortly thereafter, in response to concern expressed by the US government, the ROC government declared in a diplomatic note that it had "no intention whatsoever to develop nuclear weapons or a nuclear

---

25. *Washington Post*, Aug. 29, 1976.
26. *Washington Post*, June 13, July 16, 1976. The program was terminated six months early at the request of the State Department as the result of protests by leftist, anti-ROC students at M.I.T.
27. *Washingon Post*, Aug. 29, 1976.
28. *The New York Times*, Sept. 5, 1976.

explosive device, or to engage in any activities related to reprocessing purposes."[29]   Apparently the plan to operate the pilot reprocessing plant has been shelved because of US opposition.

It would be difficult and risky for the ROC to produce plutonium and to construct nuclear weapons secretly.   The ROC is a signatory to the treaty on the nonproliferation of nuclear weapons, which pledges it not to produce such weapons.   Although it was expelled from the International Atomic Energy Agency (IAEA) in 1972, in response to a demand from the PRC and before a safeguards agreement had been negotiated, it has placed not only the reactors and nuclear material from the United States and Canada but also its supply of South African uranium under IAEA safeguards.   Taiwan is visited regularly by IAEA inspectors, who check these facilities and materials.

The PRC, while refraining from joining the IAEA itself, has demanded that the agency cease inspecting Taiwan, apparently feeling that the disadvantage of according international recognition to the ROC by bringing Taiwan within the IAEA inspection system outweighs the disadvantage of allowing Taiwan's nuclear facilities to remain uninspected.   The US-supplied facilities and materials would be inspected in any case under a fall-back bilateral agreement, but there is no such bilateral agreement covering the Canadian reactor.[30]   The United States, however, would probably insist on extending its inspection to the Canadian reactor if IAEA inspection ceased.   Even though the ROC does not have a safeguards agreement with the IAEA requiring that all nuclear facilities on Taiwan be placed under IAEA inspection, the acquisition and use of unsafeguarded facilities to produce plutonium would jeopardize relations with the United States, the sole supplier of the enriched uranium essential to the ROC's ambitious nuclear power program.

The ROC will almost certainly continue quietly to train technicians, carry out research in the design and operation of reprocessing plants, and purchase the components needed to build them.   From the ROC viewpoint, it would be imprudent not to prepare for the eventuality that the United States might withdraw its military protection from Taiwan, so long as such contingency preparations do not jeopardize its primary objective of preserving as close a relationship with the United States as possible.   Moreover, the progress in nuclear technology re-

---

29. *Washington Post,* Sept. 23, 1976.

30. George H. Quester, "Taiwan and Nuclear Proliferation," *Orbis* 18, no. 1 (Spring 1974).   The Chief of the Public Information Section of the IAEA categorically denied that there had been any evasion of IAEA safeguards in Taiwan and any diversion of nuclear material from any facility covered by IAEA safeguards.   Letter to the Editor, *The New York Times,* Sept. 27, 1976.

quired by the ROC's extensive nuclear program will inevitably improve its capability to produce nuclear weapons, for according to one authority on the subject, "there is no real separation between the development of civil and military nuclear technology, except for work in bomb design and fabrication."[31] The same authority estimated that if a nation possesses a power reactor and a reprocessing plant and has completed its weapons design research, a weapon could be produced in less than two years.[32] However, the Carter administration has expressed strong opposition to the acquisition of reprocessing facilities by developing countries, and so long as the ROC continues to be heavily dependent on the United States for the security and prosperity of Taiwan, the possibility that its leaders will oppose the United States by building a reprocessing plant is remote.

Prospects

Once US protection was withdrawn from Taiwan, the PRC would have a wide range of military measures to use to apply pressure on the ROC. It would probably begin with measures whose military costs were low, in the hope that the political impact on Taiwan would be disproportionately heavy and could be exploited to negotiate a satisfactory settlement. If ROC resistance proved stubborn, however, and the PRC were compelled to shift to a high level of military activity, the military costs of beating the ROC into submission could become quite heavy. Although the ROC could not hold out indefinitely against a determined PRC military attack, its ability to exact a high price is a significant deterrent. The PRC might not be prepared, for example, to sacrifice up to half of its air force in action against Taiwan so long as a high level of hostility prevailed between Peking and Moscow. A decline in tension between the PRC and the Soviet Union would ease this constraint.

It will be vital for the ROC to maintain this capability to destroy a large fraction of the PRC's air force should Taiwan be attacked. In order to do so, by the 1980s, it will need more advanced aircraft and missiles to cope with the next generation of PLA aircraft, which will be built around the Spey engines. Consequently, the ROC is already giving thought to purchasing the follow-on aircraft to the F-5E from the United States. The ROC can probably improve its overall military capability

---

31. William Van Cleave, "Nuclear Technology and Weapons," in Robert Lawrence and Joel Larus, eds., *Nuclear Proliferation, Phase II* (Lawrence: University of Kansas Press, 1974), p. 33.
32. Ibid., p. 48.

for the defense of Taiwan as rapidly or more rapidly than the PRC can improve its capability to use military force against Taiwan, provided it has continued access to US spare parts and to new equipment from the United States or elsewhere. The ROC's military budget in 1974 amounted to 7 percent of the GNP, or about $800 million. This is a moderate expenditure for an embattled nation. Israel's military budget in 1974 amounted to over 30 percent of the GNP and Egypt's to nearly 20 percent.[33] Consequently, if the mutual defense treaty were terminated and the ROC felt more immediately threatened by military attack, it could divert additional resources to military expenditures, although at the expense of the standard of living and of investment in economic growth.

Not only do the potential military costs serve to deter the PRC from using military force against Taiwan, but the political costs have the same effect. Sino-Soviet tension will probably continue to inhibit the PRC from launching a large-scale attack on Taiwan. Since 1971, the PRC has sought to improve its relations with the United States and Japan as a means of strengthening its position vis-à-vis the Soviet Union. Even though neither the United States nor Japan was prepared to help defend Taiwan by military force, an attack on the island by Peking could not fail seriously to damage its relations with Washington and Tokyo. The long-term effects on Japan could be particularly serious. The willingness of the PRC to resort to force against Taiwan and to engage in battle so close to Japanese territory would drastically alter the Japanese view of the PRC as a peace-loving nation and give strong impetus to a buildup of Japan's military forces. The possibility of Japan's acquiring nuclear weapons would be considerably increased. Thus, a military conquest of Taiwan by the PRC could set in motion changes that would result in a substantial weakening of its relative international position, both politically and militarily.

The PRC is also inhibited from attacking Taiwan by the risk that Taiwan might declare the island an independent state and then produce nuclear weapons with which to defend it. ROC adherence to the "one China" concept is a valuable asset to the PRC, which it would not lightly jeopardize. Thus, PRC use of military force much beyond low-level harassment seems unlikely under the present circumstances, even if the defense treaty with the United States were to end. If the PRC's relations with the Soviet Union improved substantially and the United States were no longer willing to sell weapons and spare parts to the ROC, the probability of a larger scale use of force against Taiwan would rise.

---

33. US Arms Control and Disarmament Agency, *World Military Expenditures and Arms Transfers, 1965–74* (Washington, D.C.), pp. 24, 27, 33.

Political Maneuvering

5

The political element in the civil war between the Nationalists and the Communists was from the outset more important than the purely military element. Mao Tse-tung and his associates were able to triumph despite the relative inferiority of their military forces in numbers and armament because of superior political skills. Yet had they not been able to combine their political skill with military force, they could not have triumphed. And once prevented from using military force by the intervention of the United States, they have been unable to bring Taiwan under their control by political means alone.

The several forms of political action resorted to by the PRC, among which there has been a complex interplay, include the effort to compel or persuade the United States to withdraw its military protection from Taiwan, the drive to isolate Taiwan internationally, the campaign to build support on Taiwan for its reunion with the mainland under the PRC, and the contest with the ROC for the support of Chinese overseas. The most important of these forms of political action has been the attempt to get the United States to withdraw its military protection, for if the attempt were successful, the other three forms of political action would become more effective. The PRC leaders have refused to renounce the use of force in the Taiwan area because they believe that they have the sovereign right to use all necessary force to bring the unfinished civil war on Chinese territory to an end. To renounce, at the behest of a foreign state, the option of using force on their own territory would not only, as a matter of principle, be an unacceptable encroachment on the PRC's rights as the legitimate government of China but might also, as a practical matter, end their hopes of gaining control of Taiwan.

Contention between Peking and Taipei for the loyalty of all Chinese has been conducted in a variety of ways, including propaganda, organizational activities among overseas Chinese, the provision of advanced education to young Chinese from abroad, and the infiltration of agents into each other's territory. The PRC has had the great advantage of governing the China mainland and, since 1971, of being seated in the United Nations as the legitimate government of China. But its efforts have been hampered by its inability so far to weaken drastically US ties with Taiwan and by the ROC's success in providing effective government and economic progress to the people of Taiwan.

The Ties That Bind

The PRC has never wavered in its insistence that Taiwan is an integral part of China. Its propaganda and political action aimed at Taiwan and Chinese overseas has stressed Chinese patriotism and love for the homeland. The appeal of Chinese nationalism is a potent one, for the pressure of Chinese history, culture, and language bears heavily on all Chinese, mainland or Taiwanese. Even the overseas Chinese feel a closer attachment to the motherland than do emigrants from most other countries. Throughout the long history of China, no territories inhabited by Han Chinese ever broke away permanently from the main body of the nation. Division and civil war invariably ended in reunification. The rule of Taiwan by Cheng Ch'eng-kung (Koxinga) and his descendants from 1662 to 1683, although it denied control of the island to Peking temporarily, was not aimed at taking Taiwan out of the Chinese empire, but at defeating the Manchu usurpers and restoring the Ming dynasty. Except for Taiwan, the only sizable Chinese population in former Chinese territory not under the rule of the PRC is that in Hong Kong and Macao. The PRC claims both. The citizens of the PRC would find it difficult to conceive of any solution to the Taiwan problem that did not ultimately make the island an integral part of China, in fact as well as in theory.

Thus, the official "one China" position asserted by the ROC as well as by the PRC was firmly grounded in historical precedent. While it was in the interest of mainlanders in Taiwan to maintain this position as a justification for their continued domination of the government, it was also true that for most of them a total and final separation from mainland China would be difficult to contemplate. Even the Taiwanese,

123

although they had become accustomed to a de facto separate status and would be loath to submit to control from Peking, could not escape the ties of language, tradition, and custom that have made them Chinese. The educational system on Taiwan has served to reinforce the Chineseness of the population by its heavy emphasis on Chinese language and history. It would be a psychological wrench for most people on Taiwan to accept the view that they and their descendants would no longer be part of the stream of history now represented by the 850 million people on the China mainland.

Pride in China's growing prestige and influence, although rarely expressed openly, also made the Chinese of Taiwan reluctant to cut their ties with the mainland. They could not suppress their satisfaction when the PLA administered a drubbing to the Indians in defense of China's frontiers, and they had a fraternal feeling toward the Chinese troops who stood up to the Soviets in the north. They have cherished the hope that conditions on the mainland will change so that some day they or their children could be a part of the great China of the future.

Family connections were also an important link between the mainlanders on Taiwan and their old homes. Many lost contact entirely, but a surprising number was able to maintain a tenuous communication via Hong Kong. For those few who returned to the mainland, the desire to be reunited with parents, brothers and sisters, or children appears to have been the strongest motivation.

Measured against the potent appeal of Chinese nationalism as a bond between Taiwan and the mainland, the appeal of Communist ideology to the people of Taiwan has been insignificant. For a variety of reasons the nature of the Communist system under the PRC probably constitutes more of an obstacle to the reunion of Taiwan with the mainland than a force tending to draw them together. Its appeal would be impossible to measure, in any case, because the propagation of communism in Taiwan has been so sternly suppressed. It is possible, however, that some of those on the lower rungs of the social and economic ladder may believe that their relative position would improve under a Communist system. And some intellectuals may be attracted by the egalitarianism, the spirit of national self-reliance, and the puritanical way of life advocated by the Chinese Communist party, although these attractions must have been weakened by the ideological excesses of the cultural revolution and other evidence of political instability.

Thrust and Counterthrust

For some time after the US intervention in the Chinese civil war, the PRC was too deeply involved in the Korean conflict and other problems to develop a comprehensive political strategy toward Taiwan. In 1950, it tried to get the United Nations to oppose the US "occupation" of Taiwan, but when this move failed, it resorted to continual verbal attacks on the United States and threats to "liberate" Taiwan by force, culminating in the military attacks on the offshore islands in 1954–1955.

Soon thereafter, the PRC changed its tactics, proposing negotiations with the United States on the Taiwan issue and stressing to Taiwan itself the possibility of a peaceful resolution of the question. In July 1955, Chou En-lai declared that the PRC was prepared to negotiate directly with "the responsible local authorities" on Taiwan for its "peaceful liberation."[1] At the National People's Congress the following year, Chou presented a carefully formulated appeal to Chinese in Taiwan and elsewhere to contribute to the reunification of Taiwan with the mainland. He pledged that "the Chinese people would seek to liberate Taiwan by peaceful means so far as it is possible" and asserted that "the possibility of peaceful liberation is increasing." Warning the KMT military and political personnel on Taiwan that they were in constant danger of being stabbed in the back or abandoned by the United States, he declared: "Now, on behalf of the government, I formally state: we are willing to negotiate with the Taiwan authorities on specific steps and terms for the peaceful liberation of Taiwan, and we hope that the Taiwan authorities will send their representatives to Peking or other appropriate places, at a time which they consider appropriate, to begin these talks with us." Chou went on to make a number of promises designed to reassure and appeal to Chinese on Taiwan and abroad. Regardless of how great their crimes might have been, those who joined the "patriotic ranks" and worked for the peaceful liberation of Taiwan would not be punished for their misdeeds but would be rewarded and given appropriate jobs. Compatriots in Taiwan, who had "always been an inseparable part of the Chinese people," would be welcomed to participate in the socialist construction of the motherland. KMT military and political personnel on Taiwan would be allowed to communicate with relatives and friends on the mainland and to return for short visits with them, for which purpose they would be given assistance. So long as "the responsible KMT military and political personages on Taiwan" worked for the peaceful liberation of Taiwan, their future positions would be assured. They could send representatives to the mainland to resolve any doubts they might have as to conditions there, and the entry and departure of such representatives would be guaranteed. And finally, the KMT military personnel on Taiwan who expedited the peaceful liberation of Taiwan would be well treated, as evidenced by the treatment accorded to their military compatriots who had gone

---

1. US Consulate General, Hong Kong, *Current Background*, no. 342, Aug. 3, 1955.

over to communism on the mainland. Chou also appealed to KMT military and political personnel residing abroad and to "patriotic overseas Chinese" to promote the cause of peaceful liberation of Taiwan.[2]

Chou's formula for the "peaceful liberation" of Taiwan provided the basic guidelines for PRC policies toward Taiwan in subsequent years, except for the brief return to the use of force against the offshore islands in 1958. His effort to exploit the anxieties in Taiwan over the US negotiations then taking place with the PRC in Geneva foreshadowed the more vigorous efforts to drive a wedge between the United States and the ROC at the time of the 1958 crisis and again after Nixon's China trip in 1972. A noteworthy aspect of Chou's 1956 appeal was the way that it virtually ignored the Taiwanese, an orientation in sharp contrast to the numerous measures taken after 1972 to appeal to the Taiwanese.

Although the ROC promptly rejected Chou's proposals, he continued to urge publicly Taiwan's "peaceful liberation." In a press conference at Calcutta in December 1956, he remarked: "The Chinese Government is making all efforts for the peaceful liberation of Taiwan as well as efforts to win Chiang Kai-shek over. If Taiwan is restored to China then Chiang Kai-shek would have made a contribution and he could stay in any part of his fatherland according to his wish. You have mentioned an offer of a government position to Chiang Kai-shek would be offered a minister's post [sic]. I said a minister's post is too low."[3] But Chiang was not impressed by Chou's proposals. He denounced them as "acts of deception," and affirmed that there was "absolutely no possibility of any compromise" with Peking, since "the Chinese Government has already had too many painful experiences in negotiating with the Communists."[4]

Reverting to a combination of military and political action in the offshore island bombardment of 1958, the PRC appealed again to nationalistic feelings and tried to stimulate suspicion of the United States among Chinese on Taiwan. The flavor of this appeal came through strongly in a message broadcast by Defense Minister P'eng Te-huai to "compatriots in Taiwan" on October 25, 1958, after the blockade of Quemoy had been breached and the odd-day bombing pattern had been instituted:

We are fully aware that the overwhelming majority of you are patriots, and only extremely few among you are willing slaves

2. US Consulate General, Hong Kong, *Current Background*, no. 395, July 5, 1956.
3. US Consulate General, Hong Kong, *Survey of China Mainland Press*, no. 1430 (Dec. 13, 1956): 31.
4. Chiu, *China and the Question of Taiwan*, p. 275.

of the Americans. Compatriots! Chinese problems can only
be settled by us Chinese. If they are difficult to settle for the
time being, things can be talked over at length. The American political broker Dulles ... wants to ... order Chinese to
do this or that, to harm the interests of the Chinese and serve
the interests of the Americans. That is to say: step one, to
isolate Taiwan; step two, to place Taiwan under trusteeship ...

Friends of the Kuomintang! Do you not sense this
danger? Where is the way out? ... There is only one China,
not two, in the world. On this we agree ... Of course, we are
not advising you to break with the Americans right away.
That would be an unrealistic idea. We only hope that you
will not yield to American pressure, submit to their every
whim and will, lose your sovereign rights, and so finally be
deprived of shelter in the world and thrown into the sea.
These words of ours are well-intentioned and bear no ill-
will. You will come to understand them by and by.[5]

But the ROC continued firmly to reject all PRC proposals for negotiation.

Despite the lack of progress toward negotiations on Taiwan between the two governments, PRC leaders must have been gratified at the
determination with which Chiang Kai-shek opposed any suggestion of
a "two Chinas" resolution of the Taiwan problem. Even before President Truman interposed US military power between Taiwan and the
mainland, fears that the United States might be engaged in a scheme
to set up a separate Taiwan surfaced in Peking. As early as September
1949, Taiwanese in mainland China accused the United States of wanting to gain control of Taiwan.[6] The PRC's suspicions were strengthened by US statements that the legal status of Taiwan was undetermined,
by the increasingly close network of relations being created between the
United States and Taiwan, by proposals of American scholars for a
separate status for Taiwan, and by the impetus given the concept of
"two Chinas" in the United States and elsewhere by the offshore island
crisis of 1958.[7]

Throughout the 1960s, statements by PRC leaders and editorials in
the *People's Daily* repeatedly charged the United States with scheming
to create "two Chinas" or "one China, one Taiwan." The PRC warned
Washington that it would never accept such an arrangement and alerted

---

5. Chiu, *China and the Question of Taiwan,* pp. 288–290.
6. Chiu, *China and the Question of Taiwan,* pp. 215–217.
7. E.g. the "Conlon Report," prepared by US scholars for Senate Committee on Foreign Relations in 1959, proposed that a "Republic of Taiwan" be established under
US sponsorship.

KMT leaders in Taipei that the United States was plotting to replace them with subservient puppets who would go along with American designs. Chou En-lai asserted in 1960:

> For quite some time now, the U.S. Government has been scheming to create "two Chinas." In this regard, both the Republican and the Democratic Parties in the United States have the same policy. The United States seeks to set up what they call an "independent state" of Taiwan, or a "Sino-Formosan nation," or to conduct what they call a "plebiscite" in Taiwan, or even to place Taiwan "under trusteeship," and so on. All this is aimed at dismembering Chinese territory, violating China's sovereign rights and legalizing the seizure of Taiwan by the United States. All the Chinese people, including those on Taiwan, are firmly opposed to these schemes; even those members of the Chiang Kai-shek clique who have the slightest concern for the national interest don't approve of them.[8]

Chiang Kai-shek, for his part, treated the idea of two Chinas no less scornfully. In March 1964, he declared: "I myself and the Chinese people are resolutely opposed to the "two Chinas" concept. The Republic of China will never consent to any "two Chinas" arrangement. Meanwhile, I believe that the conspiracy for "two Chinas" can produce only a negligible effect on the free world as a whole. It can in no way affect the international position of the Republic of China." And in 1968 the ROC ambassador to the United States, Chow Shu-k'ai, presented the historical and legal justification for regarding Taiwan as an integral part of China in terms very similar to those repeatedly put forward by the PRC.[9]

The attachment of both the PRC and the ROC to the principle of "one China" caused them to share a common hostility to the Taiwan independence movement. Neither accepted it as genuinely promoting self-determination for the people of Taiwan. But they differed in their views as to who was behind the movement and what was its ultimate purpose. Peking regarded it as having been concocted by the United States, in collaboration with "Japanese reactionaries," as a means of severing Taiwan from China and bringing it permanently under US and Japanese control.[10] The fact that supporters of the

---

8. Chiu, *China and the Question of Taiwan*, pp. 301–302, 312–317, 322–327, 335–338.
9. Chiu, *China and the Question of Taiwan*, pp. 321, 322–333.
10. PRC denunciations of alleged US-Japanese collaboration in support of the Taiwan independence movement became most strident in 1970–1971, after Prime Minister Eisaku Sato in the Nixon-Sato communiqué of November 1969 declared that security

Taiwan independence movement were most numerous and active in the United States and Japan lent color to this accusation. Whether or not the PRC leaders really believed that the United States was behind the Taiwan independence movement, the charge that it was provided another convenient means by which to try to stimulate suspicion of US plans among mainlander leaders on Taiwan. The ROC, on the other hand, excoriated the Taiwan independence movement as a tool of the PRC itself. Chiang Kai-shek charged that Mao was using the movement to drive a wedge between mainlanders and Taiwanese in order to further his purpose of "liberating" Taiwan. He accused the Communists of secretly financing the movement, while overtly attacking it.[11]

The many differences that separated Taipei and Peking could not be overcome by their common adherence to the "one China" principle and their common hostility to the Taiwan independence movement. From 1950 to 1972, the PRC's various official proposals to the ROC to enter into negotiations invariably met with a stony rejection. The secret ambassadorial talks between the United States and the PRC, which began in 1955, caused misgivings in Taiwan but, even with the added military pressure on the offshore islands in 1958, did not strain Washington-Taipei relations sufficiently to cause Chiang Kai-shek to respond to PRC appeals that the divided Chinese should begin to talk with each other. The ROC continued to rely on solidifying relations with the United States and hoping for changes on the mainland that would permit the reunion of China under conditions compatible with the interests and convictions of the Chinese on Taiwan.

The PRC supplemented its official proposals for negotiation with a variety of political actions aimed at stimulating interest in them and weakening support for the ROC in Taiwan and abroad, including appeals to KMT leaders on Taiwan, propaganda broadcasts, infiltration of agents, and organizational work among the overseas Chinese. The ROC fought back with similar political weapons.

The appeals to individual KMT leaders came from relatives, friends, former subordinates, and others on the mainland. Some were broadcast; others arrived in letters, often hand-carried from Hong Kong. Like the official statements, they appealed to nationalistic feelings, but in addition they sought to assure the recipient, by reference to the writer's own experience in the PRC, that those who contributed to Taiwan's "liberation" could expect good treatment. Propaganda broadcasts to Taiwan described the virtues of "people's China" and contrasted them with the evils of preliberation China and the alleged

---

in the Taiwan area was "a most important factor for the security of Japan." Chiu, *China and the Question of Taiwan*, pp. 335–338.
11. Chiu, *China and the Question of Taiwan*, p. 338.

misery existing on Taiwan. They attacked the "Chiang Kai-shek remnant clique" as puppets of the United States, trying to alienate the people on Taiwan from the government, and the ROC from the United States.

The ROC retaliated in broadcasts that denounced the "Maoist bandits" and showed scenes of suffering on the mainland and of the good life on Taiwan. The ROC supplemented its broadcasts with propaganda balloons, some attached to food packages, which were carried inland from the offshore islands on the monsoon winds. The generally heavy-handed and unsubtle propaganda in both directions seems to have had little effect.

The number of individuals from among the elite of either side who defected after 1950 was remarkably small. A few diplomats from each side defected to the other. Several pilots from each air force have gone over to the other side. The most recent defection was the PRC squadron leader who landed his MIG-19 in Taiwan on July 7, 1977. Occasional low-ranking officials defected. The highest ROC official to go to the PRC was Li Tsung-jen, former vice-president and rival of Chiang Kai-shek, who went to Peking in 1965 from the United States, where he had lived since 1949. But he was not a genuine post-1950 defector, for he had never gone to Taiwan and had long been replaced as vice-president. His arrival in Peking provided the occasion for a renewed appeal to ROC leaders to break with the United States and return to the fatherland.[12] Given the relative freedom of travel of Taiwan residents, the small number of defections over the years suggests that the PRC has been unable to convince more than a handful of mainlanders living in Taiwan that their aspirations could be better realized on the mainland.

The relative success of covert operations mounted by each side is impossible to gauge with any accuracy. Peking and Taipei from time to time announced the arrest of agents. The Hong Kong police periodically seized KMT operatives and quantities of arms and explosives, apparently intended for acts of sabotage on the mainland. When Taipei announced the arrest of persons for treasonable activities, it was sometimes difficult to differentiate between those who might actually have been PRC agents and those connected with the Taiwan

---

12. Vice-Premier Ch'en Yi announced on Sept. 29, 1965, that Li had returned to take part in the KMT Revolutionary Committee, one of several minor parties permitted to exist under the strict control of the Chinese Communist party, and that Chiang Kai-shek and Chiang Ching-kuo would be welcome to return and take part also. All that was necessary was for them "to break away from US imperialistic control and be loyal to the motherland." Ch'en added that "the possibility of Kuomintang-Communist cooperation is great and is, moreover, increasing." Chiu, *China and the Question of Taiwan*, p. 329.

independence movement, since in the eyes of the ROC the latter were also serving Peking's purposes. Both governments were highly security-conscious and had extensive security apparatuses, although the government in Taiwan did not control all aspects of the life of the individual as the PRC did. Peking may conceivably have had some success in infiltrating agents into Taiwan to obtain intelligence, but it had little success in making the government or people of Taiwan perceptibly more receptive to "liberation."

The Struggle for Overseas Chinese

The competition for the loyalty of overseas Chinese focused principally on Southeast Asia, where 95 percent of the 12 to 15 million overseas Chinese lived.[13] Until World War II, the large two-way flow of new emigrants and returnees constantly renewed the bonds between these Chinese communities abroad and the homeland. Chinese governments traditionally reinforced these ties through government agencies created to assist overseas Chinese, especially by helping them educate their children in the Chinese language and culture. Overseas Chinese in turn demonstrated their attachment to China by remittances to their relatives in the homeland and by substantial patriotic contributions to causes, such as Sun Yat-sen's revolution against Manchu rule and the defense of China against Japanese aggression.

With the establishment of independent governments in the former European colonies of Southeast Asia after World War II, the rise of local nationalism increasingly eroded the links between the overseas Chinese and mainland China. The immigration of Chinese into Southeast Asian nations was halted. Chinese language newspapers were shut down, and Chinese schools were closed or restricted in many places. Chinese were excluded from some of their traditional economic activities and professions. Thus, after 1949, when the PRC and the ROC began to compete for the loyalty of overseas Chinese, they had to operate in an atmosphere of growing anti-Chinese sentiment.

During the early 1950s, the PRC followed the pattern established by the KMT: it set up an Overseas Chinese Affairs Commission, urged over-

---

13. There are no precise figures on the numbers of overseas Chinese because no commonly accepted definition of an overseas Chinese exists. The highest figure, 21.5 million, given by the ROC, includes dual nationals, many of whom are excluded from other estimates, and approximately 4.7 million Chinese in Hong Kong and Macao, who are treated differently from overseas Chinese by both the ROC and the PRC. *China Yearbook, 1975,* p. 380. The PRC used the figure "approximately 13 million" in the late 1950s but has not since given a figure.

seas Chinese to support the PRC, encouraged remittances to family members and to educational institutions for overseas Chinese in mainland China, created facilities for private investment in industry by overseas Chinese, provided educational materials to overseas Chinese schools in Southeast Asia, and invited Chinese youths to come to China for high school or college education. The PRC condemned the KMT for failing to protect the rights and interests of the overseas Chinese and declared that the strong new China would do a better job.

By the late 1950s, however, the PRC found that the degree of involvement in overseas Chinese affairs demanded by the traditional approach conflicted with its foreign policy objectives. It discovered that it was unable to intervene effectively to protect overseas Chinese from discrimination by local governments and that attempts to do so heightened Southeast Asian fears of intervention in their internal affairs by a powerful Communist China. Moreover, retaining the goodwill of overseas Chinese required preferential treatment for their relatives in China, which was incompatible with the PRC's domestic policies. Consequently, instead of urging all overseas Chinese to support the PRC, Chou En-lai and other leaders in Peking shifted to encouraging them to adopt the nationality of their host country or, if they wished to remain Chinese, to scrupulously respect the laws of the host country and to refrain from interfering in its politics. The preferential treatment of relatives of overseas Chinese in China was greatly diminished. Students were no longer welcomed indiscriminately to study in China. Those who were admitted were told that they would be expected to remain in China permanently once they had completed their studies. The PRC was still interested in receiving remittances from Southeast Asia but appeared to be reconciled to their inevitable decline as the older generation of overseas Chinese with close family ties in China died off. By the late 1960s, remittances had dwindled, and the number of overseas Chinese going to study in mainland China had become negligible.[14]

The ROC suffered severe losses of support relative to the PRC in overseas Chinese communities in the early 1950s, owing partly to the early enthusiasm for the "new China" among the young and partly to the PRC's success in establishing diplomatic relations with Indonesia and Burma. In these countries the PRC sought to persuade the local governments to prohibit KMT activities, outlaw the KMT, and deport KMT agents. Overseas Chinese tended to align themselves, at least outwardly, with the diplomatic relations maintained by the host country. As a result, until the 1970s Taipei was protected against more serious

---

14. Stephen Fitzgerald, *China and the Overseas Chinese* (London: Cambridge University Press, 1972); Mary F. Somers Heidhues, *Southeast Asia's Chinese Minorities* (Melbourne: Longman, 1974).

losses by the continuance of diplomatic relations with the ROC by most Southeast Asian countries.

The change in policy toward the overseas Chinese by the PRC in the late 1950s and the economic surge of the ROC in the 1960s brought some gains for the ROC, as did the suspension of diplomatic relations between the PRC and Indonesia in 1965. As remittances to mainland China declined, investment in Taiwan rose. Overseas Chinese investment in Taiwan climbed from $1 million in 1960 to $80 million in 1974.[15] While mainland China lost its attractiveness for overseas Chinese students, they continued to come to Taiwan. Encouraged by scholarships, travel grants, and other subsidies, some 9700 were studying in Taiwan in 1974, and more than 40,000 had studied in Taiwan between 1954 and 1974.[16]

Among the millions of overseas Chinese in Southeast Asia and elsewhere, only a small fraction are actively involved in the struggle between the PRC and the ROC. For the vast majority, their principal concern is how to protect their interests and improve their livelihood in the host country.[17] Assimilation is the long-term trend, but it is slow, partly because of obstacles raised by the host country and partly because of the Chinese reluctance to abandon the culture of their ancestors and become indistinguishable from others. The thousands of young Chinese still seeking a Chinese higher education in Taiwan testify to the tenacious hold of the historical and cultural bond.[18] For a long time to come, overseas communities of people who regard themselves as Chinese will continue to exist, but the number willing to involve themselves in the political struggle between the PRC and the ROC will probably continue to decline.

Over the past twenty-five years, the nature of the struggle between the PRC and the ROC in overseas Chinese communities has changed. The PRC has won the contest for international recognition as the government of China, thus gaining a far stronger position from which to claim the loyalty of the overseas Chinese. But the anti-Chinese and anti-Communist views of most Southeast Asian governments place constraints on the extent to which Chinese minorities in these countries are willing to identify themselves as supporters of the PRC.[19] Conse-

---

15. *TSDB,* p. 230.

16. *141 Questions and Answers about the Republic of China* (Taipei: Government Information Office, n.d.), p. 30.

17. See e.g. Wang Gungwu, "Chinese Politics in Malaysia," *The China Quarterly,* no. 43 (July–September 1970): 1–30.

18. See David W. Chang, "Current Status of Chinese Minorities in Southeast Asia," *Asian Survey* 13 no. 6 (June 1973): 587–603.

19. Reactions of overseas Chinese to the PRC are complex and vary from country to country. E.g. in Fiji, rather than favoring establishment of a PRC diplomatic mission,

quently, in order to avoid complicating its state-to-state relations with Southeast Asian countries, to which it has assigned a higher priority than to relations with overseas Chinese, Peking has chosen to assert in a low voice its claims to the loyalty of those Chinese who have not chosen to become nationals of the host country.

The ROC has been compelled to assume an even lower profile in its relations with overseas communities because it no longer has official relations with most of the host governments. Thus, the political struggle is now less concerned with outward signs of support, such as flying the PRC or the ROC flag on national days, and more with the practical results of the ties with the overseas Chinese communities. Both governments, for example, rely heavily on overseas Chinese to handle trade and financial transactions with the host country. Because Taiwan's survival depends greatly on foreign trade and industrial growth, these connections are important. Consequently, Taipei has found it reassuring that, even though organizations such as the Chinese Chamber of Commerce shifted from a pro-ROC to a pro-PRC orientation when the host government established diplomatic relations with the PRC, many businessmen privately assured Taipei that this was simply a necessary adjustment to local conditions, and trade with Taiwan continued as usual. Moreover, since the ROC has been deprived of official channels for dealing with most foreign governments, friendly overseas Chinese are valuable not only as traders but also as middlemen and facilitators.

The contest for influence within the overseas Chinese communities will probably have only a marginal affect on the outcome of the PRC's efforts to "liberate" Taiwan. Peking can interfere with the economic connections between Taiwan and the overseas Chinese only if it is willing to assume the onus of interfering with the host countries' external trade. Peking may be able to enlist a few intelligence agents among the overseas Chinese, who would have readier access to Taiwan than Chinese from mainland China or Hong Kong. Should talks be contemplated between the PRC and the ROC, overseas Chinese might serve as suitable go-betweens. Thus, both governments continue to devote substantial resources to the competition for the loyalty of overseas Chinese, but the shrinking numbers of overseas Chinese willing to involve themselves in the political struggle between Peking and Taipei seem unlikely to have a significant influence on its outcome.

---

which might be expected to act vigorously to protect the interests of Chinese nationals, 96 percent of the respondents to a public opinion poll among the small Chinese community opposed it, fearing that a strong and active Chinese mission would do them more harm than good, and preferring the impotent but harmless Trade Mission from Taiwan. Stuart W. Greif, "Political Attitudes of the Overseas Chinese in Fiji," *Asian Survey* 15, no. 11 (November 1975): 977.

Post-1972 PRC Campaign

President Nixon's decision to open relations with the PRC significantly strengthened Peking's hand in its political contest with Taipei. Once the PRC had been admitted to and the ROC expelled from the United Nations, most of the remaining props were removed from the ROC's claim to be the legitimate government of China. Nixon's highly publicized trip to Peking and the language of the Shanghai communiqué created the impression in Taiwan and elsewhere that the United States was planning to move fairly quickly to establish diplomatic relations with the PRC and to disengage from Taiwan. More than any action by the United States since 1950, the Nixon visit created grave doubts in Taiwan concerning the reliability of the United States as a protector of its security. Exploiting its improved position, Peking redoubled its efforts to convince the people of Taiwan that "liberation" was inevitable and would not harm their interests.

The PRC was still handicapped, however, because the United States continued to have diplomatic relations with the ROC, maintained its security treaty, and expanded its economic relations with Taiwan. Peking could not reinforce its political campaign by threats of force without alarming the United States, thereby making it less likely that the United States would consent to dimish its links with Taiwan in the manner demanded by the PRC as the condition for the establishment of formal diplomatic relations. The PRC leaders appeared to think that Taiwan's "liberation" would come in two stages. First, the military intervention by the United States would be ended. Second, the terms of Taiwan's integration into the mainland would be negotiated between the Chinese themselves, without US participation. Until the first stage had been completed, proposals for the integration of Taiwan would be couched only in the most general terms because the PRC lacked the bargaining power it would acquire in the second stage. Thus, the political campaign that was aimed at Taiwan after the Shanghai communiqué, although more intense than before in some respects, was probably not expected to produce concrete results. Rather, it was preparing the ground for the real bargaining that would come later.

A distinctive characteristic of the post-1972 political campaign was the emphasis on the Taiwanese. The early appeals to Taiwan had been aimed almost exclusively at mainlanders. No doubt the leaders in Peking recognized that family and other personal connections with the mainland were by 1972 wearing thin. Moreover, it was obvious that Taiwanese influence in governing circles on Taiwan was growing and that eventually the native-born would achieve predominance. From the PRC's viewpoint, it was vital that the Taiwanese adhere to the "one China" principle when they came to dominate the government.

Thus, the PRC began courting the Taiwanese. The Taiwan Democratic Self-Government League on the mainland received more prominent mention. Greater attention was paid to the commemoration of the February 28, 1947, uprising by Taiwanese against the mainlander government on Taiwan, which was portrayed as an aspect of the nation-wide struggle by the People of China against KMT oppression. At least two persons of Taiwan origin were elected to the Central Committee of the Chinese Communist party at the Tenth Party Congress in August 1973, and twelve delegates of Taiwan origin took part in the National People's Congress of January 1975.[20] The large official mission to Japan in April 1973, headed by Liao Ch'eng-chih, chairman of the Sino-Japanese Friendship Association, paid particular attention to persons of Taiwan origin living in Japan. Special receptions were held at the Canton Fair for persons of Taiwan origin. Tourists' services were opened in the principal cities of Fukien to take care of "compatriots from Taiwan" desiring to visit that province.

The PRC made an intensive effort to use sports to persuade young people of Taiwan origin to visit the mainland. In August 1973, a team composed of persons from Taiwan living in the United States and Japan participated in the Asia-Africa-Latin America invitational table tennis tournament in Peking. In April 1974, Taiwan-born athletes from the United States and Japan took part in the Peking trials for the selection of the PRC team at the Seventh Asian Games in Teheran. In September 1975, Taiwan-born athletes from the United States, Japan, and other countries represented Taiwan province in the Third National Games held in Peking. These athletes were received by Teng Hsiao-p'ing and other senior leaders, feted at receptions and dinners, and given a tour of the country. Those who had relatives in Fukien province were taken to visit them. In July 1977, a basketball team made up of Taiwanese living in the United States and Canada and a baseball team composed of Taiwanese in Japan visited the PRC.

The PRC's wooing of Taiwanese produced a softening in its attitude toward the Taiwanese independence movement. Instead of denouncing the adherents of the movement as tools of the United States or Japan, Peking began to treat them as persons who were misguided but capable of redemption, since they shared the Chinese Communist's antipathy to the KMT. The PRC sought to take advantage of the discouragement felt within the movement when the United States virtually ruled out support for an independent Taiwan in the Shanghai communiqué.[21]

---

20. Lin Li-yun, a participant in the February 28 uprising, and Ts'ai Hsiao.
21. *The New York Times,* Jan. 31, 1973.

During the years after the issuance of the Shanghai communiqué, senior PRC leaders gave a number of authoritative expositions of their policies toward Taiwan to visitors from the United States, including some of Chinese origin. These meetings seemed to be trying to convey to Americans and to the people of Taiwan reassurance that the "liberation" of the island would be peaceful and that subsequent economic and political change would be gradual. Chou En-lai himself spoke with such groups until he became too ill to receive visitors.

At a five-hour interview with overseas Chinese from North America in August 1972, Chou expressed understanding of the support and sympathy received by the Taiwan independence movement from Taiwanese abroad, attributing their attitude to Taiwan's long separation from the mainland and to KMT propaganda, which distorted the true nature of the people's revolution on the mainland.[22] He invited Taiwanese to visit the mainland, more than once if necessary, in order to see for themselves that the Chinese people were now their own masters. Chou defined the liberation of Taiwan in the same terms as the liberation of the mainland—to make the people of Taiwan their own masters. He added that the liberation of Taiwan was a matter of great complexity, so one should not become impatient and a military solution should be avoided.

Chou went on to stress the great importance of the role of Taiwanese in peacefully liberating Taiwan. He intimated that the recruitment of Taiwanese cadres to participate both in the liberation of Taiwan and in its subsequent administration might already be under way. Chou denied emphatically that incorporating Taiwan into the PRC would lower living standards there, pointing to the example of Shanghai, which had enjoyed the highest living standard in China in 1949 and still did. The transfer of Taiwan's private enterprise to government ownership would take longer than the seven years it required in Shanghai, and the transformation of Taiwan's social and political system would also be gradual. The PRC could negotiate with the present government for the liberation of Taiwan, Chou said, but that regime would have to be removed so that the people of Taiwan could run their own affairs. Chou did not specify whether Taiwan would be a province of China or an autonomous region, but at one point he referred to the precedent of Tibet.[23]

Other interviews by Chou followed similar lines.[24] In a con-

---

22. Joseph J. Lee, "Peking's View of Taiwan: An Interview with Chou En-lai," in Jo, *Taiwan's Future* pp. 65–70.
23. For the thoroughgoing control by Peking over Tibet, see *Washington Post,* Oct. 16, 1977.
24. See e.g. reports of Chou En-lai's interviews with Chinese from abroad in Hong

versation with an American correspondent in June 1971, Chou offered additional details about plans for Taiwan's economy after liberation. Living standards would improve, he said, because income taxes would be abolished, other taxes decreased, internal and external debts eliminated, and needed capital for construction provided by subsidies from the mainland.[25]

Despite its new emphasis on influencing the Taiwanese, the PRC did not neglect the mainlanders on Taiwan, who, after all, would continue to be the dominant element in the government of the ROC for some years to come. Appeals to them were made by Liao Ch'eng-chih and Fu Tso-yi at a meeting in Peking in 1973 to commemorate the February 1947 uprising, shortly after the United States and the PRC had announced their agreement to establish liaison offices in their respective capitals.[26] Liao warned that the general trend was now clear and that "the state of hanging on to imperialist forces to prolong one's feeble existence will never last long." Echoing previous appeals, Liao called on the military and administrative personnel of "the Chiang Kai-shek clique" to seize the opportunity to contribute to the unification of the motherland. He assured them that "we treat all patriots with due respect and forgive them for their past wrongdoings—however serious these were—provided they now support the socialist motherland and work for the unification of the motherland." Fu Tso-yi, former commander of Nationalist forces in North China, who had negotiated the surrender of Peking to the Communists and had been rewarded with a cabinet post in the Peking government, cited his own experience to his former colleagues as an example of what they might expect if they contributed to the unification of the motherland. Referring to the Shanghai communiqué and the agreement on the establishment of liaison offices, Fu warned his countrymen that they could not rely on the United States much longer. He added: "We are all Chinese... why couldn't we talk for the sake of the sacred cause of unifying the motherland?... Let us come together and talk, the sooner the better. If you are not prepared to enter into formal talks right away, then send some people to the mainland, openly or secretly, to have a look and visit relatives and friends. You can rest assured that the government will keep the matter secret, keep its word and guarantee your safety and freedom to come and go."

Kong periodical *Ch'i Shih Nien Tai* (*The Seventies*), December 1972, pp. 38, 39, April 1973, pp. 30, 31, and comments on Taiwan made to visiting Chinese by Ch'iao Kuan-hua and Lo Ch'ing-Ch'ang, May 1973, in *Ch'i Shih Nien Tai*, October 1973, pp. 63–65.
25. Seymour Topping, *Journey Between Two Chinas* (New York: Harper & Row, 1972), pp. 399–400.
26. FBIS, *Daily Report, People's Republic of China*, Mar. 1, 1973, pp. B5–B9.

In October 1974, Teng Hsiao-p'ing, who by then had taken over many of Chou En-lai's duties, met with a group of overseas Chinese and Taiwanese, for whom he summarized the current state of the campaign to liberate Taiwan:

> What method should be adopted for the liberation of Taiwan? In general, it is hoped that this can be resolved through peaceful negotiations. However, there is a problem: At present, with Chiang Kai-shek and his son in power, can peaceful negotiations be carried out? Can the negotiations be successful? There are basically no negotiations at present. What should be done if peace is impossible? What other methods could be taken if the peaceful method cannot be carried out? We should not exclude this method! We have to do out best at present and continue to make energetic efforts. The future calls for the consideration of both the peaceful and nonpeaceful methods. At this stage, prior consideration is given to the peaceful method ... We hope that through a relatively long period of work, our fellow countrymen in Taiwan will understand the conditions and policies of our country. We believe that the patriotic forces in Taiwan can be developed. The development of patriotic forces can play a part in both peaceful liberation and the nonpeaceful method. Our patriotic fellow countrymen overseas and compatriots in Taiwan will definitely produce results in doing more work. The result at the beginning is not always very great, but the work accumulated little by little will produce an effect.[27]

Meetings of high PRC officials with visiting Chinese from abroad, intended to convey authoritative views on the Taiwan issue to the people on Taiwan through personal channels, were supplemented by a barrage of broadcasts. Former Nationalist army commanders, provincial governors, industrialists, professors, journalists, diplomats, and students took to the air to convince their former friends and colleagues on Taiwan of the good life in people's China. Most of these messages came from older persons who had been prominent in Nationalist China and were directed primarily to mainlanders. A few younger people educated in Taiwan broadcast dismal pictures of the life there as compared to the mainland. The newly established intercourse between the United States and the PRC was underlined by references to the recent visits to the PRC by many Chinese from the United States.

Broadcasts attributed to individuals known in Taiwan were accompanied by larger numbers of general propaganda broadcasts. The

---

27. Ibid., Dec. 10, 1974, pp. E5–E6.

themes of these broadcasts were in the main familiar: the happiness of the mainland and the misery in Taiwan, the growing international stature of the PRC and the increasing isolation of the ROC, and the need to throw off the US yoke and complete the unification of China. But the trend of events in East Asia since 1972 gave the PRC propagandists fresh ammunition. The United States could not be relied on, they declared, both because it was in the process of normalizing relations with the PRC and because it had not come to the aid of South Vietnam and Cambodia when they were on the verge of collapse. The ROC was described as a "sinking ship" whose officials and merchants were building up bank accounts and investing in real estate abroad preparatory to fleeing. Even Chiang Ching-kuo, they pointed out, had sent his daughter and son-in-law to live in the United States.

In broadcasts referring to events in Taiwan, PRC propaganda showed greater knowledge of the situation there and an ability to respond to events there more quickly than in the past, although propagandists continued to undermine their own propaganda by gross exaggeration. Their primary emphasis was on the alleged exploitation of the island by foreign capital. Foreigners, principally Americans, were said to be taking advantage of the low wages on Taiwan, skimming off the wealth, keeping the workers in servitude, and causing inflation and recession that hurt the common people. The propagandists charged that foreign domination brought with it the decadent culture of the capitalist countries, resulting in a rise in crime and prostitution.

The PRC took another important step in its efforts to influence the people on Taiwan in 1975, when it announced the release of over 500 Nationalist prisoners, the first such act of amnesty since 1966 and by far the largest number released in a single year.[28] The first group of 293 persons was released in March 1975 as the result of a special amnesty granted by the Supreme People's Court to "all war criminals in custody." Many of those released were military commanders holding the rank of lieutenant general or major general; others were senior officers of the KMT or the Nationalist government and security services. All had been in custody twenty-five years or more. The second group, released in September 1975, consisted of 144 special agents or crew members of ROC vessels, all of them captured between 1962 and 1965 after having infiltrated PRC territory by sea or air. They were said to be the last remaining such agents in custody, the others having been released earlier. The third group, released in December 1975, was said to include "all former Kuomintang party, government, military, and

---

28. The dates of previous amnesties and the numbers released were: 1959—33, 1960—50, 1961—68, 1963—35, 1964—53, 1966—57, for a total of 296.

special agency personnel at or above county or regimental level who were held in custody." The total number in this group was not announced, but the names of 72 who were invited to Peking to take part in a "study tour" were released. Broadcasts by members of each group, directed to Taiwan, expressed gratitude for their release and a determination to work hard for the construction of the socialist motherland.[29]

The PRC's vice-premier and minister of public security, Hua Kuo-feng, declared that the release of the "war criminals" was of major significance in "promoting the patriotic struggle of the people of Taiwan against the Chiang Kai-shek clique." A broadcast to Taiwan from the Fukien Front PLA expressed confidence that the KMT military and administrative personnel in Taiwan, disillusioned with Chiang Kai-shek, would respond to the news of the release of their old colleagues by patriotically joining the Revolutionary United Front to contribute to the unification of the motherland.[30]

The "war criminals" granted amnesty were told that they could either start a new life in the PRC or, if they wished, go to Hong Kong or Taiwan. Ten of them who had elected to go to Taiwan soon arrived in Hong Kong amid worldwide publicity. The ROC was on the spot, having denounced the amnesty as a trick intended to weaken morale in Taiwan and to create a false illusion of stability on the mainland, among overseas Chinese and in the international community. It therefore hesitated to admit the ten, fearing that they would serve PRC ends, particularly as some had said that they wished only to visit Taiwan and return to the mainland. On the other hand, the ROC would look bad if it refused to accept former officials who had been jailed for years by the Communists because of their association with the ROC. In the end, caution prevailed and the ROC declined to admit them. In despair, one committed suicide in a Hong Kong hotel and several others returned to the mainland.

The PRC also offered the released special agents and crew members of the second group an opportunity to go to Taiwan. The sixty-five who elected to go were brought to Peking, where they were given a farewell dinner by the Ministry of Public Security and heard an address by an official describing the difficulties besetting "the Chiang clique" in Taiwan and stressing the hopes placed in the people of Taiwan to liberate the island and unify the motherland.

The ROC was better prepared to cope with the release of the second group than it had been with the first. It promptly broadcast to the mainland that reception centers had been prepared on Quemoy,

---

29. FBIS, *Daily Report, People's Republic of China,* Mar. 20, 1975, pp. E1–E3, Sept. 23, 1975, pp. C1–C3, Dec. 23, 1975, pp. C1–C4.
30. Ibid., Mar. 25, 1975, p. E6, Apr. 22, 1975, pp. C1–C2.

Matsu, and two of the smaller offshore islands for those who wished to return to Taiwan. Less then three weeks from the day that their release had been announced, sixty returnees arrived in Quemoy by boat from the mainland.[31] This group had closer ties with Taiwan than the "war criminals." They had all come from intelligence agencies under the direction of Chiang Ching-kuo, and over half of them were Taiwanese. By receiving them in Quemoy, the ROC could interrogate them and keep them isolated from the people of Taiwan long enough to minimize the risk that their return would contribute to the PRC's political campaign toward the island. Six additional amnestied prisoners, three each from the second and third groups, were sent by boat to Quemoy in February 1976.[32]

Despite the increased anxiety produced in Taiwan by the US government's announced intention to normalize relations with Peking, the PRC's intensified campaign since 1972 to win support in Taiwan for bringing the island under its control has had little perceptible effect. The government of the ROC has time and again rejected the idea of negotiating with the PRC. "Our stance is that we will never establish any type of contact with the Communists," Premier Chiang Ching-kuo told the Legislative Yuan in September 1976.[33] President C. K. Yen indicated that only if the government in Peking ceased to be Communist would negotiations be possible.[34] Public discussion in Taiwan of the proposals advanced by Chou En-lai for the unification of the island with the mainland has been taboo, and even private conversations on such subjects have to be conducted with care lest the participants be suspected of being pro-Communist.

Mainland broadcasts can be heard clearly in Taiwan, but it is illegal to listen. Prospective listeners seem to be deterred more by the dullness and blatant propaganda nature of the broadcasts than by the ban on listening, for there has been no report of anyone having been arrested for violating this law. Experienced political observers in Taiwan detect no significant effect of the increased propaganda beamed at Taiwan since 1972.

Unlike the propaganda broadcasts, the information about mainland China that interests the people on Taiwan, especially the mainlanders, is that which reaches them indirectly and mainly by word of mouth as a result of visits to the mainland by Chinese living in the United States and Japan. Because such visits have greatly increased since 1972, much

---

31. *The New York Times,* Oct. 9, 1975.
32. FBIS, *Daily Report, People's Republic of China,* Jan. 29, 1976, p. C1, Feb. 3, 1976, p. C3.
33. Ibid., Sept. 20, 1976, p. B1.
34. *The New York Times,* May 29, 1973.

more information has reached Taiwan through these channels than in previous years. These second- or third-hand eyewitness reports probably serve to correct some of the more flagrant exaggerations that appear in Taiwan's press concerning conditions on the mainland, but they seem unlikely to convince many in Taiwan that they would be better off if they came under Peking's control.

The political turmoil on the mainland during 1976 has had a greater impact in Taiwan than the PRC's political efforts to influence people there. The death of Chou En-lai, the downfall of Teng Hsiao-p'ing, the rioting in Tien An Men square and disturbances elsewhere in China, the death of Mao Tse-tung, the arrest of the "gang of four," the rise of Hua Kuo-feng, and the resurgence of Teng Hsiao-p'ing—this kaleidoscopic procession of events has attracted enormous attention. The ability of the PRC leaders to project an image of stability and progress has been weakened. As a result, in early 1977, people in Taiwan expressed less fear that Peking could exert effective pressure on them and more hope that the US government will be deterred from moving ahead with normalization.

Obstacles to Incorporating Taiwan in the PRC

The PRC has encountered much difficulty in establishing political rapport with people on Taiwan despite the strong bond of Chinese nationalism linking them to the mainland and the jolt administered to the ROC by the US opening to Peking. Only a small part of the PRC's difficulties can be ascribed to barriers erected by the ROC to bar entry of PRC influence. Much more important are the fundamental obstacles, both personal and institutional, to the incorporation of Taiwan into the PRC.

For civilian and military government officials in Taiwan who came from the mainland, one powerful incentive to oppose reintegration is the fear of what would happen to them if the PRC gained control of the island. Almost all have friends or relatives who stayed behind on the mainland when the Chinese Communists took over the country. Some were killed or jailed. Many of those who escaped these harsh measures and were retained in government positions were subjected to repeated "struggle sessions" and otherwise discriminated against because of their background and family connections. The PRC's promise of lenient treatment to all but a handful of top officials in Taiwan after "liberation" are not trusted. The recent release of former Nationalist officials, after twenty-five years of incarceration, is not particularly reassuring.

For more than twenty-five years, large numbers of mainlander officials in Taiwan have been sending their children to US universities. The great majority of these students stayed in the Untied States and became permanent residents or citizens. Thus, if Taiwan should be threatened with a PRC takeover, the parents could flee to their children in the United States. The existence of this escape hatch reduces the susceptibility of mainlander government officials in Taiwan to PRC threats or inducements. However, it also creates a rift between those who have the means of escape and the much larger number who do not. By spring 1976, this had become enough of an issue that Governor Hsieh Tung-min publicly denounced "toothbrushism," a term for the behavior of those who had acquired foreign passports or reentry permits which would allow them to flee Taiwan in an emergency with only a toothbrush.[35]

Taiwanese officials and businessmen to some extent share mainlander fears of what would happen to them if the PRC were to take over Taiwan, although few of them had close relatives or friends who suffered under the Communist government on the China mainland. Politically ambitious Taiwanese see their influence steadily growing in a Taiwan that remains free of PRC control. They fear that the reintegration of Taiwan with the mainland would snuff out their hopes for a Taiwanese-governed island and would impose a new set of mainlander officials on the island. Taiwanese businessmen, who own the bulk of the private enterprises on the island, fear that their properties would be confiscated and that their standard of living would deteriorate drastically.

Fear among the decision-making elite of Taiwan that they would fare badly under a Communist system is a serious barrier to Taiwan's unification with the mainland. But even if this critical personal factor were set aside, the great differences in the political and economic systems and the standards of living of the two areas would make unification difficult. Taiwan's prosperity rests on its ability to produce large quantities of consumer goods primarily for the industrial societies of the United States, Japan, and Western Europe; in return, it receives the raw materials and capital goods essential to its continued rapid growth. This foreign-trade–oriented economy can function effectively only with close and constant communication between buyer and seller, a willingness to attract foreign technology and capital by permitting direct foreign investment on favorable terms, and wide scope for initiative and freedom of action on the part of producers in anticipating and supplying market requirements.

One need only study the accounts of Western buyers of consumer

---

35. *China Post,* June 6, 1976.

goods at the Canton fair to see how different the mainland state-operated system is from the Taiwan free enterprise system. If Taiwan came under PRC control, it is difficult to imagine how Peking could permit the direct foreign investment, the freedom of travel and communication with foreign countries, or the private ownership of industry that exists in Taiwan today. To do so would have a subversive effect on the rest of the country. Yet if the PRC were to impose its economic system on Taiwan, foreign trade would drop precipitately. The China mainland could provide neither the market for Taiwan's exports nor the technology that Taiwan receives from the industrialized West.

The political systems of Taiwan and the China mainland superficially resemble each other. Each is governed by a single party whose structure derives from the Soviet Communist party. Like the Soviet party, each Chinese party periodically holds a party congress to elect a central committee to exercise authority between party congresses. Each party is a hierarchical structure—the PRC with a politburo, the ROC with a standing committee of the central committee at the top and party cells at the bottom. Each political system long had a recognized leader who held great power until his recent death. Each is now governed by a new leader who has held power for a relatively short time. By virtue of his lineage and his long experience in the central government, Chiang Ching-kuo in Taiwan is more firmly established than his mainland counterpart, Hua Kuo-feng.

Despite the superficial resemblance of their political systems, the differences between political and social conditions on the China mainland and in Taiwan are much greater than the similarities. The PRC maintains totalitarian controls over all aspects of life. In Taiwan, where the majority of the population earns its living in the private sector, the individual has much greater freedom of choice. The KMT controls over publication and political activity are far less rigid and pervasive than those maintained on the mainland by the Chinese Communist party. A large segment of the population has become accustomed to access to information from abroad and association with foreigners. Freedom to travel overseas is available on a scale unknown on the China mainland. The chances of obtaining higher education are far greater in Taiwan, where there are almost as many college students as there are on the mainland—and thousands of graduate students from Taiwan study abroad. Many more examples of the differences between Taiwan and the mainland could be cited, but these suffice to show the difficulty of absorbing Taiwan into the PRC. Radical changes in the way of life on Taiwan would be essential if the island were not to become a subversive influence on the rest of China.

The people of Taiwan are resistant to the PRC's persuasion not only because many fear that their personal situation would worsen under communism but also because few see any convincing evidence that theirs would improve. The standard of living on the mainland is well below that on Taiwan. For example, the Chinese on the mainland are gratified to be able to purchase a bicycle or a transistor radio; many citizens of Taiwan already own motorcycles and TV sets. As more people of Taiwanese origin visit the mainland, more reports filter back of the contrast between the austerity of life there and Taiwan's relative abundance. For most people in Taiwan, the improvement in their living condition over the past twenty-five years provides a strong motivation for wanting to continue and improve the present system rather than to experiment with the radically different Communist system.

Still another obstacle to reintegration is the reluctance of mainland leaders even to talk with the PRC. The PRC has made many overtures to officials of the ROC in public statements and in private letters, but ROC leaders have publicly rejected any negotiation with the PRC. Little credence can be given to the rumors of secret negotiations that have emanated occasionally from Hong Kong or Tokyo. There are compelling reasons why Chiang Ching-kuo or any other mainlander leader would not wish to negotiate with Peking. Their distrust of the Communist leaders is profound, growing out of fifty years of experience. Moreover, they would be negotiating from weakness, and no one wants to negotiate from weakness unless forced to. Were Chiang Ching-kuo to open secret negotiations with Peking, he would place his fate in the PRC's hands. Revelation of such negotiations would bring down on him the denunciations of large numbers of worried mainlanders and Taiwanese who feared a sellout. The adverse reaction of the Taiwanese, who now constitute over 90 percent of the enlisted men in the armed forces, would be particularly damaging and could fatally weaken his political position.

The Future

Current trends suggest that obstacles to the reintegration of Taiwan with the mainland are likely to grow rather than diminish. The increasing influence of the Taiwanese will tend to weaken ties with mainland China. So long as Taiwan is able to maintain its extensive trading relations with the rest of the world, the gap between living conditions on the mainland and those on Taiwan probably will also continue to widen.

The PRC faces a dilemma. The longer reunification is deferred, the more difficult it will become. The use of military force is not practicable so long as there is a risk of US intervention. Even if the United States were not prepared to intervene, the PRC's use of military force would incur a high cost in terms of its relations with the United States and Japan and would risk driving the ROC to go nuclear in desperation, if there was time, or to declare independence. Consequently, the PRC probably is placing its confidence in a middle course: persuading the United States to withdraw its military protection from Taiwan and thereafter employing a combination of political and limited military measures to convince a majority of people on Taiwan that they have no choice but to negotiate with Peking. Political threats and inducements would become more effective, once the PRC could pose a credible threat of large-scale use of force, even if it were not actually used.

But striking an effective balance between persuasion and the threat of force will be difficult. If the PRC takes too hard a line, for example, it may unintentionally undermine the ROC's commitment to the "one China" position, and preserving that commitment is important to the PRC. Chou En-lai told American visitors in 1973 that the PRC had made no effort to drive Chiang Kai-shek's troops off the offshore islands because those islands were Taiwan's link to the mainland, a refutation of any claim to separate nationhood.[36] The PRC's courtship of the Taiwanese since 1972 is an effort to counter their feeling of separateness, in recognition of their growing political importance in Taiwan.

Therefore, if PRC leaders wish to keep the door open to peaceful resolution of the Taiwan issue—and there is little doubt that they would prefer this to a military takeover—they must apply pressure with care and, as part of that pressure, present a credible plan for the association of Taiwan with the mainland—a plan that would not seriously threaten the way of life and hopes for the future of the people of Taiwan. The example of Tibet, which PRC leaders have occasionally mentioned in connection with Taiwan, is hardly a reassuring precedent.

---

36. *Washington Post*, May 25, 1973.

The Contest
for International Status

6

During the years immediately after its founding, the PRC's efforts to exert political influence on Taiwan were hampered not only by its inability to threaten credibly to use military force against the island but also by its failure to gain general recognition from the international community. After the PRC's intervention in the Korean war, the United States and the ROC cooperated effectively to exclude the PRC from the United Nations and otherwise limit its international acceptance. The ability of the ROC's leadership to sustain the morale of the people of Taiwan and to expand its foreign trade rapidly during the 1950s and 1960s rested in part on the diplomatic support of its principal trading partners, the United States and Japan, and its worldwide diplomatic relations.

But the PRC, through its control of the China mainland, held the high cards. By 1971, the principal backers of the ROC were unable to muster majority support for its international position. The PRC was seated in the United Nations; the ROC was excluded. Since that time, as nation after nation, including Japan, established diplomatic relations with the PRC and broke relations with the ROC, the ROC has been struggling to survive as an international entity. Encouraged by its diplomatic successes, the PRC has redoubled its efforts to exclude the ROC from governmental and private international organizations and to win over the few countries that still maintain diplomatic relations with the ROC. The ROC has had to resort to a variety of unorthodox methods of international intercourse in order to maintain economic relations with foreign countries on which its survival depends.

The principal target of the PRC's drive to undercut the ROC's international status has been its diplomatic relations with the United States. The PRC doubtless hopes that when the United States shifts its diplomatic relations from Taipei to Peking, not only will the ROC find itself in a diplomatic limbo, but also the people of Taiwan will become far more susceptible to the PRC's insistence that there is no future for the island except through incorporation into the PRC. With such a shift in US relations, the future of the ROC would depend on its skill in devising unorthodox ways to maintain international economic relations and on the PRC's ability to interfere with such relations. If all else failed, the ROC might declare itself an independent state or seek to establish a relationship with the Soviet Union, although for the present neither of these is a realistic option.

Battle for the UN Seat

Early in January 1950, three months after the founding of the PRC, Chou En-lai cabled Secretary-General Trygve Lie, demanding the expulsion of the ROC from the United Nations. The ROC was a charter member of the United Nations and one of the five permanent members of the Security Council. When a Soviet resolution calling for the ouster of the ROC was defeated, the Soviet representative walked out of the Security Council, declaring that the Soviet Union would not participate in its deliberations or accept any of its decisions so long as the ROC representative remained.

The absence of the Soviet representative and the strong influence of the United States on the majority of UN members made possible the passage in late June of two resolutions in the Security Council: a call for withdrawal of the North Korean forces that had invaded South Korea and an appeal to UN members to aid South Korea. The Soviet representative, recognizing that his absence placed the Soviet Union at a tactical disadvantage, returned to the United Nations in early July. He supported an Indian resolution in the General Assembly to seat the PRC and presented a resolution of his own to expel the ROC. Both were defeated by substantial margins.[1]

In August 1950, Chou En-lai cabled Yakov Malik, the Soviet repre-

---

1. See *China and U.S. Foreign Policy*, 2nd. ed. (Washington, D.C.: China Quarterly, 1973), p. 103.

sentative, then president of the Security Council, and Trygve Lie, accusing the United States of having committed armed aggression against Chinese territory by sending the Seventh Fleet to the Taiwan Strait and US air force units to Taiwan. He urged the UN Security Council to condemn the US government and to take immediate measures to cause the withdrawal of US forces from Taiwan and other Chinese territory. At the invitation of the Security Council, General Wu Hsiu-ch'uan appeared before it in November to present the PRC's case. By this time, however, PRC forces had intervened massively in Korea, and the Security Council rejected a Soviet resolution incorporating Peking's charge of aggression by the United States. The Soviet Union then vetoed a six-power resolution calling on the Chinese to withdraw from Korea. After General Wu's departure, no PRC representative appeared at the United Nations until 1971, after the PRC had been seated and the ROC expelled.

The Korean war not only caused the United States to reverse overnight its hands-off policy toward the Chinese civil war but also greatly handicapped the PRC's efforts to secure the seat held by the ROC in the United Nations. In 1951, the United States, overcoming the reluctance of allies and the opposition of neutralists such as India, pushed through a UN General Assembly resolution condemning the PRC as an aggressor for having attacked US and allied forces acting under the aegis of the United Nations in defense of South Korea. Under these circumstances, the United States was able to obtain a sizable majority for its resolution "not to consider" any change in Chinese representation in the world body. This so-called moratorium on debating the issue was renewed year after year until 1961, although with diminishing majorities.

Throughout the 1950s, "the administration, the Congress, and the overwhelming majority of the American people were united in their opposition to Communist China's representation in the United Nations."[2] The Committee of One Million, including many members of Congress, was organized in 1954 to rally public opinion against seating the PRC in the United Nations and opposing any action by the US government that might weaken the position of the ROC. Every year from 1950 through 1970, the Congress expressed its opposition to seating the PRC in the United Nations in provisions attached to appropriations bills and enacted into law.[3] Every year before and during the UN General Assembly session, the Department of State pressed friendly governments to support the US-sponsored resolution to extend the moratorium on debating the China issue for another year.

Despite continuing strong US public and congressional opposition

---

2. Dulles, *American Foreign Policy Toward Communist China*, pp. 183–184.
3. *China and U.S. Foreign Policy*, p. 53.

to seating the PRC in the United Nations, the voting majorities in the General Assembly for the moratorium resolution gradually eroded. A growing number of countries, including some of the new members entering the organization in large numbers, thought that the issue of the Chinese representation should be debated and voted on. By 1960, the vote on the moratorium had slipped to 42 for, 34 against, and 22 abstentions, as compared to 1954 when it had been 43 for, 11 against, and 6 abstentions. It was becoming risky to continue to rely on the moratorium tactic.

Consequently, in 1961 the Kennedy administration, in consultation with the government of the ROC and other friendly governments, devised a new tactic to continue excluding the PRC. Whenever a resolution was proposed by one of the Communist states to seat the PRC and expel the ROC, it would be voted on, but at the same time a second resolution, declaring that any change in the representation of China was an important question requiring a two-thirds majority for approval, would also be put forward. In 1961, this second resolution was passed by a vote of 61 for, 34 against, and 7 abstentions, while the Soviet-sponsored resolution to oust the ROC and seat the PRC was defeated by a vote of 37 for, 48 against, and 19 abstentions.

Although the United States, as the main buttress of the effort to exclude the PRC from the United Nations, expended significant amounts of diplomatic capital annually in persuading friendly nations to support this position, the ROC was by no means standing idly by. It maintained a sizable diplomatic establishment throughout the world and invited a stream of influential foreign visitors to Taiwan to enjoy Chinese hospitality and to observe the progress being made by the ROC. The most effective effort undertaken by the ROC to bolster its position in the United Nations was its program of technical assistance to other developing countries, particularly in Africa and Latin America. Beginning in 1961 with a 15-man agricultural demonstration team in Liberia, the ROC rapidly expanded its program until at its peak in 1970 a total of 702 technicians were in 23 African countries on short-term or long-term missions. That same year, Taipei had 111 other technicians working in Iran, South Vietnam, Thailand, the Dominican Republic, Brazil, Chile, Mexico, Panama, Peru, Ecuador, and Guyana.[4] In addition, from 1954 to 1975, over 7500 technicians from 50 countries received training in Taiwan.[5]

The bulk of the technical cooperation extended by the ROC was in agriculture, but many other fields were represented, including fisheries, veterinary work, handicrafts, sugar milling, and highway engineering.

---

4. *TSDB*, pp. 232–233.
5. *141 Questions and Answers about the Republic of China*, p. 41.

The ROC's technicians were welcome and useful because the levels of technical skills and education in Taiwan were considerably higher than in most of the countries aided, yet not so high as those of the industrialized nations. Consequently, ROC technology often was more easily applied in other developing countries than that offered by European nations or by the United States. Moreover, the standard of living of the visiting technicians from Taiwan was closer to that of the local people. During the 1960s, although US influence on the nations concerned continued to be the decisive factor in most cases, the technical aid programs administered by the ROC helped significantly in persuading African and Latin American states to maintain diplomatic relations with Taipei instead of Peking and to support the ROC on the Chinese representation issue in the United Nations.

Despite the vigorous diplomatic efforts by the ROC and the United States, support for exclusion of the PRC from the United Nations continued to decline. France's decision in 1964 to break relations with Taipei and establish diplomatic relations with Peking had wide repercussions. By 1965, the vote on the resolution to oust the ROC and seat the PRC had dropped to 47 for, 47 against, and 20 abstentions. Moreover, support for requiring a two-thirds majority vote to decide the Chinese representation issue was also declining. The 1965 vote on that resolution was 56 for, 49 against, and 11 abstentions. Peking's xenophobic behavior during the cultural revolution temporarily reversed the voting trend in its favor, but not for long. In 1970, the proposal to oust the ROC and seat the PRC was supported, for the first time, by a majority of those voting. The vote was 51 for, 49 against, and 25 abstentions. But the two-thirds majority requirement blocked its passage. That requirement was supported by a vote of 66 for, 52 against, and 7 abstentions.

American opinion was also changing: many were coming around to the view that the PRC should be seated in the world organization, if the ROC was also seated. In 1971, for the first time in twenty years, the US Congress did not adopt the traditional statement opposing the entry of the PRC into the United Nations. Sensitive to the changing public mood and the greater scope it offered for diplomatic flexibility, President Nixon in July 1971 announced his agreement with the government of the PRC to visit China the following year. The US government also withdrew its opposition to seating the PRC in the United Nations but continued to oppose the expulsion of the ROC. The PRC, however, firmly rejected any suggestion that it might participate in the United Nations alongside the ROC. Consequently, in October 1971, those countries desiring to bring the PRC into the organization voted, some of them reluctantly, to expel the ROC as the only way of accomplishing this end.

For this vote the General Assembly rejected the resolution requiring a two-thirds majority by a vote of 55 for, 59 against, and 15 abstentions. The vote on ousting the ROC and admitting the PRC was then 76 for, 35 against, and 17 abstentions.

Bilateral Diplomatic Relations

The relative international status of the PRC and the ROC was measured not only by the support each was able to muster for membership in the United Nations but also by the number of states that recognized and maintained diplomatic relations with each.[6] The Soviet Union had been the first to recognize the PRC, on October 1, 1949, the day after the announcement of its establishment. Other Soviet bloc states quickly followed suit. Burma, India, Pakistan, the United Kingdom, Norway, Ceylon, Denmark, Israel, Afghanistan, Finland, Sweden, and Switzerland all recognized the PRC during the winter of 1949–1950. By January 1950, 26 countries had established diplomatic relations with Peking; 53 still retained relations with Taipei.

The outbreak of the Korean war gave the ROC a respite in the decline of its international position. From the time of Indonesia's recognition of the PRC in the spring of 1950, no other state recognized the PRC until Nepal in 1955. Thereafter, although the PRC gained ground, the ROC more than recouped its losses by establishing diplomatic relations with many newly emerging nations, particularly in Africa. By 1963, the tally stood at 42 for the PRC and 58 for the ROC.[7] French recognition of the PRC in 1964 was a heavy blow, but it did not result in a stampede by former African colonies to establish relations with Peking. A few followed the French example, but many preferred to maintain relations with the ROC, which by that time had sent technical assistance missions to nearly a dozen African countries.

The French break was partially compensated for by the suspension of diplomatic relations between Peking and Jakarta as a result of the abortive coup in Indonesia in the fall of 1965. By 1966, the PRC's diplomatic relationships had climbed to 50, but the ROC's had also advanced slightly, to 60. Twenty-one countries had relations with neither.[8] The cultural revolution slowed the PRC's progress, but only temporarily.

6. See Donald Klein, "Formosa's Diplomatic World," *China Quarterly*, no. 15 (July–September 1963): 45–50.
7. Ibid., p. 49.
8. UN Association of the USA, *China, the United Nations, and United States Policy* (New York, 1966), pp. 56–58.

In 1970, the PRC made a critical breakthrough, winning over two close allies of the United States: Canada and Italy. Thus, on the eve of the shift in US policy toward the PRC, one count showed 53 nations recognizing the PRC, 68 recognizing the ROC, 2 recognizing both, and 14 recognizing neither.[9] Not all countries that recognized the PRC established diplomatic relations with it, but most did.

The contest for international recognition was unequal, in that by most customary tests the PRC clearly qualified as the government of China. The ROC's ability to maintain so strong a position for twenty years can be ascribed to a variety of factors: the PRC's intervention in the Korean war and its condemnation by the United Nations as an aggressor; the inclination in many countries to follow the lead of the United Nations; strong anti-Communist views on the part of the governing elites of some countries; fear of PRC-instigated subversion by leaders in countries with large overseas Chinese minorities; and actions by the PRC, especially during the cultural revolution, which provoked anger and suspicion in certain countries. The ROC's active diplomacy also contributed to the maintenance of its relatively strong position for so long, but the most important single factor was the strong opposition of the United States to recognition of the PRC. Many countries felt that they would lose more than they would gain by taking an action sure to provoke strong resentment in the United States.

Many countries would have established diplomatic relations with both Peking and Taipei had it been possible to do so, but the adamant opposition by both the PRC and the ROC to any "two Chinas" arrangement forced countries to choose. The only country that had some form of official relations in Peking and in Taipei was the United Kingdom, which kept open its consulate in Taiwan—accredited to the provincial government, not the national government—after it had established diplomatic relations with the PRC. But the British were penalized for this transgression against the "one China" principle by being allowed only a chargé d'affaires in Peking. Not until the British consulate in Taiwan was closed in 1972 did Peking and London exchange ambassadors.

Once the President of the United States announced his intention to visit China in July 1971 and the PRC replaced the ROC in the UN Security Council and General Assembly in October of the same year, the barriers against shifting diplomatic relations from Taipei to Peking came crashing down. By February 1973, 85 countries had established relations with the PRC, whereas only 39 maintained relations with the ROC. Four years later, the balance in the PRC's favor had shifted further: 111 to 23. Only 11 of those countries that had diplomatic relations with the

---

9. *The New York Times,* Oct. 14, 1970.

ROC maintained diplomatic missions in Taipei; the others accredited their ambassadors in Tokyo concurrently to Taipei. Although the trend since 1971 has run strongly against the ROC, it did succeed in establishing diplomatic relations with three newly independent states—Tonga, Western Samoa, and Barbados—and raised its representation in South Africa from a consulate general to an embassy.[10]

Representation in International Organizations

The struggle for the UN seat and the competition for bilateral diplomatic relations were the most important and visible aspects of the contest between the PRC and the ROC for international status, but the right to represent China was contested in many other international organizations, both governmental and private. In 1950, the UN General Assembly passed a resolution calling on agencies associated with the United Nations to "take account" of the assembly's attitude toward Chinese representation. Although this resolution carried considerable weight with the members, it was not legally binding on UN-associated agencies, such as the United Nations Educational, Scientific, and Cultural Organization (UNESCO) or the World Health Organization (WHO), each of which had the right to decide its own membership. When PRC-supporters raised the representation issue in these agencies, as frequently happened, the challenge to the presence of ROC representatives was rejected by the memberships on the ground that this was a political issue to be decided by the UN Security Council or General Assembly.

In those international organizations in which the delegates were private citizens rather than government officials, some delegates advocated universality of membership. In scientific organizations especially, a cogent case could be made for the benefits to scientific inquiry from having both "Chinas" represented. Consequently, many scientists, as well as representatives of Red Cross societies and members of the International Olympic Committee (IOC), would have preferred to put aside political considerations and welcome representatives from both the PRC and the ROC, but efforts to do so were frustrated by the refusal of either country to sit down with the other. It proved impossible to exclude political

10. Western Samoa and Barbados later broke relations with the ROC. As of May 1977, the following countries still maintained diplomatic relations with the ROC, of which those in italics also maintained a diplomatic mission in Taipei: (Europe) *Holy See;* (Africa) Ivory Coast, Lesotho, Libya, Malawi, South Africa, Swaziland; (Americas) Bolivia, *Colombia, Costa Rica, Dominican Republic,* El Salvador, *Guatemala,* Haiti, Honduras, *Nicaragua, Panama,* Paraguay, *Uruguay, United States;* (Asia and Pacific) *Saudi Arabia, South Korea,* Tonga.

considerations. In those organizations to which the ROC already belonged, it had the advantage of being first on the ground. The PRC supporters were compelled to propose the expulsion of ROC representatives in order to seat those from the PRC. Even members sympathetic to the PRC were reluctant to expel the ROC representatives, because the ROC was a member in good standing of the United Nations, was recognized by many nations of the world, and had been active in many of the organizations for years.

When the ROC was ejected from the United Nations, PRC representatives promptly replaced those from Taiwan in the Security Council, the General Assembly, the Economic and Social Council, and other organs of the United Nations itself. The PRC demanded that all reference to the ROC or Taiwan be excluded from UN publications. Hence, even basic compilations of statistics such as the *Statistical Yearbook* and UN trade and demographic reports contain no data on Taiwan from 1972 on. Most of the intergovernmental organizations related to the United Nations, including UNESCO, WHO, the Food and Agricultural Organization, the World Meteorological Organization, the International Hydrographic Organization, the Intergovernmental Civil Aviation Organization, the International Telecommunications Union, and the International Maritime Consultative Organization, one by one expelled the ROC and seated the PRC. The International Labor Organization and the International Atomic Energy Agency expelled the ROC, but the PRC chose not to enter.

As of mid-1977, the ROC remained a member of the principal international financial institutions: the International Monetary Fund (IMF), the World Bank, and the Asian Development Bank. The PRC had notified the IMF as early as August 1950 that the PRC was the only legal government representing China and demanded the expulsion of the representatives of the "Chinese Kuomintang reactionary remnant clique." In September 1973, the PRC foreign minister, Chi Peng-fei, in a message to the managing director of the IMF, called attention to the action of the United Nations expelling the ROC and demanded that the IMF follow suit. He sent a similar message to the president of the World Bank.[11] In September 1976, the People's Bank of China sent a message to the managing director of the IMF referring to earlier messages and again demanded the expulsion of the ROC representatives. The message warned that all China's assets in the IMF belonged to the people of China, that only the People's Bank of China had the lawful right to deal

---

11. FBIS, *Daily Report, People's Republic of China,* Sept. 26, 1973, p. A1, Sept. 27, 1973, p. A1.

with these assets, and that any illegal disposal of them would be null and void.[12]

Even before it was expelled from the United Nations in 1971, the ROC had taken the precaution of withdrawing from the IMF $60 million in convertible currency to which it was automatically entitled. Prior to the annual meetings in September 1972, it withdrew from the boards of directors of the World Bank and the IMF, and it refrained from voting at the meetings.[13] From the time of its expulsion from the United Nations, the ROC also refrained from applying for new loans from the World Bank. Its policy has been to be as inconspicuous as possible in both the World Bank and the IMF so as to avoid providing an occasion for the Chinese representation issue to be raised.

Neither the World Bank nor the IMF has acted on the PRC's demand to oust the ROC. The system of weighted voting in the financial institutions, favoring the large contributors, makes it more difficult for the PRC to muster the necessary votes to expel the ROC than it was in other organizations. The World Bank would have a particular problem if it expelled the ROC, for it has $310 million in loans outstanding in Taiwan. Many members of both organizations are reluctant to expel the ROC unless the PRC indicates that it would be prepared to take the ROC's place, which it has not yet done. The PRC probably is unwilling to meet the IMF's requirements that members both provide extensive data on foreign trade, national income, and foreign exchange reserves and consult regularly with staff members of the IMF concerning economic conditions in the country. In January 1977, the IMF had to decide whether or not it would return some $15 million in gold to the ROC in the process of returning to each member a proportion of its original deposit. In a compromise between those who would have returned the gold to Taipei and those who would have held it for Peking, the gold was placed in escrow.[14] As of September 1977, its disposition was undecided.

At a meeting of the UN Economic Commission for Asia and the Far East (ECAFE) in Tokyo in April 1973, the first attended by a PRC representative, the PRC called attention to the ROC's continued membership in the Asian Development Bank and declared that ECAFE should urge the bank to expel it.[15] But the PRC made no move to join that bank either. In March 1976, the president of the Asian Development Bank stated that although the PRC, as a major Asian nation, should

---

12. Ibid., Sept. 30, 1976, p. A1.
13. *The New York Times,* Sept. 28, 1972.
14. *Washington Post,* Jan. 11, 1977.
15. FBIS, *Daily Report, People's Republic of China,* Apr. 25, 1973, p. A8.

have joined the bank long before, it had not applied to do so. Under these circumstances, he explained, the bank could hardly expel Taiwan, which had $90 million in loans outstanding.[16]

The PRC not only attacked the ROC's position in intergovernmental organizations but also sought its exclusion from all kinds of private international organizations. It tried to utilize the leverage acquired from its membership in the intergovernmental agencies related to the United Nations to place pressure on nongovernmental organizations related to these agencies. For example, in November 1974 it prevailed on the eighteenth general conference of UNESCO in Paris to pass a resolution urging the over three hundred international nongovernmental organizations maintaining relations with UNESCO to exclude immediately and break off all relations with "bodies or elements linked with Chiang Kai-shek."[17] Not all organizations followed UNESCO's advice, and the PRC representative found it necessary to obtain passage of a similar resolution by the nineteenth general conference in Nairobi in November 1976. Complaining that "a few leaders of certain international organizations have hitherto continued to permit the Chiang bodies or elements to carry out illegal activities in these organizations in violation of the resolution adopted by the UNESCO general conference at its 18th session," he declared that "the bodies or elements linked with it [the ROC] have no right whatsoever to join any international organizations, whatever name they may use."[18]

The PRC took similar action in the governing bodies of other intergovernmental organizations related to the United Nations. Resolutions urging associated nongovernmental organizations to expel groups or individuals linked to the ROC were passed by the WHO in January 1974 and by the Intergovernmental Civil Aviation Organization in April 1976. The PRC representative called on the congress of the World Meteorological Organization to take similar action in May 1975 but apparently failed to get a resolution passed.[19]

The International Council of Scientific Unions (ICSU) proved unusually resistant to PRC persuasion. Many scientists took the view that, since science was a nonpolitical activity, bona-fide scientists or scientific organizations should be permitted to take part in the work of international scientific bodies regardless of where they came from. In November 1976, the general assembly of the ICSU passed a resolution embodying this universalist view with regard to Chinese scientists, which provoked an angry reaction from Peking. The Scientific and Technical

16. FBIS, *Daily Report, East Asia and Pacific,* Mar. 2, 1976, p. A1.
17. FBIS, *Daily Report, People's Republic of China,* Nov. 25, 1974, p. A12.
18. Ibid., Nov. 24, 1976, p. A3–A4.
19. Ibid., Feb. 3, 1975, p. A10, Apr. 7, 1976, p. A3, and May 28, 1975, p. A1.

Association of the PRC charged "a few leading officials of the ICSU" with framing the resolution publicly creating "two Chinas" and "one China, one Taiwan" and pointed out that this action ran counter to the resolution passed by UNESCO. It also spoke approvingly of the recent decision of the International Union of Geological Sciences to cancel the membership of "the Chiang gang" and admit the Geological Society of the PRC.[20]

Potentially more serious than the ROC's loss of membership in most other international organizations was its expulsion from the International Telecommunications Satellite Organization (INTELSAT) in September 1976.[21] It is not necessary, however, to belong to INTELSAT in order to receive its services, and the ROC arranged through the Communications Satellite Corporation (COMSAT), the executive agent of INTELSAT, for the continued handling of messages to and from its ground station, as the PRC has also done since 1972. The PRC joined INTELSAT in September 1977 but has given no indication whether it will attempt to interfere with the ROC's use of COMSAT facilities.

International sports organizations have also seen frequent PRC efforts to exclude sportsmen from Taiwan. The hardest-fought and lengthiest battle has been waged over the Olympic Games. Until the summer of 1976, ROC teams competed and PRC teams stayed away. The IOC holds the view that political considerations should be excluded from the games, and host countries are required to agree to admit all contenders approved by the committee. But neither the ROC nor the PRC would accept such an arrangement as that which enables teams from both East Germany and West Germany to compete. Before the opening of the Olympic Games in Montreal in 1976, the PRC asked the Canadian government to refuse admission to athletes from Taiwan. The Canadian government declined to go so far to accommodate the PRC but did notify the IOC that the team from Taiwan would not be allowed to compete under the name of the ROC, fly its national flag, or play its national anthem. The president of the IOC denounced the Canadian action as a violation of its assurance that Canada would admit all parties representing national Olympic committees recognized by the IOC. The Canadian government later withdrew its ban on the use of the ROC flag and anthem, but the team from Taiwan, still denied the right to use the name of the ROC, withdrew from the games.

The representatives of the PRC were admitted to the International Basketball Federation and those from Taiwan expelled in August 1976.

---

20. Ibid., Nov. 29, 1976, p. Cl.
21. Knowing it lacked the votes to retain membership, the ROC notified INTELSAT just before the meeting that it was withdrawing, but the expulsion was voted before the withdrawal became effective.

Similar action was taken by the International Badminton Federation in May 1977. The PRC lost a vote, however, in the International Federation of Football Associations in June 1974 because, even though a majority voted for the PRC, the organization requires a three-fourths vote of the membership to decide such matters. In October 1976, the Australian government, following the precedent established by the Canadians at the Olympic Games, refused to allow the Taiwan team at the second Asian taekwondo (a sport similar to karate, which originated in Korea) tournament to use its official name, national flag, or national anthem, and again the Taiwan team withdrew.

In 1975, the Australian government indicated that it would refuse entry to delegates from Taiwan attending the Pacific Area Travel Association's conference, but it then admitted them after the association had threatened to cancel the conference in Australia because of the organization's rules that host countries must admit delegates from all member countries.[22] In May 1977, the Philippine government, under pressure from the PRC embassy in Manila, refused to allow the delegation from Taiwan to enter the Philippines to attend a convention of the Pacific Asian Congress of Municipalities. The government then relented and allowed the delegates from Taiwan to attend, but only after the American organizers of the meeting threatened to move it to another city.[23]

These developments since the ROC lost its seat in the United Nations suggest that the PRC has made substantial progress in further isolating the ROC. The ROC retains diplomatic relations with only a handful of countries, most of them small and uninfluential, with the notable exceptions of the United States and Saudi Arabia. It has been excluded from nearly all intergovernmental organizations, with the important exception of financial institutions.[24] It is gradually losing ground in international nongovernmental organizations, although as of the end of 1974 it was still affiliated with 245 such bodies.[25] The PRC's goal is thus not merely to prevent the ROC from claiming to represent China in the international community but also to eliminate representatives from Taiwan from all international organizations, whether such representatives use the name "China" or not. From the PRC's viewpoint, it is just as necessary to oppose "one China, one Taiwan" as it is to oppose "two Chinas."

---

22. The ROC and the Soviet Union belong to the Pacific Area Travel Association and attend its conferences, but the PRC does not. *Far Eastern Economic Review,* Jan. 21, 1977, pp. 36–37.
23. FBIS, *Daily Report, East Asia and Pacific,* May 24, 1977, p. P3.
24. As of the end of 1974, the ROC still belonged to only ten nonfinancial intergovernmental organizations. *The China Yearbook, 1976,* pp. 374–375. It has since been expelled from two of these, INTELSAT and the International Hydrographic Organization.
25. Ibid., p. 375.

Informal Methods of International Intercourse

The ROC's position in the world cannot, however, be accurately measured by the formal criteria of bilateral diplomatic relations and membership in international governmental and nongovernmental organizations. Informal relationships have greatly increased since 1971. At the end of 1976, the ROC was trading with over one hundred countries, and total foreign trade had nearly quadrupled in total value. The number of foreigners and overseas Chinese visiting Taiwan each year had increased more than 50 percent. Merchant ships, aircraft, and fishing vessels under the ROC flag plied between Taiwan and other countries in increasing numbers. These informal bilateral relations between Taiwan and other countries are far more difficult for the PRC to interfere with by diplomatic or political means than its formal relations are. In addition, the ROC has devised an array of unorthodox substitutes for the diplomatic relations that have been severed, few of which had any direct bearing on Taiwan's ability to survive as an autonomous political entity in the world. To date, the PRC's efforts to isolate the ROC have had little effect on the substantive informal relations vital to survival.

Taiwan's principal economic relations are with the United States, where formal diplomatic relations still exist. In 1975, the United States took 34 percent of Taiwan's exports and supplied 28 percent of its imports. Americans furnished 46 percent of total foreign direct private investment.[26] The US Export-Import Bank, with its $1.7 billion in loans and guarantees outstanding, is the only foreign governmental agency supplying capital to Taiwan, except for the Saudi Arabian Fund for Development.[27]

Japan, Taiwan's second largest trading partner, took 13 percent of Taiwan's exports and supplied 30 percent of its imports in 1975. The severance of diplomatic relations in September 1972 had little effect on trade, for Taiwan's exports to Japan, which had amounted to $245 million in 1971, increased to $694 million in 1975. Imports from Japan increased from $827 million in 1971 to $1.8 billion in 1975.[28] Although Japan ceased extending governmental loans to the ROC after relations were broken, the flow of Japanese private capital, after a pause in 1972–1973, recovered in subsequent years, and new Japanese investments exceeded those from the United States in the first half of 1976. Japanese

---

26. *TSDB*, pp. 189, 191; *Fortune*, Jan. 1976, p. 87.
27. In December 1976, the Saudi Fund extended a 20-year loan of $30 million to the ROC to finance railway electrification, with a 5-year grace period and 4 percent annual interest. FBIS, *Daily Report, East Asia and Pacific*, Jan. 3, 1977, p. B3.
28. *TSDB*, pp. 184, 189, 191.

visitors to Taiwan also increased from 278,000 in 1972 to 419,000 in 1975.[29]

Although by 1976 the ROC's only diplomatic relations in Europe were with the Holy See, its European trade increased from $400 million in 1971 to $1.6 billion in 1975.[30] The ROC leaders have recognized the importance of diversifying Taiwan's overseas markets and sources of supply in light of the uncertainties and difficulties looming ahead, and they have placed special emphasis on Western Europe because of its importance as a potential market, source of technology, supplier of capital, and even, conceivably, as an important future supplier of military equipment. Although the absence of diplomatic relations has hindered the expansion of trade, the trade figures show that progress is being made. In 1974, Europe was Taiwan's third largest market and supplier, accounting for 15 percent of both exports and imports.

The ROC has also placed increased emphasis on the Middle East. Imports from Kuwait, with which the ROC has had no diplomatic relations, increased from $45 million in 1971 to $412 million in 1975; and exports to Kuwait increased from $5 million in 1971 to $43 million in 1975. Similarly, trade with Saudi Arabia, with which the ROC still has diplomatic relations, increased. Imports from Saudi Arabia rose from $5 million in 1971 to $228 million in 1975, and exports from $8 million in 1971 to $117 million in 1975. Higher oil prices account for only part of these increases. In May 1977, Saudi Arabia agreed to purchase one million metric tons of cement from Taiwan annually. Moreover, Saudi Arabia has become a supplier of capital on favorable terms.

Trading partners other than the United States took 66 percent of Taiwan's exports in 1975 and supplied 72 percent of its imports. In order to maintain these vital economic relations, almost all of which were with countries that had broken diplomatic relations with the ROC, unorthodox methods for promoting trade, facilitating travel, and encouraging investment had to be devised, tailored to the requirements of individual countries. In 1970, the ROC established the China External Trade Development Council (CETDC) to take the place of commercial attachés in diplomatic missions or official trade missions. It is a private organization supported by compulsory donations from exporters of 0.06 percent of their foreign earnings. Through its staff of 236 in Taipei as well as thirty-three overseas offices, the CETDC offers a variety of services to businessmen in Taiwan and abroad engaged in foreign trade. Its overseas offices go by a variety of names: the Oficina Commercial de Taiwan in Buenos Aires, the CETDC Correspondent in Mel-

29. Ibid., p. 117.
30. Ibid., p. 193.

bourne, the Far East Trading Co., Ltd., in Montreal, the CETDC Representative's Office in Jakarta, and the CETDC Branch Office in New York. In countries where the use of the word "China" might cause problems, the overseas offices report back to the Far East Trade Service, Inc. (FETS), established in 1971, most of whose personnel are identical with those working for the CETDC. The overseas offices bear such names as the FETS Honorary Representative in Kuwait, the FETS Representative Office in Zurich, Switzerland, and the Tokyo Office of the FETS.[31] The CETDC, in addition to providing services to individual businessmen, presents exhibits of Taiwan products at its exhibition hall in Taipei, organizes overseas trade missions, of which there were forty-six in 1975, and participates in international trade fairs.

Trade cannot be promoted effectively unless freedom to travel exists, especially for the traders themselves, but also for officials who must negotiate solutions to problems with which the private businessman cannot cope. The ROC has had to work out substitute arrangements with countries where it lacks diplomatic or consular relations for the issuance of visas to permit travel to and from Taiwan. The ROC Ministry of Foreign Affairs has shown considerable flexibility and ingenuity in resolving the problem. In Tokyo, visas for travel to Taipei bearing the stamp of the Chinese Embassy, Seoul, Korea, are issued by a private East Asia Relations Association, staffed by professional foreign service officers. In Frankfurt, West Germany, travelers can obtain from the Taiwan Travel Service stamped and sealed "letters of recommendation" that are exchanged for entry visas when the traveler arrives at Taipei airport. Similar arrangements are in effect in France, the Netherlands, Switzerland, Australia, and elsewhere.[32] In New Zealand, letters of introduction are available from the Trade Span (N.Z.) Ltd. branch office in Auckland.[33] In Manila, visas are issued by the Pacific Economic and Cultural Center, set up after the severance of diplomatic relations and headed by a former ROC ambassador.[34] In Malaysia and Thailand, visas are issued by China Airlines. Judging by the statistics on foreign visitors in recent years, the severance of diplomatic relations has not significantly interfered with freedom to travel to Taiwan. The number of Japanese visitors has increased spectacularly. Although the number of visitors from Canada, Australia, and New Zealand declined somewhat in 1974 as compared to 1970, during the same period visitors from France nearly tripled, those from West Germany more than doubled, and those from

---

31. See *1976 Directory of Taiwan* (Taipei: China News, 1976), pp. 113–117; *Far Eastern Economic Review,* May 14, 1976, p. 46.
32. *Washington Post.* Oct. 5, 1974.
33. *China Yearbook, 1975,* p. 344.
34. *Far Eastern Economic Review,* July 30, 1976, p. 28.

Belgium, Italy, and the United Kingdom all increased substantially, which suggests that factors other than the lack of access to visa facilities accounted for the decline in visitors from the Commonwealth countries.[35]

Taiwan residents can still travel without serious inconvenience to a number of countries with which diplomatic relations have been severed. The Interchange Association in Taipei, staffed by professional Japanese diplomats, takes visa applications and provides visas bearing the stamp of the Japanese Consulate General, Hong Kong. The Taipei offices of the Malaysian Airlines System and Thai Airways have been authorized to issue entry permits for their respective countries. But some countries have not been willing to provide such irregular facilities for Taiwan residents. Consequently, travelers from Taiwan have to apply for visas at the consular offices of those countries in Japan, Hong Kong, or the United States and suffer travel delays. On the whole, traveling businessmen are not subject to serious inconvenience, but ROC officials sometimes face long delays or even refusal of entry by countries that are highly sensitive to possible PRC protests on the ground that they are pursuing a "two Chinas" policy when they admit ROC officials, particularly if the mission of the official is negotiating some problem between Taiwan and the country concerned.

The severance of diplomatic relations by many countries seems to have created no significant impediments to carrying out financial transactions related to trade. Branches of eight American banks operate in Taiwan, as well as branches of the Dai-Ichi Kangyo Bank of Tokyo, the Bangkok Bank of Thailand, the Metropolitan Bank and Trust Company of the Philippines, and the Toronto Dominion Bank of Canada.[36] Thus, Taiwan is well plugged into the international network of financial institutions, for not only do these banks provide the necessary facilities for conducting foreign trade, but they also make loans for economic development in Taiwan. The Continental Bank made a loan of $200 million to the China Steel Corporation; the Chemical Bank lent the ROC $100 million for use on several of the Ten Major Projects; a consortium of five banks—Chase Manhattan, Chemical, First National City, Bank of America, and Toronto Dominion—lent $50 million for the construction of a petrochemical plant by Union Carbide.[37]

Economic relations with countries with which Taiwan does not have diplomatic relations are facilitated in other ways. Some countries have

---

35. *TSDB*, p. 117.
36. The American banks are American Express International Banking Corp., Bank of America, Chase Manhattan Bank, Chemical Bank, Continental Bank, First National City Bank, Irving Trust Co., and United California Bank.
37. *Fortune,* January 1976, p. 87.

established offices in Taiwan to promote trade, such as the National Export Trading Corporation of the Philippines, the Anglo-Taiwan Trade Committee, and the Japanese Interchange Association. In March 1977, the ROC vice-minister of foreign affairs signed a trade agreement with Ecuador.[38] In cases where a substantial purchase by Taiwan is involved, the absence of diplomatic relations may be no bar to agreements entered into by officials of both sides, as when Wong Yi-ting, director general of the Chinese Board of Foreign Trade, signed an agreement on July 6, 1977, with the president of the Thai Department of Foreign Trade for the import of 200,000 tons of corn from Thailand during the 1977–1978 crop year.[39] Trade delegations visit Taiwan from time to time; for example, a 28-member Swedish trade mission spent six days there in November 1975 at the invitation of the CETDC.[40] Aircraft from a dozen foreign airlines continue to provide services to and from Taiwan. Where government-to-government agreements concerning such services have had to be terminated because of the severance of diplomatic relations, agreements for the continuance of reciprocal landing rights have been worked out between China Airlines and the foreign airline concerned.

Although trade statistics show that the ROC has successfully overcome many of the obstacles to the promotion of economic relations with countries where it no longer has diplomatic relations, problems remain. For example, officials cannot negotiate quotas for textile exports to the European Economic Community (EEC) countries, which places the ROC at a disadvantage relative to its principal competitor, the Republic of Korea. Quotas on imports of textiles from Taiwan are unilaterally imposed by the EEC countries. The ROC organized a Taiwan Textile Federation in 1976 to allocate quotas among Taiwan's exporters and to represent them in negotiations with EEC countries. Another problem is the refusal of some countries to allow Taiwan the trade preferences given other developing countries or to permit Taiwan to participate in trade fairs.

The difficulty of negotiating solutions that require government action for problems impeding trade is a continuing headache for ROC officials. Foreign officials may refuse to see ROC officials because of their sensitivity to possible PRC reactions or, in extreme cases, may even refuse to admit ROC officials to the country. ROC officials travel on ordinary passports and receive no diplomatic privileges or immunities in countries with which Taiwan does not have diplomatic relations. Even when ROC officials are able to see the appropriate foreign officials, their representations are weakened by their lack of official status in the eyes of

38. FBIS, *Daily Report, East Asia and Pacific,* Mar. 22, 1977, p. B1.
39. Ibid., July 11, 1977, p. B3.
40. Ibid., Nov. 13, 1975, p. B1.

the foreign government. Consequently, ROC officials must rely more heavily than the representatives of most other countries on personal connections and influence to accomplish their purposes.

Until now, the PRC has not launched a sustained and intensive campaign to interfere with the ROC's foreign economic relations. Yet there are scattered examples of such interference. The Mexican government responded to PRC representations by closing the ROC's commercial office in that country. The Toronto Dominion Bank was struck off the list of banks in the United States through which trade with the China mainland could be conducted, apparently in retaliation for the bank's having opened a branch office in Taipei in February 1975.[41] For a time, PRC banks stopped accepting American Express travelers' checks, and the Union Carbide Corporation was not invited to join a delegation of chemical firms touring the China mainland. Both actions seems to have taken because these companies joined the USA-ROC Economic Council, established in the United States in 1976 to promote trade with Taiwan.[42] In June 1976, the Philippine government, reportedly under PRC pressure, ordered the Philippine Asian Exchange Center in China, set up in Taipei after the severance of diplomatic relations and headed by a retired Filipino ambassador, to stop issuing visas.[43]

In addition to the economic relations which are vital to its survival, the ROC maintains an extensive network of information and cultural centers, such as the Sun Yat-sen Center in Madrid, as well as a worldwide news-gathering organization, the Central News Agency (CNA). These activities, while probably not essential to the ROC's survival, help to combat the PRC's continuing efforts to isolate Taiwan. Activities directed from Taiwan are supplemented by associations organized by persons friendly to the ROC in various countries, such as the Australia-Free China Society. Some of the public relations activities of the ROC, particularly those featuring the name "Republic of China," are more and more likely to become the object of protests by PRC embassies to local governments. The Philippine government, which established diplomatic relations with the PRC in June 1975, has already instructed newspapers and radio and television stations to eliminate references to the ROC "in order to maintain the cordial relations that now exist between the Philippines and the People's Republic of China." It has also reportedly ordered off the air a Chinese-language television program that occasionally used footage from Taiwan.[44] Other evidence of the responsiveness of some governments to PRC pressures is a directive

41. *Far Eastern Economic Review,* Sept. 5, 1975, p. 10.
42. *Washington Post,* Nov. 21, 1976.
43. *Far Eastern Economic Review,* July 30, 1976, p. 28.
44. Ibid., pp. 28–29.

from the British Foreign Office to theatrical impresarios and organizers of sporting events in the United Kingdom, stating that "some Taiwan groups are not welcomed by Her Majesty's Government as visitors to the United Kingdom, and this could lead to difficulties about their entry to this country ... we are keen to discourage visits of groups claiming to represent the 'Republic of China.' "[45]

The CNA, which was reorganized as a private corporation after the United Nations withdrew accreditation from its correspondents, has been quite successful in maintaining offices in the principal cities of the world. The PRC's efforts to dislodge it in countries with a traditionally free press and where the CNA has been long established have been particularly unsuccessful. In Tokyo, for instance, where the New China News Agency (NCNA) correspondent tried to get the CNA correspondent ejected from the Foreign Correspondents' Club so that he could join, the CNA correspondent's right to membership was upheld by an overwhelming majority.[46] The CNA correspondent was refused admission, however, to another journalists' organization in Tokyo, the Japan Reporters' Club, because of the opposition of PRC journalists, who had joined earlier.[47] In Ottawa, the NCNA correspondent failed to get the CNA correspondent expelled from the group of journalists covering Parliament. In Ethiopia, on the other hand, the government accommodated the PRC by expelling the CNA correspondent.

The most critical and sensitive of all relationships that the ROC maintains with foreign countries is the military relationship, which has been almost exclusively with the United States. There is some evidence, however, of limited relations with others in the military field. In March 1975, the ROC was reported to be selling military equipment to the Philippines.[48] In January 1977, Lieutenant General de V. du Toit, chief of intelligence for the South African Defense Forces, was decorated in Taipei with the Order of Cloud and Banner "for his contributions to promoting friendship and military cooperation between the two countries."[49] In the same month, a request by the ROC to purchase "a substantial number" of Rapier surface-to-air missiles was turned down by the British government.[50]

---

45. The circular was quoted by an outraged citizen who questioned the right of the Foreign Office to interfere with those wanting to bring foreign performers or athletes into the UK, regardless of what they called themselves. *The Times* (London), Dec. 1, 1976.
46. David Nelson Rowe, *Informal "Diplomatic Relations": The Case of Japan and the Republic of China, 1972–1974* (Hamden, Conn.: Shoestring Press, 1975), p. 64.
47. FBIS, *Daily Report, East Asia and Pacific,* June 2, 1977, p. B2.
48. *The New York Times,* Mar. 12, 1975.
49. FBIS, *Daily Report, East Asia and Pacific,* Jan. 18, 1977, p. B1.
50. *The New York Times,* Jan. 18, 1977.

The most extensive military relationship, except for that with the United States, is the military cooperation with Singapore. Singapore has never had diplomatic relations with either the PRC or the ROC and rigidly excludes propaganda, educational materials, and political agents from either side. It does not want the Chinese civil war extended to its territory, where 75 percent of the population is of Chinese ancestry. But it trades extensively with both the PRC and the ROC. Visitors to Singapore can compare the array of goods from the China mainland and from Taiwan in the small department stores that each has established on adjacent floors of a building in a downtown shopping center. Despite Singapore's evenhandedness in excluding politics and in welcoming trade from both the China mainland and Taiwan, it worked out a deal with Taipei in 1975 to train its military forces, because Taiwan had the open space that Singapore lacked, and the Chinese-featured soldiers from Singapore, dressed in ROC uniforms, would be inconspicuous. A Singapore Airlines jumbo jet arrived weekly in Kaohsiung rotating the troops, while ships brought in the tanks, artillery, and ammunition. Prime Minister Lee Kuan-yew visited Taiwan privately on several occasions. In the spring of 1977, however, the training program was reportedly transferred to the Philippines, perhaps as the result of Lee's conversations during his Peking visit in May 1976.[51]

The Soviet Option

Taipei's growing diplomatic isolation and the virulence of the Sino-Soviet dispute prompted the question whether Moscow might not seek a relationship with the ROC as a further step in strengthening its ties with governments on the periphery of China. Ever since the Soviet journalist Victor Louis visited Taiwan in 1968, outside observers have speculated that some relationship between the ROC and the Soviet Union was under consideration by the two governments. Officials of the ROC flatly denied such rumors, but speculation was fed by occasional shreds of information: the statement by Foreign Minister Chow Shu-kai in March 1972 that the ROC was willing to develop economic and other relations with Communist countries if they were not "puppets of Communist China," the report in February 1973 that the ROC would lease a naval base in the Pescadores to the Soviet Union if the United States recognized the PRC, the transit of the Taiwan Strait

---

51. *Far Eastern Economic Review*, Aug. 15, 1975, pp. 45–46, May 14, 1976, p. 24, Oct. 8, 1976, p. 5, Dec. 3, 1976, p. 5; FBIS, *Daily Report, East Asia and Pacific*, Jan. 28, 1976, p. B1.

for the first time since 1949 by a squadron of Soviet warships in May 1973, the rumors of additional trips by Victor Louis, occasional contacts between Soviet and ROC diplomats, and occasional references to the ROC in the Soviet press. Although this was pretty thin fare, the logic of "my enemy's enemy is my friend" helped keep the speculation alive.[52]

The PRC appears to have taken seriously the possibility of collaboration between Moscow and Taipei. Chou En-lai in August 1972 praised Chiang Kai-shek for the spirit of national independence he had showed in rejecting a Soviet feeler concerning the possible use of the Pescadores by Soviet ships, but expressed doubts that Chiang Ching-kuo would show the same regard for national sovereignty and the interests of his Taiwanese compatriots.[53] Then in January 1973, Chou accused the Soviets of harboring ambitions to occupy Taiwan and claimed that Soviet ambitions would be opposed not only by the PRC but also by the United States.[54] Fu Tso-yi in his 1973 statement warned his compatriots in Taiwan against "dreaming of relying on someone else" when the United States turned out to be unreliable. Later Fu explained that at the time he had been referring to a possible linkup between Chiang Ching-kuo and the Soviet Union, although he expressed confidence that the United States would not permit such an eventuality.[55]

The speculation about possible links with the Soviet Union was awkward for the ROC, because there were divided counsels on the subject within its leadership. Those favoring the firmest possible anti-Communist position deplored any hint of contacts with the Soviets. They argued that such contacts would not only be morally wrong but also undermine support for the ROC in the United States. Others saw diplomatic advantages in hints of flexibility toward the Soviet Union. The hardliners won the debate, however, and one of the advocates of flexibility, Chow Shu-kai, lost his position as foreign minister.

There is no evidence that the development of substantial relations with the Soviet Union is being seriously considered by the present ROC leadership. Those who favored hints of flexibility saw such a change as a useful way of conveying a subtle warning to the PRC not to push too hard rather than as a foreshadowing of a major shift in foreign policy. The ROC is inhibited from pursuing a relationship with the Soviet Union in several respects. First, ROC leaders are deeply suspicious of

---

52. *The New York Times,* Mar. 8, 1972; Hong Kong, *South China Morning Post,* Feb. 17, 1973; *Washington Post,* May 14, 1973; *Far Eastern Economic Review,* June 27, 1975, p. 5.
53. *Ch'i Shih Nien Tai,* Dec. 1972, p. 38.
54. Ibid., Apr. 1973, p. 30.
55. Conversation with Yale University professor Howard H. S. Chiao, *Asahi* (Tokyo), July 10, 1973.

the Soviet government. They do not wish to become dependent on the Soviet Union, for they suspect that Moscow would dump them unceremoniously if it ever served Moscow's purposes. Second, developing a relationship with the Soviet Union runs counter to their policy of maintaining the closest possible relations with the United States and Japan. Both of these countries would be highly suspicious of a significant and expanding relationship between Taiwan and the Soviet Union. Third, the Soviet Union itself has so far shown no evidence that it would like to develop a significant and lasting relationship with Taiwan. In fact, after Mao's death the Soviet Union probed the possibility of improved relations with Peking. Although PRC leaders showed no inclination to respond favorably and the Soviet Union resumed its verbal attacks on the PRC, it is still too early to judge the course that Sino-Soviet relations will take during the next several years. So long as Moscow is interested in a degree of reconciliation with Peking, it is unlikely to jeopardize that possibility by taking serious steps to develop relations with Taiwan.

Thus, under the present circumstances, seeking to establish relations with the Soviet Union does not seem to offer the ROC leaders a promising counter to the PRC efforts to isolate Taiwan. It would be attempted only in desperation, if the ROC leaders felt that they were being abandoned by the United States. Even then such a move would be practicable only if the Soviets had given up hope of improving relations with Peking and were willing to face the intensified hostility from the PRC that Soviet intervention in Taiwan would provoke.

The Independence Option

Although it is possible, as the ROC has demonstrated, for a political entity to survive and prosper in the international community without wide recognition as a state, this is not easy. The disadvantages and difficulties are numerous. Consequently, declaring Taiwan an independent state appears increasingly attractive to some. Support for this alternative will almost certainly grow as the influence of Taiwanese in the central government increases.

Under the present circumstances, however, there is nothing to gain and much to lose by declaring Taiwan's independence. Neither the United States nor Japan would be likely to recognize the new state formally because of the damage it would do to their relations with the PRC. The PRC would regard US recognition of the new state as proof that the United States had engineered the move in direct contravention of the spirit if not the letter of the Shanghai communiqué. If the United States and Japan declined to recognize the new state of Taiwan, few other countries would be likely to do so. Thus, by declaring independence, Taiwan would have hurt rather than improved its international position. Even worse, by its own action it would have terminated the existing treaties and agreements between the ROC and other countries, and the other countries might not choose to renegotiate those arrangements with the new government. The United States, for example, probably would not choose to conclude a security treaty with the new government given the situation today.

A declaration of independence by Taiwan would also be seen by the PRC as a challenge, thereby increasing the danger that the PRC would abandon all alternatives but the use of military force to gain possession of Taiwan. Those within the PRC who had argued for patiently working toward a peaceful resolution of the Taiwan problem would be discredited. The threat that Taiwan might be declared an independent state is a deterrent to a PRC military attack on Taiwan only so long as the threat is not carried out.

As a result of their own analysis of the situation and probably also of warnings by the US government, ROC leaders undoubtedly are well aware of the disadvantages of declaring Taiwan independent. Thus, a declaration of independence would seem inadvisable to them, except for three possible circumstances: the United States was disengaging from Taiwan so unmistakably and totally that the ROC had nothing to lose; US relations with the PRC had deteriorated so seriously that the United States was no longer concerned about the effect of recognition of a new state of Taiwan on its relations with the PRC; or relations with the United States and Japan had become so important to the PRC that its leaders believed they had to tolerate those nations' recognition of an independent state of Taiwan. A new leader who came to power by a coup in the course of a succession struggle might also proclaim independence as a means of mobilizing popular support without giving much thought to the international consequences of his act. None of these contingencies seems likely, but all need to be kept in mind by the United States, the PRC, and Japan as they formulate their policies toward Taiwan and toward each other.

The Struggle for Survival

The ROC has been engaged since 1949 in a struggle for survival. The advantage it held in international relations in the 1950s, resulting from Peking's intervention in Korea and the adoption by the United States of a policy of containment of the PRC, could not last so long as the PRC held the China mainland. Recognition of the PRC as the legitimate government of China by the great majority of nations was inevitable sooner or later. Moreover, the PRC's control of almost all of China's territory and population placed it in a strong position to insist that it would accept diplomatic relations only with those nations that broke relations with the ROC.

In its continuing struggle for survival, the ROC possesses important assets. Its population is larger than that of two-thirds of the members of the United Nations and its people are more highly educated than those of most developing countries. It has built a strong and diversified economy, based on large-scale trade with many countries, despite an absence of diplomatic relations with most of those countries in recent years. It has devised ingenious unorthodox substitutes for diplomatic relations and has earned the sympathy of many people in the United States, Japan, and elsewhere. Up to the present the PRC's efforts to isolate Taiwan, while complicating the island's international relations, have not significantly weakened its ability to survive and prosper independently. The opposition of the people of Taiwan to being incorporated into the PRC also seems substantially unaffected.

The ROC's most difficult test lies ahead: adjusting to the impact on its economy and international relations of the normalization of relations between Washington and Peking. Almost all of those nations that still maintain diplomatic relations with Taipei probably would follow the United States in severing relations. The PRC might take advantage of the ROC's weakened diplomatic position to institute new forms of pressure on Taiwan's foreign trade. How effective such measures would be would depend heavily on the reaction of Taiwan's trading partners, particularly the United States and Japan, to the PRC's attempts to interfere with their trade with Taiwan. The ROC's option of declaring independence and the possibility that the United States might recognize the new state are important deterrents to excessive PRC pressures.

Japan's Relations with Taiwan

7

Geographical proximity, economic interests, historical connections, and US policy combined to create strong ties between Japan and Taiwan. Only the United States surpasses Japan as an economic partner and political supporter of Taiwan. Yet the relationship between Japan and Taiwan has been an uneasy one, resting on ambivalent Japanese attitudes toward China and buffeted by the swirling undercurrents of Japanese domestic politics.

Japan's fundamental policy toward the two parts of China, which it has followed consistently since emerging from US occupation, has been to develop as fruitful relations as possible with both of them. In following this policy, Japanese governments have been constrained by deep differences among the political parties concerning relations with China and constant domestic conflict over this issue, compounded by varying pressures from Washington, Taipei, and Peking. Until 1972, Japan's diplomatic and other official relations were only with Taipei, but trade was conducted with both Chinas. After the establishment of diplomatic relations with the PRC in September 1972, the situation was reversed. All official relations were with the government of the PRC, but Japan continued to trade with both mainland China and Taiwan. In order to conduct trade and a wide variety of people-to-people contacts in the absence of diplomatic relations, the Japanese devised a number of unique institutions and techniques, first to deal with the PRC and later with the ROC. Neither the PRC nor the ROC accepted in principle the concept of "separating politics and economics" used by the Japanese government to justify its policy, but they went along with that concept in practice.

Japan's relations with Taiwan since 1972 merit close study by the United States as it considers the choices before it. Officials of the PRC have privately pointed to the Japanese model as a precedent for US relations with Taiwan after the normalization of relations with the PRC. There are obvious differences, however, in the past relations of the two countries with Taiwan that diminish the usefulness of Japan's experience. Unlike the United States, Japan assumed no obligation for Taiwan's security. The Japanese government, while acknowledging that security in the Taiwan area was important to the security of Japan, relied on the United States to ensure it. Moreover, there were important differences in the attitudes of the American and Japanese peoples toward the two parts of China, as well as in the forms of economic and other interests in Taiwan pursued by each country. Japan's relations with Taiwan nevertheless provide a key to the extent to which the United States could follow the Japanese model in readjusting its own relations with Taiwan after establishment of diplomatic relations with the PRC, as well as to the possible effect of that readjustment on Japan's future relations with Taiwan.

Legacy of the Past

For the past hundred years or more, the association between the Japanese and the Chinese has been close but troubled. While respecting China as the source of much of their own culture, the Japanese took a condescending view of China's failure to respond to pressure from the West with the unity and vigor that Japan itself displayed. The Chinese, compelled by the military superiority of the Western nations to make concession after concession, found the modernizing Japanese to be an even more dangerous threat to China's integrity. As early as 1879, Chinese statesman Li Hung-chang warned that "the Japanese are of a proud and overbearing nature; extremely ambitious and wily, they advance step by step."[1] The disdainful Japanese view of China after Japan had defeated it in the war of 1894–1895 and acquired Taiwan is reflected in the objection of a Japanese diplomat to Australia's exclusion of the Japanese along with the Chinese as if they were "on the same level of morality and civilization."[2]

---

1. Harley Farnsworth MacNair, *Modern Chinese History: Selected Readings* (Shanghai: Commercial Press, 1927), p. 511.
2. Takaaki Kato, Japanese minister in London about 1900, quoted in T. B. Millar, "Japan and Australia, Partners in the Pacific," *Pacific Community* 8 (October 1976): 29–30.

Animosity between Chinese and Japanese reached its height in the destructive war that began with the Japanese conquest of Manchuria in 1931 and ended in 1945. The suffering of the Chinese in that conflict left them with a distrust of and wariness toward the Japanese that persist to this day. As a Chinese leader candidly told Japanese Premier Kakuei Tanaka when he visited Peking to normalize relations between the two countries in 1972: "Pre-war militarism inflicted great losses to the Chinese continent. There are more than a dozen million people who had their relatives or family members killed. There are some people who are not happy about your visit to China."[3] The victories won by the Japanese troops in China reinforced the Japanese convictions of their superiority to the Chinese but also gave to many Japanese a sense of guilt for their country's aggression against China.

During the fifty years of Japanese colonial administration of Taiwan, the Chinese in Taiwan retained their distinctive Chinese characteristics but came to have a degree of rapport with and understanding of the Japanese shared by few of their mainland compatriots. They resented the domination of the island by the Japanese and the often brutal retaliation by Japanese police and soldiers for acts of resistance. Yet they benefited from the improvements in public health, agriculture, education, and industry, which gave them a higher standard of living than enjoyed by any province of mainland China.[4] After the suppression of the 1947 uprising by the newly installed mainlander-dominated government of Taiwan and the discovery by Taiwanese that they were to be excluded from positions of power in that government, many Taiwanese came to view the Japanese colonial period through rose-colored glasses that softened its harsher features. Thus, Japanese visiting Taiwan found a warmer welcome than they encountered in Korea, where resentment and bitterness toward Japan remained strong.

US Influence and Japanese Politics

Although the Japanese government had its own reasons for wishing to maintain links with Taiwan in the postwar period, its pronounced tilt toward the ROC was a response to US pressure. Immediately after signing the treaty at San Francisco in 1951 with forty-

---

3. *Asahi*, Oct. 1, 1972.
4. There were about 2.6 million Chinese in Taiwan in 1900, increasing to about 6 million by 1945. See George H. Kerr, *Formosa: Licensed Revolution and the Home Rule Movement, 1895–1945* (Honolulu: University Press of Hawaii, 1974).

eight nations—not including the Soviet Union, the PRC, or the ROC—which formally ended the Pacific phase of World War II, Japan placed itself under US protection by signing a bilateral mutual security treaty, which gave the United States the right to maintain bases in Japan for the defense of Japan and other uses. Before either of the treaties had been acted upon by the US Senate, Prime Minister Shigeru Yoshida indicated to the Japanese Diet that he would be willing to establish official Japanese offices in both Taipei and Shanghai, provoking a large number of US senators to express concern about the possible recognition of the PRC by Japan. In order to reassure them, Yoshida wrote to Secretary of State John Foster Dulles, in what became known as "the Yoshida letter," that Japan had no intention of concluding a bilateral treaty with the Chinese Communist regime and that, as soon as it could legally do so, the Japanese government would conclude a peace treaty with the ROC. That treaty was signed in April 1952, the day on which both treaties concluded at San Francisco came into effect.[5] Thus, the Japanese government had given a pledge that limited its freedom of action with respect to the PRC even before it had gained freedom to conduct its own foreign relations.

During the years that followed, the Japanese government felt constrained not to provoke American anger by diverging too far from US policy toward China. The advantages to Japan's economy and security from the close connection with the United States were too important to risk for the uncertain gains to be derived from moving closer to the PRC. Trade with the China mainland was allowed, because it would have been politically impossible for a Japanese government to maintain a total embargo on trade with China, as the United States did. But in 1952, Japan joined the Coordinating Committee (COCOM) and its China Committee (CHINCOM), which had been established by the United States and other industrial nations to control the shipment of strategic materials to Communist countries. The Japanese government cooperated closely with the US government in supporting the position of the ROC in the United Nations. It maintained an embassy in Taipei and refrained from establishing any official office on the China mainland.

The Japanese government hewed closely to the China policy pursued by the United States, despite much criticism by the opposition

---

5. Chae-jin Lee, *Japan Faces China* (Baltimore: Johns Hopkins University Press, 1976), p. 27. Neither the PRC nor the ROC had been invited to the San Francisco conference because the countries recognizing one or the other could not agree on which to invite. The peace treaty of Japan with the ROC applied only to territories that were then or might thereafter come under ROC control. It formally ended the state of war as far as the ROC was concerned but was denounced as null and void by the PRC.

parties and even by some persons within the ruling Liberal Democratic party (LDP) itself. It also had to resist pressures from Peking, which found ways of exploiting to its own advantage the divisions over China policy among Japanese politicians. Taipei was quick to protest any Japanese government action that seemed to enhance the status of the PRC. Japanese leaders, bolstered by the LDP's comfortable parliamentary majority, threaded their way among these conflicting pressures. Some worried, especially after the United States had initiated ambassadorial-level talks with the PRC, that the United States would establish dipomatic relations with Peking first, leaving Japan in the lurch. Nevertheless, the predominant view was that Japan had to follow Washington's lead.

Sharp differences over China policy among Japanese politicians were closely linked to the more fundamental differences over Japan's relations with the United States. The conservatives, who governed Japan throughout almost the entire postwar period, strongly supported the US-Japan security treaty and the deployment of US forces in and around Japan. They generally followed the lead of the United States in their policies toward China and the Soviet Union. The Japan Socialist party (JSP) and the Japan Communist party (JCP), on the other hand, bitterly attacked the security treaty and advocated closer relations with the Communist states. The JSP, which was the largest opposition party, favored unarmed neutrality for Japan, its security to be protected by nonaggression pacts with the big powers.

Views on China were further complicated by splits within each of the major parties. Pro-PRC figures in the LDP crticized government policy and pressed for closer relations with the PRC. Differences developed between pro-Chinese and pro-Soviet factions within the JSP after the break between Peking and Moscow. The quarrel between the Communist parties of Japan and China in 1966 left the JCP highly critical of the Chinese Communist party, which promptly shifted its support to a tiny Marxist splinter party in Japan. Thus, differences within and between political parties in Japan offered opportunities to the PRC, but also presented it with difficulties.

Most Japanese felt some uneasiness about the absence of normal relations with their big neighbor. This uneasiness was increased by the PRC nuclear explosion in 1964. The lack of diplomatic relations with Peking hindered the full-scale development of the "peace diplomacy" to which the Japanese people were deeply committed. Pan-Asian sentiment, cultural affinities with China, and a sense of guilt for the harm done to the Chinese by Japanese aggression added to the vague and usually mild yet widely shared dissatisfaction with Japan's relation with China during much of the 1950s and 1960s.

Pressure for better relations with the PRC also came from Marxist-influenced intellectuals and much of the media, which often expressed uncritical admiration for the PRC's domestic policies, except in periods of turmoil such as the Great Leap Forward and the cutural revolution. The strongest attraction China had for the Japanese, however, was the lure of China trade. Many small businessmen longed for the trade they had enjoyed in prewar China and had high expectations of expanded trade with the PRC if political obstacles could be removed.

In a climate in which better relations with the PRC were widely desired, the Japanese government was often placed on the defensive. But the desire was rarely turned into pressure on Diet members at the ballot. For the great majority of voters, the China issue was remote and low on their list of priorities. As a result, the government was able to maintain its policy of separating economics from politics by relatively minor tactical moves that underscored its determination to promote trade with mainland China.

Moreover, there were countervailing political pressures from influential quarters that made difficult any departure from the policy of rejecting official relations with the PRC. At least until 1970, big business was generally skeptical about the prospects for large increases in trade with China. Until 1964, two-way trade with Taiwan exceeded trade with the China mainland, and Japanese exports to Taiwan exceeded those to China in every year from 1958 to 1970, except for the three years 1964–1966. Taiwan also offered opportunities for profitable investment that were unavailable in the PRC. A sizable group of LDP politicians had close ties with Taiwan. Strongly anti-Communist, they believed that Japan should work closely with ROC leaders to prevent the spread of communism in Asia. They reminded their fellow country-men of the magnanimity demonstrated toward Japan by Chiang Kai-shek when he renounced reparations and declined to participate in the occupation. They urged Japan to continue to show gratitude for these favors. Economic and personal links with Taiwan and a sense of obligation to Chiang Kai-shek thus reinforced the distrust that anti-Communist members of the LDP felt toward the PRC.

Backdoor Relations with the PRC

The LDP leaders who governed Japan in the postwar period were conservative and anti-Communist, but they were also pragmatic. They did not reject relations with the PRC on ideological grounds. On the contrary, they sought relations that would promote Japanese national interests, as they conceived those interests, and would protect their personal political positions. Consequently, the LDP leaders permitted extensive travel to and from China and encouraged the expansion of private trade. Their policies were influenced not only by the United States and by domestic political pressures but also by the policies of the PRC.

The PRC's principal objectives toward Japan during the 1950s and 1960s were to weaken its ties with the United States, to gain greater influence on the Japanese government, and ultimately to establish official relations with it. During the 1950s, trade with Japan was used almost entirely as a means toward these ends, but after the Sino-Soviet split, trade also became an end in itself, as the PRC was forced to turn to non-Communist trading partners in order to pursue its economic development. Peking's policies toward Japan, which varied from hard to moderate, employed a wide variety of tactics, including the cultivation of ties with opposition parties and critics of the government within the LDP, the esablishment of Sino-Japanese friendship associations, and a wide variety of people-to-people activities aimed especially at the numerous pro-PRC journalists, trade unionists, young people, and academics. Manipulation of the trade link was a favorite PRC technique, as no Japanese politician could afford to be against expanding trade with China, given the public consciousness of Japan's vital dependence on foreign trade.

Initially, Peking took an extremely hostile view of the Japanese government, encouraging its violent overthrow by the Japanese Communist party, joining with the Soviet Union in an alliance directed against Japan, and condemning Premier Yoshida for collaborating with the United States in the Korean war and for signing a peace treaty with the ROC. Soon after the Korean war, however, the PRC moderated its policy toward Japan in line with the "peaceful coexistence" theme that was to dominate its foreign policy during the mid-1950s. Chou En-lai took several initiatives to encourage the Japanese to begin negotiations on the establishment of diplomatic relations. Although the Japanese government rejected proposals for official discussions, informal relations multiplied. Unofficial agreements on trade, fisheries, cultural exchange, and the repatriation of Japanese war criminals were concluded during 1955 and 1956.[6] Trade grew rapidly, although it was still relatively small in 1956 at $150 million.

From 1957 to 1960, relations between the PRC and Japan deteriorated. Peking shifted to a radical line domestically with the Great Leap Forward and to a more militant policy toward the United States

---

6. Lee, *Japan Faces China*, pp. 33–34.

that coincided with the accession to office of Prime Minister Nobusuke Kishi, a strong supporter of the US-Japan security treaty. Mao Tse-tung and Chou En-lai welcomed to Peking an official delegation from the JSP, the principal Japanese opposition party, which resulted in a joint communiqué stating that Taiwan was an internal Chinese matter and that Japan should establish formal diplomatic relations with the PRC as soon as possible. The LDP was highly critical of this intervention by the JSP in foreign policy and rejected its views as unrealistic. Kishi became the first Japanese prime minister to visit Taiwan. He also visited the United States, where he warned against PRC expansion in Asia. The PRC's attacks on Kishi increased, while the LDP expressed its resentment of Chinese interference in Japanese domestic politics. Thus, polemics and suspicion between Peking and Tokyo were on the rise when, in 1958, a minor incident involving the tearing down of a PRC flag at a stamp exhibit in Nagasaki was seized on by Peking as an excuse to sever all economic relations with Japan, as well as all cultural exchanges and negotiations on the repatriation of Japanese nationals.

The drastic PRC move was apparently intended to influence the forthcoming Japanese general election and the debate on the revision of the US-Japan security treaty planned for 1960. But Peking's actions failed to prevent an LDP election victory, and the PRC's support of Japanese opponents of the treaty with funds, propaganda, and mass demonstrations throughout China did not thwart the adoption of a revised security treaty. Instead, Peking's action produced several years of tenuous relations between the two countries. Trade slumped to less than $25 million in 1959 and 1960, and it did not reach the 1958 level again until 1964, despite an initiative by Chou En-lai in 1960 that opened trade with Japanese firms considered by the PRC to be "friendly."[7] The policies toward the PRC followed by Kishi's successor as prime minister, Hayato Ikeda, differed radically in style, although not greatly in substance. Ikeda, who soon came under a Chinese propaganda attack, maintained a low profile, avoiding polemical exchanges.

The PRC, swinging away from the ideological excesses of the late 1950s, sought better relations with Japan. It stepped up its cultivation of faction leaders in the LDP who were critical of the government's failure to improve relations with mainland China. In 1962, one of those

---

7. This lengthy slump in Sino-Japanese trade coincided from 1960 with a decline in the PRC's overall foreign trade, resulting from internal economic difficulties and confusion attending the shift of the bulk of the PRC's foreign trade from the Soviet bloc to non-Communist states, so that it can be attributed only in part to the PRC's punitive policy toward the Japanese government.

leaders, Matsumura Kenzo, reached an agreement with Chou En-lai that created a framework for long-term trade between Japan and China. The most important provision of the agreement set up trade offices, known as the Liao Ch'eng-chih Liaison Office in Tokyo and the Takasaki Liaison Office in Peking after the Chinese official and the LDP dietman who had negotiated the implementing agreement. Those who staffed the liaison offices, although not recognized as representatives of their governments, were in fact government officials and carried on a variety of quasi-diplomatic functions.

Through the twin channels of "friendly firm" trade and the transactions concluded under the Liao-Takasaki agreement, known after 1968 as "memorandum trade," both exports and imports grew substantially after 1963, although they suffered a temporary setback during 1967–1968, the years of the cultural revolution. The PRC's "people-to-people" diplomacy flourished in the early and middle 1960s, but it too was hampered by the cultural revolution. Pro-Peking groups in Japan, such as the Japan-China Friendship Association, which had been vigorously supported by the JSP and the JCP, split and fell into disarray when both the JCP and the right wing of the JSP entered into bitter disputes with the Chinese Communist party.[8]

In its effort to respond to the domestic demand for increased trade with the PRC without having official relations with that government, the Japanese government sometimes faced severe pressures from both the PRC and the ROC. A graphic illustration of this problem was the Kurashiki Rayon Company incident of 1963–1964. Prime Minister Ikeda's approval of Export-Import Bank funding of the export to China of a $22 million vinylon artificial fiber plant by that company provoked a strong reaction from Taipei. Chiang Kai-shek withdrew his ambassador from Tokyo, halted government purchases of Japanese goods, and threatened to sever diplomatic relations, accusing the Japanese government of giving official assistance to the ROC's chief enemy. In order to mollify the ROC, Ikeda sanctioned a "private" letter from the former prime minister, Yoshida, to Chang Ch'un, secretary-general of the Presidential Office in Taipei, containing assurances that Export-Import Bank funds would not be used in the future to finance exports to the PRC. When in early 1965 the newly installed prime minister, Eisaku Sato, indicated his intention to honor these assurances, the PRC withdrew from negotiations with a number of Japanese companies for the purchase of industrial plants and ships. Thus, the Japanese government did not always succeed in establishing a sharp distinction

---

8. See Lee, *Japan Faces China*, pp. 65–82.

between official and unofficial relations in dealing with the PRC and the ROC. The gray area between these extremes concealed political pitfalls.

During the period from 1950 to 1970, Japanese relations with the PRC were more extensive than those of any other non-Communist country, but they were plagued by tension and controversy. The root of the problem was the abnormality of continuing to treat the government of the ROC as the legitimate government of all China when PRC authorities clearly controlled the China mainland. The logic of the situation favored the PRC, which used its strong position to press for a normalization of relations with Japan by exploiting both the political division within Japan and the high priority that nearly all Japanese attached to the expansion of foreign trade. The PRC would probably have been more successful had it not been for the domestic turmoil in China and for the ill-chosen policies adopted toward Japan in the Great Leap Forward and the cultural revolution. The LDP government, generally on the defensive against pressures for expanded relations with the PRC even from within its own ranks, went as far as it could to permit extensive unofficial relations within the constraints imposed by Japan's dependence on the United States.

Front-Door Relations with the ROC

The 1952 peace treaty between Japan and the ROC ended the state of war between those two governments and began two decades of official relations. Japan maintained an embassy in Taipei, and the ROC maintained one in Tokyo, as well as consular offices in Yokohama, Osaka, and Nagasaki. Two Japanese premiers made official visits to Taiwan—Kishi in 1957 and Sato in 1967. Numerous other high officials visited back and forth. Japan became one of the chief supporters of the ROC's position in the United Nations, along with the United States. In 1965, the Japanese government provided the ROC with a five-year yen credit amounting to $150 million for industrial projects, a dam, and harbor improvements.[9] The Japanese government sent technical experts to Taiwan and received technicians from Taiwan for training in Japan under the Technical Cooperation Program. Japan and the ROC became members of the Asian and Pacific Council, a political grouping of Asian and Pacific countries that did not maintain diplomatic relations with the PRC. Thus, the Japanese government

---

9. Lawrence Olson, *Japan in Postwar Asia* (New York: Praeger, 1970), p. 168.

did not hesitate to enter into a broad range of official relations with the ROC, despite frequent criticism of its actions by the PRC.

Strictly official relations were supplemented by contact between private, politically oriented organizations in both countries. These organizations had many influential members. The leading group was the Committee on Japan-China Cooperation, created in 1957. The principal aim of this committee was to promote economic activities between the two countries, but speeches made and, to a lesser extent, communiqués issued at the annual meetings frequently contained language critical of the PRC. The Japanese membership of the committee numbered Kishi as well as LDP Diet members and prominent businessmen, including the president of the Keidanren or Federation of Economic Organizations, the most influential business association in the country to which all of its largest companies belonged. On the Taiwan side, members included leading businessmen and senior KMT figures, such as Ho Ying-ch'in, an adviser to Chiang Kai-shek. Another such private organization, avowedly political in purpose, was the World Anti-Communist League, originally called the Asian-Pacific Anti-Communist League, whose annual meetings were attended by anti-Communist politicians from Japan and Taiwan. The conferences of the Inter-Parliamentary Union provided other opportunities for politically influential Japanese and Chinese from Taiwan to meet. Through the frequent meetings of these and other organizations, a fairly large group of persons who held important positions in Japan and Taiwan and had a common interest in promoting relations between the two countries came to know each other well. These connections served to mitigate the impact of the severance of official relations, when it occurred, and helped in developing substitutes for those relations.

Purely private relations between Japan and Taiwan also flourished. Japanese exports to Taiwan in most years exceeded Japanese exports to the China mainland. By the end of 1970, 394 Japanese investments in Taiwan, amounting to $99.6 million, had been approved by the ROC. Japanese firms had entered into 42 technical cooperation agreements with companies in Taiwan, and 22 Japanese firms had opened branch offices there.[10] In 1969, Japanese trading companies were reportedly handling over half of Taiwan's exports to third countries.[11] Between 1965 and 1972, the number of Japanese visiting Taiwan annually swelled from 38,000 to 278,000.[12] Cultural delegations traveled back and forth, and several hundred students from Taiwan studied in Japanese educational institutions. Perhaps the strongest ties of all were

10. Information provided by American Embassy.
11. *The New York Times*, Sept. 22, 1969.
12. *TSDB*, p. 117.

between the 50,000 Chinese residents in Japan, most of whom were Taiwanese, and their friends and relatives in Taiwan.

The attitudes of Chiang Kai-shek and other ROC leaders toward Japan were complex and ambivalent. They recognized that the expanding economic relations between Japan and Taiwan were essential to the island's rapid economic growth, but they were disturbed by the heavy trade imbalance in Japan's favor and tried, with little success, to reduce it. They feared Japanese economic domination, but at the same time they saw the political advantage of increasing Japan's economic stake in Taiwan. They relied on Japan's support in the United Nations, but they were deeply worried about the strength of pro-PRC sentiment in Japan. They knew that they could not prevent trade and other forms of unofficial relations between Japan and the China mainland, but whenever the Japanese government seemed about to confer a more official character on those relations, as in the Kurashiki Rayon case, they sought to check the drift by taking a strong stand and by mobilizing the influence of pro-ROC politicians and businessmen in Japan. They were helped in this effort by the fact that some senior ROC officials, including Chiang Kai-shek himself, had studied in Japan, and a few could speak Japanese.

The often cordial relations between Taiwanese and Japanese also worried ROC mainlander leaders. They recognized the advantages of these established connections for encouraging trade and investment. Moreover, certain Taiwanese businessmen who were both close to the government and well-connected in Japan were indispensable 'as intermediaries for handling delicate political matters. On the other hand, ROC leaders suspected that Japanese businessmen were supporting the Taiwan independence movement, which had its headquarters in Tokyo. The mainlander-dominated government of the ROC feared that too intimate a relationship between Japanese and Taiwanese might be dangerous both in building support in Taiwan for the Taiwan Independence Movement and in serving as a conduit for pro-Communist ideas. Consequently, Japanese publications were excluded from Taiwan, and the commercial circulation of Japanese movies and popular songs was strictly controlled.

The Reversal of Relations

As the turmoil of the cultural revolution in China subsided, Sino-Japanese trade resumed its upward trend. So did international support for seating the PRC in the United Nations. As a result, increasing numbers of LDP members joined with the opposition in criticizing Prime Minister Sato's China policy.

That policy had become a prime target for Peking propaganda as well, for a number of reasons. Sato had made an official visit to Taiwan. He had declined formally to nullify the unofficial guarantee to the ROC not to finance exports to the PRC, which the PRC had demanded as a prerequisite to the resumption of whole plant purchases from Japan. He had also signed a joint communiqué with President Nixon in November 1969 declaring that security in Korea and the Taiwan area was important to Japan's security. The PRC, fearing that the Nixon doctrine and the reversion of Okinawa to Japan involved the Japanese assumption of military responsibilities toward Korea and Taiwan, launched a vituperative campaign against Sato, accusing him of reviving Japanese militarism. The LDP dietman who visited Peking annually to renew the memorandum trade agreement was compelled to agree to communiqués harshly denouncing the Sato government's policies. Representatives of "friendly firms" visiting China publicly attacked the Japanese government in even stronger terms.

In 1970, Chou En-lai laid down four "principles" for Sino-Japanest trade: the PRC would not trade with any Japanese firms that assisted South Korea against North Korea or supported the ROC's mainland recovery policy, had large investments in South Korea or Taiwan, aided US military operations in Indochina, or were US joint ventures or US subsidiaries in Japan. Chou's announcement caused a flurry among Japanese businessmen. Producers of fertilizer and steel, Japan's chief exports to mainland China, promptly accepted the principles. Many other Japanese companies followed their example, particularly after the Canton fair in the spring of 1970, at which the PRC refused to deal with companies deeply involved in Taiwan and even canceled some contracts with such companies.

Although Peking's action caused a temporary slowdown in Japanese investment in Taiwan, it had little apparent effect on the level of Japanese trade with the ROC, which continued to increase. Chou En-lai's vague criteria were never clearly defined, and after the first few months, the PRC did not attempt to enforce them rigorously. Japanese companies that announced their acceptance of the conditions were able to trade with the PRC but were not prevented from trading with or investing in Taiwan through subsidiaries or affiliates. Many Japanese investors in Taiwan were small firms that had no trade with the mainland anyway. The principal value of Peking's acton was to make the heads of Japanese firms more cautious about sizable investments in Taiwan and to cause a number of companies that had been active in the Committee on Japan-China Cooperation to withdraw from that organization.

The growth of Japanese trade with the PRC and international trends favoring the PRC stimulated leading Japanese businessmen and pro-PRC politicians to press more vigorously for a change in Japan's China policy. The pressures increased when Canada and Italy, both close allies of the United States, established diplomatic relations with the PRC. Japanese business leaders, disturbed by the intensity of Peking's attacks on Sato, feared that countries recognizing the PRC would gain a competitive advantage over Japan in trade. The decisive factor, however, setting Japan irreversibly down the road to recognition of the PRC, was President Nixon's surprise announcement in July 1971 that he planned to visit China soon. The US government's failure to consult with the Japanese government before taking this momentous step shocked the Japanese and undermined Sato's influence within the LDP. His position in the country slipped further when a resolution cosponsored by Japan, the United States, and other countries and aimed at preventing expulsion of the ROC from the United Nations was defeated and the PRC took the ROC's place. These developments loosed an irresistible flood of opinion favoring the early normalization of relations between Japan and the PRC. Peking had played its cards well, ensuring that normalization would be the first order of business for Sato's successor, whose way to it was smoothed by Peking's easing of its attacks on Japanese militarism and redoubling of its cultivation of Japanese big business.

The terms for Japan's future relations with Taiwan remained to be agreed upon with the PRC. Japanese politicians from several parties and business leaders did much of the preparatory work for negotiating the terms through unofficial conversations in Peking. By means of this arms-length technique, PRC leaders gradually formed a judgment about the concessions that they could expect from the Japanese government, while Japanese leaders reached conclusions on the extent of Peking's flexibility. Consequently, after Kakuei Tanaka became prime minister in July 1972, he was able to work out a consensus on Japan's position within the LDP, and in September, he set out for Peking to negotiate the normalization of relations.

In the preliminary discussions with Japanese unofficial envoys to Peking, the PRC had laid down three principles that the Japanese government would have to accept in order to normalize relations between the two countries: the government of the PRC was the sole legitimate government of China; Taiwan was an inseparable part of Chinese territory; and the peace treaty of 1952 between Japan and the ROC was illegal and must be abrogated. The first of these principles presented no problem for the Japanese government, but the other two had been debated hotly in Japan, and Tanaka had to tread warily. After five days of sometimes difficult negotiations, a compromise formula was agreed upon, which was incorporated in a joint communiqué issued in September 1972.[13] The communiqué included four points: the Japanese government acknowledged that, in seeking the normalization of relations, it proceeded from the stand of "fully understanding the three principles for the restoration of diplomatic relations put forward by the People's Republic of China"; the Japanese government recognized the government of the PRC as the "sole legal government of China"; the Japanese government "fully understands and respects" the PRC's view that "Taiwan is an inalienable part of the territory of the People's Republic of China" and promised to comply with Article 8 of the Potsdam Proclamation, thereby reaffirming the Cairo Declaration which supported the restoration of Taiwan to the ROC; and finally, the Japanese government and the government of the PRC agreed to establish diplomatic relations.

The peace treaty of 1952 between the ROC and Japan was not referred to in the joint communiqué, but Foreign Minister Masayoshi Ohira, in accordance with an understanding reached during the negotiations, announced at a press conference just after the release of the communiqué that the treaty with the ROC was "understood as having ended."[14] Shortly before leaving for Peking, Tanaka had also made clear that establishing diplomatic relations with Peking would require ending diplomatic relations with Taipei.[15] The Japanese government, while complying reluctantly with the PRC's demands for termination of the peace treaty and diplomatic relations with the ROC, was nevertheless anxious to preserve Japan's extensive economic and other relations with Taiwan. In the course of the negotiations, the Japanese specified their intentions in this regard, to which the Chinese made no objection. When Ohira returned to Tokyo, he reported to his LDP colleagues: "There are strong and deep ties between Japan and Taiwan. Consequently, even if diplomatic relations are severed, administrative relations must be respected and treasured. So long as they do not touch upon the very roots of the maintenance of Japan-China relations, we intend to devote utmost efforts for the maintenance of administrative relations between Japan and Taiwan."[16]

13. *The New York Times*, Sept. 30, 1972. See also Shinkichi Eto, "Japan and China —A New Stage?" *Problems of Communism* 21 (November–December 1972): 1–17.
14. *Asahi*, Oct. 1, 1972.
15. *Washington Post*, Sept. 22, 1972.
16. *Asahi*, Oct. 1, 1972.

The Japanese government avoided explicitly acknowledging in the communiqué that Taiwan was part of the PRC's territory, limiting itself to the statement of understanding and respect for the PRC's position as well as the ambiguous reference to the Potsdam Proclamation. Although the Japanese government stopped short of express agreement with the PRC on the status of Taiwan, it went somewhat further than the Canadian government, which simply "took note" of the PRC's position. The relationship between the US-Japan security treaty and the defense of Taiwan, a sensitive subject, was also left out of the communiqué but may have been touched upon at least obliquely in the negotiations. The question was whether Japan would permit the United States to use its bases in Japan to carry out its defense commitment to the ROC. Queried about the security treaty on his return to Tokyo, Tanaka replied: "The treaty will not be invoked, China will not resort to arms, and Taiwan will not use arms against the mainland ... The United States... will engage in negotiations for the future. The days of no dialogue are over. Thus, no unfavorable situation will break out. It is safe to say that no undesirable situation can arise."[17]

In Taipei, as it became evident that the Japanese government was preparing to establish diplomatic relations with the PRC, the ROC government issued stern warnings and hawkish legislators threatened economic retaliation. Etsusaburo Shiina, vice-president of the LDP and a former minister, was sent to Taipei to try to gain understanding for Japan's projected move, but he was coldly received. As soon as the news that diplomatic relations between Japan and the PRC had been established reached Taipei, the ROC government announced that it was severing diplomatic relations with Japan. Angry mobs gathered outside the Japanese embassy, and students called for a boycott of Japanese goods. But ROC leaders, despite their resentment at what they saw as an unprincipled Japanese action, recognized that relations with Japan were too important to be jeopardized by retaliation based on emotion. They protected Japanese property, toned down the press attacks on Japan within a few days, and prepared to adjust to the new situation.

Thus, Japan's relations with the PRC and the ROC were reversed. Japan now had full diplomatic relations with Peking and unofficial relations with Taipei. The PRC represented China in the United Nations; the ROC had been ousted. Throughout the world the PRC was increasingly recognized as the legitimate successor to the ROC as the government of mainland China. Its legal position for pressing its claim to Taiwan had been immensely strengthened. There was speculation

---

17. FBIS, *Daily Report, East Asia and Pacific,* Oct. 3, 1972, p. C1.

that Peking would now step up the pressure on Japan to reduce its remaining relations with Taiwan.

So far, the PRC has generally tolerated Japan's informal relations with Taiwan and the substantial growth of their trade and tourist travel since 1972. The PRC has probably exercised this restraint because it feels that it must strengthen relations with Japan and the United States in order to offset the Soviet threat. Moreover, so long as Peking proffers the Japanese formula of relations with Taiwan as an inducement to the United States to accept its conditions for normalization, it cannot afford to mar the attractiveness of the model. Pressure on Japan to reduce relations with Taiwan also presents tactical difficulties. Once the Japanese government had established diplomatic relations with the PRC, the PRC's ability to influence Japanese domestic politics declined sharply, for the leverage provided by the government's failure to establish diplomatic relations no longer existed. Most Japanese see the present state of relations with mainland China and Taiwan as serving Japanese interests well, and there is little political pressure for further change. Moreover, a significant group of pro-ROC members of the LDP Diet would oppose actions to reduce Japan's relations with Taiwan.

The Japanese Model

In September 1972, when diplomatic relations between Japan and Taiwan were severed, the two governments had to agree promptly and informally on certain provisional measures to ensure the continuation of trade and other private relations. Quick action was essential, as the Japanese government took the view that the severance of diplomatic relations automatically terminated all existing government-to-government agreements.

The first step was to reach an understanding between Tokyo and Taipei that their diplomatic missions would continue to issue visas and to carry on other routine operations for several months, or at least until an official substitute mechanism could be devised. The most-favored-nation treatment for Taiwan's exports to Japan, which had been provided for in the now-defunct peace treaty, was continued by specifying "Taiwan" in place of the "Republic of China" on the list of countries qualifying for most-favored-nation treatment that was part of the Japanese customs regulations. With respect to visits by each other's ships and aircraft, although neither party any longer had a legal obligation to admit them, the practical need to continue services on the existing basis was recognized, and appropriate instructions were issued to port and airport authorities. The Japanese government decided that no further Export-Import Bank loans could be made to the government of the ROC or to government corporations in Taiwan, but arrangements were made for existing loans to be serviced in accordance with previous agreements. The Export-Import Bank indicated that it was prepared to consider on a case-by-case basis applications by Japanese exporters for loans covering future exports to Taiwan.

By December 1972, three months after diplomatic relations had been severed, Tokyo and Taipei reached agreement on the creation of an unofficial mechanism for conducting bilateral relations. Since that time, an institution known as the Interchange Association (ICA), based in Tokyo with offices in Taipei and Kaohsiung, has acted on behalf of Japanese interests, and one known as the East Asia Relations Association (EARA), based in Taipei with offices in Tokyo, Osaka, and Fukuoka, has acted on behalf of Taiwan.[18] The chairman of the board of the ICA is Teizo Horikoshi, vice-president of the Keidanren, and the president is Osamu Itagaki, a former ambassador to Taipei. The chairman of the board of the EARA is Chang Yen-t'ien, board chairman of the Taiwan Sugar Corporation, who attended the graduate school of Tokyo Imperial University, and the president is Koo Chen-fu, a native of Taiwan, a graduate of Taihoku (Taipei) Imperial University, and president of the Taiwan Cement Corporation. The overseas offices of the two organizations are staffed principally by foreign service officers detached from the foreign ministries but also include officials from other government departments. The EARA office in Tokyo is headed by Ma Soo-lay (Ma Shu-li), a member of the Legislative Yuan in Taiwan and a KMT Central Committee member. The ICA office in Taipei was at first headed by the diplomat who had been deputy chief of mission in Taipei at the time that diplomatic relations were severed. He was later replaced by Toshio Urabe, former Japanese ambassador to the Philippines.

The functions of the ICA and the EARA are outlined in an agreement signed on December 16, 1972.[19] The agreement assigns a broad range of functions normally carried out by diplomatic and consular officials to the two associations, including the protection of the persons and property of nationals of one country residing in the other, the arrangements for entry into and residence in each country by the nationals of the other, and the education of nationals resident in the other country. In addition, the associations are authorized to conclude

---

18. See Rowe, *Informal "Diplomatic Relations."*
19. Rowe, *Informal "Diplomatic Relations,"* pp. 80–82.

nongovernmental agreements on trade, investment, and technical co-operation. They are entrusted with completing official technical coopera-tion agreements left unfinished at the time of the severance of relations and with facilitating the repayment of loans extended under previous official loan agreements. They are called on to promote trade and tourism; to foster academic, cultural, and athletic interchange; and to ensure the safety of ships, aircraft, and fishing boats entering the terri-tory of the other country. A maximum of thirty persons can be assigned to the overseas offices of each association, not including locally hired assistants.

As is evident from the comprehensive nature of the agreement, the associations perform most of the functions of diplomatic missions. Al-though the personnel of the association offices are not legally entitled to diplomatic or consular immunities and privileges, both governments use administrative action to go as far as their laws and the principle of reciprocity permit to grant staff members the rights and privileges neces-sary to the performance of their functions. Each association office is presumably permitted to communicate with its headquarters by coded telegrams and a secure mail pouch, the latter probably carried by the national airline of each country.[20]

Association personnel understand the need to carry out their func-tions discreetly, so as to avoid causing the Japanese government un-necessary problems with the PRC. Negotiations between association personnel and government officials of the other country are conducted away from the offices of either party to avoid press attention. When the ICA and the EARA hold trade conferences in Tokyo, carrying out their trade promotion function, ROC officials come on ordinary pass-ports and attend the conferences in the capacity of advisers to the dele-gation from Taiwan. The lack of normal diplomatic status naturally handicaps ICA and EARA office directors and staff members in carrying out their quasi-official duties. Since they cannot rely on the existing body of law, regulations, and precedent governing diplomatic and consular relations, they must improvise. Nevertheless, the unorthodox system has worked quite well so far, as attested by the expansion of trade, travel, and other forms of interaction that has occurred despite the lack of diplomatic relations. Because of the importance that each government attaches to the relationship, there is a strong political will to make the system work, and the bureaucracy consequently finds the way.

The ICA and the EARA have devoted much of their time to assist-ing their resident or visiting countrymen. The ICA offices in Taipei

---

20. Ibid., p. 17.

and Kaohsiung are responsible for some four thousand Japanese residing in Taiwan, mostly businessmen and their families, as well as tourists and other visitors. The Japanese community maintains a primary school for Japanese children. The ICA offices furnish consular-type services for residents and visitors.

The EARA offices in Japan theoretically have responsibility for the 50,000 Chinese residents in Japan, as well as for the visitors from Taiwan, who numbered 80,000 in 1976. But the resident Chinese are divided in their loyalties. A Japanese official estimated that about one-fifth are pro-PRC and one-fifth are pro-ROC, while the remainder are either neutral or play both sides.[21] A constant struggle is under way within the overseas Chinese community in Japan between the pro-PRC forces, aided by the PRC embassy, and the pro-ROC forces, aided by the EARA. The overseas Chinese had long been organized in local associations, which in turn belonged to a United General Association of Overseas Chinese Resident in Japan. After the establishment of the PRC in 1949, pro-PRC Chinese began to leave the existing organizations, which supported the ROC, and to set up their own rival associations. These new associations have tried, without much success, to gain control of the real properties owned by the pro-ROC associations. Pro-PRC groups seized one of two Chinese schools in Yokohama some years ago, and in 1975, they physically occupied and thus gained control of the office of the pro-ROC Chinese association in Kyoto. Officials of the pro-ROC association sought to recover the property through legal action, but as of mid-1976, the case was still in the courts. An attempt to seize the office of the pro-ROC Chinese association in Yokohama in May 1976 failed when the seventeen persons who had occupied the building were arrested by the Japanese police and charged with trespassing.[22] The PRC embassy demanded the release of those arrested, but the demands were turned down by the Japanese government on the grounds that the property was owned by private individuals and that by trespassing on it the prisoners had violated Japanese law.

In addition to working to maintain the ROC's influence among Chinese residents in Japan, the EARA also works closely with pro-ROC Japanese organizations. The most important of these is the

---

21. Another estimate for the total overseas Chinese community is 58,000—19,500 pro-PRC, 17,600 pro-ROC, 21,000 neutral—but this includes an unspecified number (10,000 according to another source) of naturalized Japanese, Yuzo Ohno, "Recent Characteristic Moves of Overseas Chinese in Japan," *Koan Joho*, August 1975. According to an official source in Taipei, about 15,000 Chinese in Japan, most of them of Taiwan origin, hold ROC passports.

22. FBIS, *Daily Report, East Asia and Pacific,* May, 25, 1976, p. C1. See also *China News* (Taipei), May 26, 1976; *China Post* (Taipei), June 16, 1976.

Japan-ROC Dietmen's Consultative Council, consisting of 117 LDP members of the upper and lower houses and headed by Hirokichi Nadao. This organization, established in March 1973, seeks to strengthen Japan's relations with Taiwan and to prevent actions by the Japanese government detrimental to these relations. It has sent large delegations to Taiwan on ceremonial occasions, such as Chiang Kai-shek's birthday and his funeral. Another pro-ROC Japanese organization is the Japan-China Cultural Association, established in April 1973 and headed by a Tokyo University professor of Chinese history, Seiicho Uno. Together with its counterpart, the Sino-Japanese Cultural Association in Taiwan, headed by General Ho Ying-ch'in, a graduate of the Tokyo Military Academy, it sponsors cultural exchanges between the two countries. Less important are the local chapters in Japan of the Japan-China Friendship Association[23] and the Japan-China assemblymen's associations in various prefectures. Both of these organizations periodically sponsor visits to or from Taiwan.

Trade conferences provide another important channel for unofficial contacts. The ICA and the EARA have sponsored two such conferences, the latest in Tokyo in March 1977. The Japan-Republic of China Businessmen's Conference has held annual meetings to discuss trade between Japan and Taiwan since 1973, alternately in Tokyo and Taipei. Tourist travel between Japan and Taiwan has been promoted by the Japan-Republic of China Travel Association and its fifty-four travel service company members.[24]

Judging by the results in terms of trade, travel, and investment—the three essentials for Taiwan's continued economic health—the Japanese formula of relations has worked well. Two-way trade, which stood at $1 billion in 1971, was scarcely affected by the break in diplomatic relations. In 1976, it reached $3.5 billion, some $500 million above Japan's trade with the PRC. The rising curve in the number of Japanese visitors to Taiwan, which topped 256,000 in 1971, flattened noticeably in 1972, probably because of uncertainty about the treatment that Japanese would receive in Taiwan, but by 1976, it had soared to 520,000. Japanese investment in Taiwan suffered more from political uncertainties than did trade or travel, but only temporarily. It dropped from $28 million in 1970 to $12 million in 1971, probably as a result of Chou En-lai's warning against investing in Taiwan. In 1972, it dropped further to $8 million. But in 1973, it rebounded to an all-time high of $45 million, responding to the buoyant state of Taiwan's economy. The subsequent de-

---

23. Not to be confused with the pro-PRC organization of the same name in English mentioned earlier. In Japanese, the names are different.
24. Rowe, *Informal "Diplomatic Relations,"* p. 51.

cline in 1974 to $39 million and in 1975 to $23 million seems related more to the recession in Japan and Taiwan than to political factors. Total Japanese investment at the end of 1975 exceeded $200 million.[25]

The Japanese model has evolved in practice as a complex but effective working arrangement. Both the Japanese government and the ROC government have been interested in preserving as extensive relations as could be managed and have shown much ingenuity and flexibility in working out procedures that would maintain the substance of relations without creating serious difficulties with the PRC. The Japanese government is the dominant partner. It decides which arrangements will conform to Japanese legal requirements and will be defensible if questioned by the PRC. The ROC's bargaining power is relatively weak. Officials of the ROC must often swallow their pride and accept a mode of operations less favorable to the status of the ROC than they would like. Yet so long as ROC officials maintain a low profile, they can exert considerable influence through powerful Japanese politicians and businessmen who appreciate the advantages that Japan derives from its trade and other relations with Taiwan. Hence, the Japanese Foreign Ministry gives consideration to the sensitivities of ROC officials and has become skilled at going as far as possible to satisfy the needs of the ROC without provoking the PRC.

Japan's Aviation Relations

The only serious disruption in substantive relations between Japan and Taiwan since 1972 was the suspension of flights between the two countries by their national airlines between April 1974 and the autumn of 1975. The communiqué announcing the establishment of diplomatic relations between Japan and the PRC in September 1972 had provided for the negotiation of agreements on trade, navigation, aviation, and fisheries, as well as for a treaty of peace and friendship. The negotiations on an aviation agreement began promptly, with both governments thinking that this would be the first operational agreement between them and expressing the hope that it might be concluded in time for the newly appointed ambassadors to Tokyo and Peking to proceed to their posts on direct flights. The negotiations turned out to be much more difficult than expected, however, and agreement was not reached until April 1974.

The major difficulty had to do with the flights between Japan and Taiwan by Japanese Airlines (JAL) and China Airlines (CAL), the ROC

---

25. *Tokyo Shimbun,* May 21, 1972; *Japan Times,* Mar. 27, 1976.

company. Although the government-to-government agreement under which these airlines had originally operated became invalid when diplomatic relations between Japan and the ROC were severed, the services continued through informal arrangements. The large number of travelers on this route made it a lucrative one: JAL had thirty-seven flights weekly to and from Taiwan, and CAL had twenty-one. Indeed, for JAL, the Taiwan run was more profitable than any other except its service to and from Hawaii.

Early in the negotiations, PRC officials objected to Japan's allowing CAL aircraft to use the same airports as they did. Liao Ch'eng-chih, chairman of the Sino-Japanese Friendship Association in Peking, argued that it would be ridiculous for airplanes of the Civil Aviation Administration of China (CAAC), displaying the flag of the PRC, to stand on the ramp at Haneda airport next to airplanes from Taiwan called China Airlines and displaying the ROC flag.[26] Hoping to meet PRC objections, the Japanese considered restricting CAL flights to Okinawa or having CAL change its name and remove the flag from its aircraft, but the ROC flatly refused. The Japanese also considered routing CAAC aircraft to the new international airport for the Tokyo area, which was under construction at Narita, and keeping CAL aircraft at Haneda, but it was apparent that the Narita airport would not be ready for a long time.

Negotiation of the air agreement with Peking soon became an issue in Japanese domestic politics. Members of the Japan-ROC Dietmen's Consultative Council, already resentful at what they considered excessive concessions to the PRC in the negotiations on normalization, strongly backed ROC resistance to any substantial change in existing aviation relations between Japan and Taiwan. A small but vociferous group of young right-wing legislators, known as the Seirankai, took a similar position. Most of the opponents of concessions to the PRC on aviation relations with Taiwan were from the Fukuda faction or other nonmainstream factions of the LDP. In addition to being pro-ROC, they had political reasons for using the aviation issue to make life difficult for Prime Minister Tanaka and Foreign Minister Ohira, the heads of the principal mainstream factions.

For more than a year, the Foreign Ministry conducted negotiations with the PRC and, through the ICA, the EARA, and other unofficial channels, with the ROC. Gradually the differences narrowed. The PRC dropped its insistence that CAAC and CAL use different airports or that CAL change its name or remove its flag. The Japanese government agreed that service to Taiwan would be taken over by an airline other than JAL. The ROC agreed that aviation relations between Japan

---

26. *Asahi,* Feb. 28, 1973.

and Taiwan could be governed by a private agreement. But Peking continued to demand that the Japanese government not recognize CAL as a national airline or its flag as a national flag and asked that CAL ground services in Japan be turned over to a Japanese agent. The Japanese government suggested to Taipei that it would use the designation "China Airlines (Taiwan)" in signs and other references to CAL.

The ROC, however, considered the proposals a slight to national dignity and continued to reject them. On April 11, 1974, the ROC foreign minister, Shen Ch'ang-huan, formally reiterated earlier warnings that, if the Japanese government should unilaterally change existing aviation relations between Japan and Taiwan in ways "inimical to our national dignity and interests," the government of the ROC would not hesitate to halt CAL flights to Japan and to ban JAL aircraft from landing in Taiwan or flying through the Taipei flight information region and air defense identification zone.[27] The ban on overflights would add forty to fifty minutes to JAL's flying time between Japan and Hong Kong.

Despite the Japanese government's ability to persuade the ROC government to accept Japan's planned concessions to Peking, Ohira went ahead with the final phase of negotiations with the PRC, apparently in the belief that the ROC would come around in the end and not carry out its threat. On April 20, 1974, Ohira announced that an air transport agreement had been signed that day in Peking by the Japanese ambassador and the PRC foreign minister, similar in form and substance to those which Japan had signed with other countries. He added: "The air transport agreement between Japan and the People's Republic of China is a governmental agreement and flights between Japan and Taiwan are non-governmental regional air traffic. On the basis of the joint statement of the two governments, the Japanese government since its publication does not recognize the emblem on the Taiwan aircraft as a so-called national flag nor does it recognize the "China Airlines (Taiwan)" as an air firm representing a state." The government of the ROC immediately ordered CAL and JAL to halt all flights between Japan and Taiwan. Foreign Minister Shen Ch'ang-huan, denouncing the Japanese government for "accepting Peiping's unreasonable demands," charged that Ohira, "in his outrageous statement, cast reflection upon the national flag of the Republic of China thereby impairing seriously the dignity and interests of the Republic of China."[28]

In retrospect, it seems evident that both Japanese and ROC leaders miscalculated. The hard-line opponents of Tanaka and Ohira, in urging

27. FBIS, *Daily Report, East Asia and Pacific,* Apr. 11, 1974, p. B1.
28. FBIS, *Daily Report, People's Republic of China,* Apr. 22, 1974, pp. A1, B2.

the ROC to stand firm, probably exaggerated the influence of ROC firmness on the Japanese government. They may even have convinced ROC officials that the rupture of the air link would cause the Tanaka government to fall. They were more interested in damaging their factional adversaries than in promoting a compromise solution to the airlines dispute. In the emotionally charged atmosphere that developed in Taipei, the advice of moderate specialists on Japan was disregarded. Similarly, in Tokyo the political leaders and the Foreign Ministry misjudged the ROC's determination. The Japanese government was inadequately informed on the political forces operating in Taiwan and, until the last minute, refused to believe that the ROC would carry out its threat to halt airline services.[29]

Almost immediately, the Japanese began to search for a way to repair the damage and restore the air services. Ohira was quoted as saying he thought that flights between Tokyo and Taipei would be resumed within ten days.[30] But in fact the negotiations took over a year. After the initial confusion caused by the sudden suspension of JAL and CAL service, other national airlines operating between Japan and Taiwan took over their profitable business, and the volume of travel was little affected, but JAL lost $170 million per year during the period of suspension and CAL lost $30 million.[31]

From Taipei's viewpoint, the prime requirement for restoration of the air link was a political act by the Japanese government that would ease the sting of Ohira's "outrageous" statement. Foreign Minister Kiichi Miyazawa, Ohira's successor, responding to a question in the House of Councillors Foreign Affairs Committee on July 1, 1975, provided the way out. Miyazawa expressed regret that the government's statement on the flag issue the previous spring had led to misunderstanding. It could not be denied, he said, that countries which maintain diplomatic relations with Taiwan do regard the "sun in the blue sky" flag as a national flag. The insult to the ROC's dignity having been thus redressed, representatives of the ICA and the EARA signed an agreement on July 9 providing for the restoration of air services. The agreement specified the routes that each party's airline would be authorized to fly, stated that the standards and procedures of the International Civil Aviation Organization would govern the operations, and provided that the airlines concerned should promptly conclude a "business agreement" between them concerning the number of flights, type of equipment, fares, and other details.[32] In Peking, Liao Ch'eng-chih criticized the

---

29. See *Asahi*, Apr. 22, 1974; *Far Eastern Economic Review*, May 27, 1974, p. 5.
30. *The New York Times*, Apr. 25, 1974.
31. *The New York Times*, June 16, 1974.
32. *Asahi*, July 10, 1975.

Miyazawa statement, charging that it was a statement "which regards China with hostility and which means putting 'two Chinas' into actual practice."[33] The PRC did not, however, formally protest the Miyazawa statement, nor did it attempt otherwise to interfere with the resumption of air services by the airlines of Japan and the ROC.

By the summer of 1976, airlines of the two countries were again in full operation. Japan Asia Airways (JAA) was organized as a fully owned subsidiary of JAL to operate from Tokyo and Osaka to Taipei, Kaohsiung, and onward to Hong Kong and Manila. Operations to Tokyo and onward to the United States, as well as to Fukuoka, were resumed by CAL, which had been excluded from Osaka as a result of the Japan-PRC aviation agreement. Both CAL and JAL were operating cargo and passenger services: JAA had twenty flights a week between Japan and Taiwan, while CAL had twelve. Although the flights were fewer than before the rupture, the planes were larger and the number of passengers carried was about the same. The airlines wanted to add flights, but it was difficult to do so without encroaching on the six-hour interval that the Japanese government wished to maintain between CAL and CAAC flights, to avoid having planes of both airlines at Haneda at the same time. At the time CAAC was operating two scheduled flights weekly to and from Tokyo, with occasional special flights. JAA serves as the sole agent for the ground operations of CAL in Japan, and CAL acts in a similar capacity for JAA in Taiwan. The public address system at Haneda airport refers to CAL as "China Airlines based in Taiwan," a happy choice of words to which neither the PRC nor the ROC has objected.

With the opening of the new Narita International Airport, now planned for 1978, the Japanese government plans to resolve the problem of keeping ROC and PRC planes apart by having CAAC use the new airport, while CAL continues to use Haneda. But this plan has posed new problems. Some foreign airlines have protested that CAL will have an unfair advantage if it is the only foreign airline still allowed to land at Haneda, which is much closer to Tokyo than Narita. CAL itself is disturbed by the Japanese government's plan to provide immigration service at Haneda for only eight hours each day because of the fact that only one foreign airline will be serviced there. If the plan is carried out, the ROC will probably retaliate by restricting JAL's use of Taiwan's airports to eight hours daily.

Negotiations on a shipping agreement between Japan and the PRC began in the spring of 1973 and proceeded simultaneously with the negotiations on the aviation agreement. Unlike aircraft, which could

---

33. *Mainichi,* July 15, 1975.

not begin regular flights until after the agreement had been concluded, ships from Japan and the PRC had been calling at each other's ports for years under nongovernmental agreements. Japanese port authorities had taken care that ships flying the PRC flag and those flying the ROC flag were not berthed at the same pier. After the aviation agreement was signed, it became known that PRC negotiators were insisting that ships from Taiwan not be allowed into Japanese ports flying the "sun in blue sky" flag. They cited as a precedent Ohira's statement concerning that flag in connection with the aviation agreement.[34] The talks were suspended in August 1974 because of differences over this issue but were later resumed, and the agreement was signed on November 13 without any reference to the question of the ROC flag.[35] Officials in Taipei concluded that the ROC's firm stand on the airline question had helped to stiffen Japanese resistance to PRC pressure in the shipping negotiations.

The seriousness with which the PRC and the ROC regarded the national flag issue was illustrated by an incident in Latakia, Syria, in January 1977, when a ship flying the ROC flag, chartered by a Japanese line, was berthed alongside a ship flying the PRC flag. The political officer on the PRC ship persuaded the port authorities to order the ROC captain to lower his flag before the ship could be unloaded. The captain refused and pulled out of the berth; at the same time, the local agent of the Japanese shipping company and the Japanese embassy took the matter up with the Syrian government in Damascus. After eight days' delay, the ROC freighter was permitted to unload with its flag flying.[36]

Since the signing of the aviation agreement with the PRC, Japan's relations with Taiwan have caused no serious problems between Tokyo and Peking. The PRC embassy in Tokyo monitors these relations closely, being quick to protest if it detects any tendency on the part of the Japanese government to confer official standing on the activities conducted in Japan by representatives from Taiwan. But the PRC seems more concerned with form than substance. Tokyo and Taipei have worked out ways of conducting their business effectively by methods labeled unofficial.

Thus, differences over Taiwan have not prevented the steady expansion of bilateral ties between Japan and the PRC. Trade grew from $1.1 billion in 1972 to $3.0 billion in 1975, a substantial growth even when discounting the rise in world price levels during the period. Japan strengthened its position as China's leading trading partner, accounting for over a quarter of China's total trade. Japan also led all other nations in the steadily growing number of visitors interchanged with mainland

---

34. *Yomiuri,* July 28, 1974.
35. FBIS, *Daily Report,* East Asia and Pacific, Nov. 13, 1974, p. C1.
36. Ibid., Feb. 14, 1977, p. B1.

China, although these were only a small fraction of the number traveling between Japan and Taiwan. In addition, Japan negotiated a number of official agreements with the PRC.

For the past several years, the PRC's principal concern in its relations with Japan has been to strengthen these relations at the expense of the Soviet Union. It has sought, so far without success, to persuade the Japanese to sign a treaty of peace and friendship, incorporating a clause opposing hegemonism, patently aimed at demonstrating that Japan inclines to the PRC side in the Sino-Soviet dispute. In the spring of 1977, the PRC began to invite Japanese with military backgrounds and connections to tour PRC military installations and to meet senior military officials, evidently hoping to encourage the Japanese in the view that Japan and China have a common interest in strengthening their respective military establishments and in exchanging views on opposing "Soviet expansionism." Concern over Japan's relations with Taiwan has receded into the background as Peking has sought to enhance its influence on Japan relative to that of the Soviet Union.

Implications for the United States

The Japanese model of unofficial relations with Taiwan is grounded in Japan's unique historical experience with mainland China and Taiwan. Its characteristics were shaped by geography, cultural affinities, and Japan's twenty years of experience in "backdoor" relations with the PRC. The American cultural heritage is different. Americans place greater emphasis on law and find it more difficult than Chinese and Japanese to deal with problems and people indirectly and through unorthodox channels. Americans prefer arrangements to be clear-cut and spelled out in written form; they are leery of oral understandings and tacit agreements. Consequently, although pragmatic Americans may be able to devise a workable way of handling the Taiwan problem, it is likely to be less indirect and flexible than the Japanese model, which can serve only in a very general sense as an example for future US relations with Taiwan.

The fundamental difference between American and Japanese relations with Taiwan is the US commitment to Taiwan's security through a security treaty and the ROC's reliance on the United States for equipping and training its armed forces. Japan had no comparable relationship. Consequently, any formula for the normalization of relations worked out between Washington and Peking must break new ground in this area; it cannot draw on the Japanese experience.

Economic relations between the United States and Taiwan are also different from those between Japan and Taiwan in two important respects. The US Export-Import Bank has played a far more important role than has the Japanese Export-Import Bank in financing Taiwan's industrialization. Were such loans denied Taiwan, Taiwan's planned expansion of capital-intensive industry would become far more difficult. The future of Taiwan's electric power system is critically dependent on its continuing access to the supply of enriched uranium promised by the United States in the thirty-year government-to-government agreement signed in 1972. Further economic growth in Taiwan will thus require a greater degree of governmental involvement by the United States than by Japan.

Because the people of Taiwan have regarded the United States as their principal friend and protector in the world, to sever diplomatic relations with the United States would affect them more severely than did the severance of diplomatic relations with Japan. From their viewpoint, it would be the long-feared ultimate blow to their international relations. When Tokyo worked out its unofficial relations with Taipei, it did so under the umbrella of continuing US diplomatic and security relations with Taiwan. The United States not only has a more intensive pattern of relations to provide for through unofficial agreements but also would have to work out these agreements in an atmosphere of greater uncertainty.

Contributing to the uncertainty would be the question of whether the Japanese model would itself begin to come apart once the PRC had persuaded the United States to break diplomatic relations and to end the security treaty with the ROC. Would Peking then become less tolerant of Japan's extensive trade and other relations with Taiwan? The answer to this question depends on the relative weight that PRC leaders would attach to progress toward the "liberation" of Taiwan as compared to their need for improved relations with the United States and Japan. Although the Japanese model cannot be adopted in toto by the United States, and would not in any case meet all US needs, the Japanese experience will help the United States to formulate appropriate questions for its own future relations with Taiwan. The Japanese experience with the ROC offers hope that with patience and ingenuity these problems can be resolved, provided that the cost to the PRC of disrupting US and Japanese relations with Taiwan remains unacceptably high.

The Normalization Issue

8

In the Shanghai communiqué, the United States and the PRC agreed that "progress toward the normalization of relations between China and the United States is in the interests of all countries." They also agreed that "a senior US representative" would visit Peking "from time to time for concrete consultations to further the normalization between the two countries."[1] Normalization is an imprecise and elastic term. It is sometimes used as a synonym for "the establishment of diplomatic relations," sometimes for an improvement of relations that includes but goes beyond the simple establishment of diplomatic relations, and sometimes for the improvement of relations between two countries that already have diplomatic relations with each other but whose relations are otherwise abnormal. For example, Japan's normalization of relations with the PRC in 1972 included the establishment of full diplomatic relations, but in addition, it ended the abnormal conditions that had existed between the two countries for many years as the result of the Sino-Japanese war. The Soviet Union has full diplomatic relations with Peking, but uses normalization to mean a return to a more normal state of bilateral relations than the hostility that has prevailed between the two countries in recent years.

Which meaning of normalization was implied in the Shanghai communiqué was not spelled out at the time. A year later, Assistant Secretary of State Marshall Green described it as "a simple, common-sense concept relating to substance not form." It is normal, he said, for countries to trade, to encourage travel and the exchange of information,

---

1. See Appendix.

and above all, to discuss problems with the aim of resolving them or at least making them more manageable. Green added: "The channels of communication are open, and are being used not only to lessen the risk of confrontation through accident, miscalculation, or misunderstanding, but to move positively to identify areas of common interest where cooperation in the cause of peace will be possible. This is the substance of normalization."[2] On a visit to Peking a few days before Green's speech, Secretary of State Henry Kissinger had agreed with the PRC on the need for "accelerating the normalization of relations" by expanding trade, broadening scientific, cultural, and other exchanges, and establishing liaison offices in the two capitals to help carry out these agreements.[3] In a broad sense, then, the normalization of US relations with China meant replacing past confrontation and hostility with the kinds of interaction that ordinarily occur between nations at peace. Recently, however, the term has been used increasingly in the narrow sense of the establishment of full diplomatic relations.[4] In this sense, the expansion of trade, travel, and other forms of relations may represent progress toward normalization, but the process will not be complete until the United States and the PRC have exchanged embassies.

The problem is complicated by the fact that the liaison offices exchanged by Washington and Peking in 1973 already function in most respects as diplomatic missions. Officials of the liaison offices are accorded diplomatic immunity, and the offices have been granted the right to send coded messages, to use a diplomatic pouch, and to enjoy other privileges normally reserved to diplomatic missions. The two governments regard these arrangements as constituting a form of diplomatic relations. The importance of normalization does not lie in the relatively minor advantages of an embassy over a liaison office in the conduct of diplomatic activities. It lies in the formal recognition by the United States of the PRC rather than the ROC as the sole legitimate government of China and in the implications that this recognition would have for the future of US-PRC relations and for Taiwan.

There is a danger that too narrow a focus on the establishment of

---

2. Marshall Green, "Address on U.S.-China Relations—Progress Toward Normalization," *Department of State Press Release,* no. 43, Feb. 20, 1973.
3. *The New York Times,* Feb. 23, 1973.
4. Note the exchange between a questioner and Secretary of State Cyrus R. Vance: Q: I notice that you keep referring to that term—that ambiguous term—"achieve normalization." What does that mean, really? Does that mean recognition? A: It means exactly what it says. Q: No, but it has a history. A: Yes, and that is why it means exactly what it says. Q: And its beauty lies in its ambiguity. But does it mean recognize diplomatically the People's Republic of China? A: Yes, that is what it means ultimately. *Department of State Press Release,* no. 37, Feb. 3, 1977, p. 6. Diplomatic recognition is not always followed by an exchange of embassies, but it is difficult to believe that either Peking or Washington would consider relations to be normalized without such an exchange.

full diplomatic relations between Washington and Peking, as well as on the obstacles to accomplishing that goal, will inflate the importance of such relations and will create exaggerated expectations as to what might as a result be achieved in regard to other issues between the United States and the PRC. The establishment of full diplomatic relations needs to be viewed in perspective. It will be important symbolically as marking the end of a prolonged period during which the United States and the government ruling mainland China have not had full diplomatic relations. Moreover, the limitations on US relations with Taiwan that will have to be agreed to by the United States as a condition for exchanging embassies with the PRC—such as, for example, the severance of diplomatic relations or nullification of the security treaty—will set the ground rules for the management of continuing differences among the United States, the PRC, Taiwan, and Japan about the future of the island and its people. Thus, an exchange of embassies between Washington and Peking that results from mutual concessions in regard to US relations with Taiwan will not resolve the Taiwan problem. It will place Peking in a somewhat stronger position to resolve the problem eventually on terms acceptable to itself and will probably also make the problem easier for the United States and the PRC to live with. Moreover, an exchange of embassies is likely to facilitate the improvement of relations between the two countries in other respects. The establishment of full diplomatic relations is thus a key that will open the door to a new stage in US relations with the PRC, but it will not remove other obstacles from the path beyond that door. It is an important step in a continuing process, but should not be regarded as a panacea for resolving differences between the United States and the PRC.

The difficulties preventing the establishment of full diplomatic relations with the PRC and the possible ways of overcoming those difficulties need to be analyzed. The normalization issue, as a short-term problem, can and should be resolved within two or three years if both Washington and Peking concentrate on their fundamental, long-term interests. An important problem thereafter will be the management of the differences between Peking and Washington over Taiwan that will surely continue to exist even after the normalization issue has been resolved.

Progress Toward Normalization

During his 1972 visit, President Nixon reportedly told Chou En-lai that he intended to normalize relations with the PRC during his second term.[5]   Secretary of State Kissinger has pointed out that although the Shanghai communiqué set no deadline for normalization, it did contain a commitment "to the achievement progressively of the normalization of relations."   He went on to say that the timing and conditions under which it could be achieved would have to be negotiated, as no "meeting of the minds" had been reached on these points.[6]   During the five years since Nixon's visit to China, the relations between the United States and the PRC have improved in various ways.   There has been substantial trade and cultural exchange between the two countries.   Liaison offices have been established in each capital, and reciprocal diplomatic privileges have been granted.   Communications have improved, and the atmosphere prevailing between the two countries has radically changed for the better.   Two US Presidents, three US secretaries of state, various congressional delegations, and thousands of other Americans have visited China.   The United States is complying with its pledge in the Shanghai communiqué by withdrawing US military personnel stationed in Taiwan. The head of the PRC liaison office in Washington has been accorded greater access to the President and the secretary of state than has the ROC ambassador.   United States spokesmen have referred to improvements in relations between the United States and the PRC as progress toward the normalization to which the United States committed itself in the Shanghai communiqué.

The general improvement in the state of relations between Washington and Peking may represent progress toward normalization in the sense of creating a better atmosphere for negotiating the establishment of full diplomatic relations.   But it could also be argued that the more relations improve in the absence of embassies, the less need there is for them.   Consequently, PRC officials have stressed that the lack of full diplomatic relations does impose limits.   Until embassies are exchanged, no high-level Chinese official will visit the United States, no long-term scientific or student exchanges can take place, and no American newsmen can be stationed in Peking.   Negotiations on the disposition of US claims against the PRC for confiscated property and PRC claims against the United States for frozen assets seem to have reached a stalemate pending the establishment of diplomatic relations, and American businessmen are frequently told that trade will increase after that step is taken.   Until the claims are resolved, US and PRC ships and planes cannot enter each other's ports or airports and trade exhibits cannot be exchanged, as Americans with claims against the PRC could petition the courts to attach PRC property in this country to satisfy their claims.

---

5. *The New York Times,* Apr. 11, 1976.
6. *Department of State Bulletin* 76 (Jan. 31, 1977); 87.

The PRC Position

The Shanghai communiqué did not specify the PRC's terms for normalization of relations with the United States, but it provided clues. Chou En-lai had earlier spelled out the terms more precisely in a conversation with American journalists in June 1971:

> "If the United States withdrew all its armed forces from Taiwan and the Taiwan Strait and no longer regarded Chiang Kai-shek as the representative of China, then the logical result would be that Chiang Kai-shek and Taiwan would be matters of Chinese internal affairs. This would constitute recognition of the People's Republic of China as the only lawful government representing China. There cannot possibly be two Chinas, or one China and one Taiwan. Therefore the treaty concluded with Chiang Kai-shek, signed in 1954 and ratified in 1955, known as the United States-China Mutual Defense Treaty, would become null and void."[7]

He used similar language when speaking with an American correspondent in August 1971, shortly after Nixon's prospective visit to China had been announced.[8]

Chou emphasized the withdrawal of US military personnel and the recognition of the PRC as the sole legitimate government of China. He took the view that these actions would render the defense treaty invalid without an express act of abrogation by the United States. After all, the Japanese government, without formally abrogating its peace treaty with the ROC, announced that it had lost its validity. Thus, when Chinese officials began suggesting that the United States should follow the Japanese model, they implied that the security treaty might be stripped of its validity in a similar fashion.

Spokesmen for the PRC subsequently restated Chou's view in various forms, but by 1975, they had evolved a crisp formula which they referred to as the three "principles" for normalization. The United States would have to break diplomatic relations with the ROC, withdraw all military personnel from Taiwan, and annul the security treaty in order to have full diplomatic relations with the PRC.[9] The spokesmen then usually referred to the Japanese model as a pattern for US relations with Taiwan after it had met these conditions.

---

7. Topping, *Journey Between Two Chinas,* p. 401.
8. *The New York Times,* Aug. 10, 1971.
9. See e.g. US Congress, Senate, *The United States and China, A Report to the Senate Foreign Relations Committee and the House International Relations Committee,* 94th Cong., 1st Sess., Oct. 28, 1975, p. 11.

For the PRC, "principles" are not negotiable, but the implementation of principles often permits considerable flexibility. For example, Japan was able to avoid explicitly agreeing to Peking's view that Taiwan was an inseparable part of its territory. Consequently, there is scope for negotiation on precisely how the United States might accept the PRC's principles. There is also scope for negotiation on the reciprocal conditions that the United States might ask Peking to meet.

It is difficult to judge how much importance the PRC leaders attach to completing normalization quickly. The signals from Peking have varied. Until Kissinger's sixth visit to Peking in November 1973, the PRC seemed well satisfied with the pace at which relations were expanding. But during 1974, visitors to mainland China reported increasing expressions of disappointment by PRC officials because of the slowness of the progress toward normalization. Dissatisfaction may have resulted at least in part from the appointment of a new US ambassador to the ROC that year and the approval of several new ROC consulates in the United States, actions that were protested officially by Peking. The complaints of a loss of momentum, however, were apparently not translated into representations to Kissinger.[10] Moreover, in talking with American visitors, senior PRC officials usually placed heavy emphasis on the importance of opposing Soviet expansionism and indicated that the Taiwan issue was much less important and urgent. By 1975–1976, PRC leaders recognized that the US government was inhibited from moving ahead toward normalization by Watergate, the collapse of South Vietnam, and the presidential elections. Consequently, the dominant view expressed by PRC officials during this period was disappointment with the lack of movement but willingness to wait until the United States was free of these hindrances.

Western observers have attempted to gauge the current importance that the PRC attaches to the early completion of normalization by weighing the relative emphasis that PRC spokesmen placed on a gradual and peaceful resolution of the Taiwan problem or on the possible need to use military force.[11] Thus, the PRC's emphasis on the hard line—that force may have to be used—is sometimes interpreted as an effort to urge the United States to move more quickly. But PRC leaders almost certainly know that threats of force against Taiwan are likely to reduce a US

---

10. *The New York Times,* Sept. 5, 1974.
11. Chou En-lai and Teng Hsiao-ping have been the principal spokesmen, usually in conversations with overseas Chinese or in pronouncements directed at Taiwan, for a peaceful resolution of the Taiwan problem, although neither excluded the use of force. Chang Ch'un-ch'iao, Chang Hsiang-shan, Chi Teng-k'uei, Li Hsien-nien, and Vice-Foreign Minister Yu Chan have stressed, usually in conversations with American or Japanese visitors, the PRC's right to use force. See *Mainichi,* Jan. 22, 1977; *Yomiuri,* May 16, 1977; *Washington Post,* Aug. 12, 1976, June 2, July 5, 1977; *Wall Street Journal,* Oct. 3, 4, 1977.

President's flexibility and make it more difficult to reach a compromise on the normalization issue. Therefore, conclusions about PRC policy shifts based on isolated statements published out of context are not necessarily valid. Without a verbatim text of the conversation, which is rarely available, it is often impossible to determine whether the Chinese spokesman or the American or Japanese visitor raised the Taiwan issue. Any PRC spokesman would be compelled to stress that the PRC reserved the right to use force against Taiwan if pressed on this point by a visitor. The emphasis given might also be affected by the current state of political maneuvering within the PRC leadership. Consequently, the apparent shifts back and forth from a soft line to a hard line during the past five years are unreliable guides either to the position the PRC might take in actual negotiations on normalization or to the degree of urgency of their drive toward normalization.

If the shifting signals reflect conflicting views within the PRC leadership, it is impossible from the data available to deduce who holds what view and how strongly. An analysis of the policy choices from Peking's viewpoint suggests that all leaders would favor an early normalization if the price were right, but that many probably would prefer to wait rather than to pay a high price in concessions. The PRC leaders have made clear that the US connection is important primarily because of the PRC's confrontation with the Soviet Union. Although the early normalization of relations with the United States would somewhat strengthen the PRC's position relative to the Soviet Union, it is not essential to that end. The liaison office arrangement provides a mechanism for improving and expanding bilateral relations well beyond where they stand today, should Peking see overriding geopolitical reasons for wanting to do so. In most respects, it is the PRC that has been holding back, not the United States. If PRC leaders wish to increase trade, expand cultural relations, or improve bilateral relations in other ways, the United States would clearly be willing. Not even the sale of US military equipment would be excluded by the lack of full diplomatic relations, should the PRC want to buy and the United States decide that it was in its interest to sell.

The principal pressure on the PRC to seek early normalization is probably concern that over time Taiwan will become stronger militarily and industrially and will become tied even more closely to the United States and Japan. Moreover, Taiwanese political influence will grow, while mainlander links with the mainland, already tenuous, will erode further. Domestic politics might also, in some conceivable circumstance, place significant pressure on leaders to show progress on normalization.

Yet as the PRC itself grows stronger, its ability to strike a favorable bargain over Taiwan will improve. At present, its leverage is relatively weak. It lacks the military strength to pose a credible threat to Taiwan, and the utterance of military threats tends to reduce American willingness to make concessions. The principal form of leverage employed by Peking so far, delay in the improvement of bilateral relations with the United States pending normalization, tends to weaken its own ability to draw on the US connection to strengthen its position relative to the Soviet Union. Its trump card, threatened or actual progress toward a rapprochement with the Soviet Union, is a difficult one to play. Such a rapprochement would require Moscow's willingness to come halfway and probably would require concessions by Peking to Moscow as difficult to make as those that the United States would propose on Taiwan. Thus, some in the PRC may oppose particular concessions now to either the United States or the Soviet Union on the ground that the PRC will be in a stronger bargaining position with respect to both countries some years hence. On balance, the pressures on the leadership in Peking to bring about the normalization of relations with the United States quickly are probably not strong.

The US Position

The United States, which has been more reticent than the PRC in stating its terms for normalization, has declared its determination to "complete the normalization of relations with the PRC on the basis of the Shanghai communiqué" and has accepted in principle the PRC's demand that all US military personnel and installations be withdrawn from Taiwan.[12] It has not, however, set a date for total withdrawal and has linked such a withdrawal with the "prospect" of "a peaceful settlement of the Taiwan question by the Chinese themselves," as expressed in the Shanghai communiqué.[13] It has also not agreed to sever diplomatic relations with the ROC or to annul the security treaty. The basic problem for Washington has been how to meet the PRC's terms while assuring the security of the people of Taiwan. Both President Jimmy Carter and Secretary of State Cyrus R. Vance have underlined the continuing responsibility felt by the US government for Taiwan's security.[14] If there

---

12. Statement of Phillip C. Habib before Special Subcommittee on Investigations of House Committee on International Relations, *Department of State Bulletin* 74 (Jan. 26, 1976): 106–109.
13. See *Washington Post* and *The New York Times*, Mar. 2, 1972.
14. See e.g. Carter's statement of May 12, 1977: "The one obstacle—major obstacle—obviously is the relationship we've always had with Taiwan. We don't want to see the Taiwanese people punished or attacked. And if we can resolve that major difficulty I would move expeditiously to normalize relationships with China. But I can't put

is a possible compromise that will satisfy both Peking's principles and Washington's concern for Taiwan's security, it is more likely to be arrived at in private negotiations than in public exchanges. Hence, the US government has not yet stated the terms for normalization.

The US government has good reason to hesitate, for the PRC is demanding unprecedented concessions. The United States has never broken diplomatic relations or abrogated a security treaty with a friendly government. Moreover, the United States is being asked to pay a concrete and immediate price for gains which, although of great potential importance, are long-term and uncertain. The administration would have difficulty defending such concessions before the Congress and the American people.

There is strong support in the Congress and among the American public for normalization, but there is also strong opposition to "sacrificing" or "abandoning" Taiwan. In early 1976, 218 members of the House of Representatives signed a resolution, sponsored by Representative Dawson Mathis, which called on the US government, "while engaged in the lessening of tension with the People's Republic of China, to do nothing to compromise the freedom of our friend and ally, the Republic of China and its people."[15]

In a poll taken by the Gallup Organization in April 1977, 62 percent of the respondents considered that establishing full diplomatic relations with the PRC was very or fairly important; only 21 percent thought it unimportant. But the responses shifted radically when the respondents were asked: "Suppose that in order to establish diplomatic relations with Mainland China, President Carter urges that we end diplomatic and defense treaty relations with Taiwan while at the same time we continue our interest in the security of the people of Taiwan?" Only 28 percent were strongly or fairly strongly in favor of this policy, as compared to 47 percent who were very strongly or fairly strongly opposed. When the latter were asked their reasons for opposing, 29 percent said, "We should not turn our backs on our friends."[16]

Another poll, conducted by the Foreign Policy Association among its members in early 1977, produced similar results: 53 percent of the respondents opposed breaking diplomatic relations with the ROC and ending the security treaty to gain full diplomatic relations with the PRC, while only 33 percent favored it, either strongly or "without enthusiasm."

a time limit on it." *The New York Times,* May 13, 1977. See also Carter's press conference of June 30, 1977, *The New York Times,* July 1, 1977.
15. House Concurrent Resolution 360, 94th Cong., 1st Sess., 1975.
16. Ralph N. Clough, Robert B. Oxnam, and William Watts, *The United States and China: American Perceptions and Future Alternatives* (Washington, D.C.: Potomac Associates, 1977), pp. 31–33.

Asked whether they favored continuing the present policies toward the PRC and the ROC, 42 percent said yes without qualification, while an additional 26 percent were willing to "go along without enthusiasm." Thus, a total of 68 percent supported the status quo, and only 19 percent opposed it.[17]

The two most influential newspapers in the field of foreign affairs, which have long favored improved relations between the United States and the PRC, have warned of the need to protect Taiwan. The *Washington Post* declared in July 1976: "The real problem is ... to ensure that effective if tacit arrangements for Taiwan's security remain in place even after formal diplomatic and defense ties with the island are ended. The United States can alter the nature of its relationship with Taiwan, but it cannot abandon Taiwan. That would be an intolerable demonstration of cynicism and unreliability."[18] *The New York Times* stated in August of the same year: "Taiwan's prosperity, its attraction to foreign investors and the political future of 14 million Taiwanese, who don't want to be under Communist rule, depend on its military security. The American defense treaty cannot be abrogated, as Peking now demands, unless Peking refrains from open threats of force and tacitly accepts viable substitute arrangements, including continued supply of arms for Taiwan's military forces and some less explicit unilateral American commitment to Taiwan's defense."[19] The *Washington Post* noted further in August 1977: "The trick is to end the formal American link with Taiwan without diminishing its actual security. It will take some work with diplomatic mirrors to get requisite assurances from Peking, but it can be, and should be, done ... Taiwan still commands the loyalties of a substantial number of Americans. An even greater number, including ourselves, would object to diplomatic moves that eroded its security."[20] Thus, American views as expressed in the Congress, in public opinion polls, and in the press suggest that it will not be easy for the President to mobilize public support for meeting the PRC's conditions. To do so, he would have to make a persuasive case that the proposed compromise was in the US interest and that the security of the people of Taiwan would indeed be protected.

Another problem the President faces when seeking to strike a bargain on normalization is its effect on US relations with other allies in the

---

17. *Asia Mail,* July 1977, p. 6.
18. *Washington Post,* July 8, 1976.
19. *The New York Times,* Aug. 9, 1976. On Aug. 18, 1977, *The New York Times,* in endorsing proposals by Senator Edward Kennedy for normalization of relations with the PRC, expressed confidence that the treaty could be ended and Taiwan protected by continued arms sales and unilateral US declarations of concern for the island's security, even though the PRC refused to renounce the use of force against it.
20. *Washington Post,* Apr. 20, 1977.

region. There is already considerable uneasiness in Japan and strong opposition in South Korea to President Carter's proposed withdrawal of US ground forces from South Korea over the next four to five years. Completing normalization, particularly if it requires the abrogation of the security treaty with the ROC, would be seen by many as one more step in an irreversible withdrawal of US power from the western Pacific. Right-wing politicians in Japan warn Americans bluntly against taking this step. Even Foreign Minister Kiichi Miyazawa expressed the hope to Senator Mike Mansfield, in July 1976, that the United States would go slowly and cautiously in proceeding toward normalization.[21]

The legal and technical problems of continuing economic and other relations with Taiwan after severing diplomatic relations are still another difficulty facing the United States. If the government of the ROC is no longer formally recognized as a government, it will raise a host of complications as to how the ROC should be treated in terms of American law.[22]

Despite the difficulties, the prevailing view within the US government is that making a serious effort to complete normalization would be in the US interest. There is no assurance that the passage of time will make a satisfactory compromise on a normalization formula easier to arrive at; current trends in fact suggest the opposite. During 1976 and 1977, Americans opposing acceptance of the PRC's three conditions became more outspoken, and the line taken publicly by PRC spokesmen hardened. Yet both the United States and the PRC are interested in strengthening their relations in order to improve their positions relative to the Soviet Union. Neither wishes to resume the hostile and sterile confrontation of the past. They share an interest in maintaining a confident security relationship between the United States and Japan. There is room for hope that, as in 1972, these common interests will enable both the PRC and the United States to continue to regard Taiwan as a secondary issue and to find a new formula for keeping it on the back burner.

If US relations with Taiwan and the PRC remain as they are indefinitely, the Taiwan issue may again rise in importance in the eyes of PRC leaders, especially as the PRC's industrial and military strength grows. Relations with the United States could then deteriorate, and Peking's option of seeking better relations with the Soviet Union could appear more attractive. The risk of a future military confrontation between the United States and the PRC would increase. Finding a satisfactory formula for normalization, one that protects Taiwan's security

---

21. *Sankei* and *Yomiuri,* July 13, 1976.
22. See Victor H. Li, *De-Recognizing Taiwan: The Legal Problems* (New York: Carnegie Endowment for International Peace, 1977).

but enhances the prospects for an ultimate resolution of the Taiwan problem by the Chinese themselves, would make it easier for the United States and the PRC to pursue their common interests and reduce the risk that the Taiwan issue would again produce a confrontation between them. The difficulties on both sides in agreeing to a mutually acceptable formula are great, but the potential rewards make trying to find one worthwhile.

The ROC Position

The ROC is totally opposed to the establishment of full diplomatic relations between the United States and the PRC on Peking's terms. Nationalist officials understand the broad geopolitical interests that led Nixon to create the opening to Peking, but they denounce the action because it seriously damaged the ROC's international position. They fear that US acceptance of the PRC's terms for normalization would make it still more difficult for Taiwan to survive as an almost universally unrecognized member of the international community. They have grave doubts that the United States will insist on conditions that would in fact assure Taiwan's security and prosperity. They suspect that once the United States had severed relations with the ROC, the PRC would re-double its efforts to isolate Taiwan. Moreover, they question whether the United States and Japan would stand up firmly to such pressures. Some of the more pessimistic Nationalist leaders, dismayed by the US withdrawal from Vietnam, suspect that Washington's ultimate objective is to disengage from Taiwan and to find a politically defensible way of relieving the United States of responsibility for Taiwan's future.

Officials of the ROC have been working unsparingly to impress on the American people the importance to the United States of maintaining its connections with Taiwan. Numerous members of Congress, congressional staffs, and scholars have been invited to visit Taiwan. Particular efforts have been made to invite those who have recently visited mainland China so that they can compare conditions. In December 1976, a US-Republic of China Economic Council was formed under the chairmanship of David Kennedy, a Chicago banker who was secretary of the treasury in the Nixon administration, to promote increased trade and investment between the United States and Taiwan. Most American companies with important interests in Taiwan have joined. As of mid-1977, the Council had about 130 members, including some of the largest corporations in the United States, such as Gulf Oil, National Distillers, Corning International, Rockwell International, American Cyanamid, General

Electric, Union Carbide, and Bechtel Power Corporation. ROC officials and the press in Taiwan intently follow developments in the United States bearing on the normalization issue. Arguments against normalization are marshaled and put to American visitors and residents.[23] They range from simple appeals not to abandon old friends to sophisticated analyses aimed at demonstrating how much the costs of normalization to the United States would outweight its presumed benefits.

The ROC leaders confront dilemmas in dealing with the normalization issue. They would like to dissuade the United States from completing normalization or at least persuade it to delay action. Consequently, speeches and editorials in Taiwan are filled with warnings that proceeding with normalization would be a grave error. But ROC leaders recognize that, in spite of their best efforts, the United States may go ahead. If the people of Taiwan are not kept aware of that possibility, the shock will be greater and more difficult to counteract when it happens. Therefore, the local press carries news articles from the United States showing that the possibility of breaking relations with the ROC and ending the security treaty is being seriously discussed. The leaders of the ROC would also like to convince Americans that either action would have a disastrous impact on Taiwan. Consequently, in private talks the potential damage is sometimes painted in lurid terms by ROC officials. But the government cannot take the same view in the Taiwan media. To do so would make the citizenry more nervous, increasing the risk of the flight of both people and capital should the worst happen. Thus, the ROC government stresses the goal of self-reliance and expresses confidence in the increasing capability of Taiwan to weather difficulties that the future may hold. Typical of the views expressed in the Taiwan media is the editorial in the privately-owned Chinese-language *United Daily News* (*Lien Ho Jih Pao*) of May 5, 1977. Commenting on the announcement that talks on frozen assets had resumed between Washington and Peking, it advised:

We must respond to this new development with the most proper actions, and we must also be prepared for the worst. We must manage to prolong the talks between the United States and the bandits and in the meantime properly plan our reaction. If, however, the United States and the bandits one day reach agreement in their talks and their relations are "normalized," we should do whatever is necessary to cope with

23. See editorials appearing on successive days in the English-language *China News* (Taipei), May 31–June 9, 1976, whose publication coincided with the presence in Taipei of some 40 American China scholars attending the fifth annual Sino-American Conference on Mainland China.

the situation. In short, we must not sit idle . . . we must take the initiative in carrying out diplomatic activities to oppose the "normalization" between the United States and the bandits.[24]

Formulas for Normalization

Although the US government has not proposed terms for normalization, American scholars have suggested a variety of formulas.[25] At one extreme is the German formula, so called because under it the United States would maintain embassies in both parts of China, just as it does in both parts of Germany.[26] At the other extreme, is the Japanese formula, under which the United States would conform to Peking's three principles and make no counterdemands other than the right to continue economic relations with Taiwan through quasi-official arrangements like those devised by the Japanese. Most China scholars favor a negotiated compromise lying somewhere between these extremes.

The German formula is appealing, for it would bring US diplomatic relations with the two parts of China in line with the reality that the PRC and the ROC have functioned as separate states in all but name for nearly thirty years. It is also attractive to many Americans because it would require no change in present relations with Taiwan. The ROC would protest the establishment of formal diplomatic relations between Washington and Peking, but ROC leaders and the people of Taiwan would in fact be relieved that the US connection with the island was to continue unchanged.

---

24. FBIS, *Daily Report, East Asia and Pacific,* May 10, 1977, p. B1.
25. See Mike Mansfield, "U.S./Taiwan Relations: Untying the Gordian Knot," *World Issues* (April/May 1977): 5–7; A. Doak Barnett, *China Policy* (Washington, D.C.: Brookings Institution, 1977), pp. 22–23; Allen S. Whiting, *China and the United States: What Next?* (New York, Foreign Policy Association, Headline Series, April 1976), pp. 39–44; Michel Oksenberg and Robert B. Oxnam, *China and America: Past and Future* (New York, Foreign Policy Association, Headline Series, April 1977), pp. 60–63; Robert A. Scalapino, *Asia and the Road Ahead: Issues for the Major Powers* (Berkeley: University of California Press, 1975), pp. 234–241; *United States-Soviet Union-China: The Great Power Triangle,* US Congress, House of Representatives, Hearings before Subcommittee on Future Foreign Policy Research and Development of House Committee on International Relations, October–December 1975, March–June 1976, 94th Cong.; *United States-China Relations: The Process of Normalization of Relations,* US Congress, House of Representatives, Hearings before Special Subcommittee on Investigations of House International Relations Committee, November–December 1975, February 1976, 94th Cong.; Jerome Alan Cohen, "A China Policy for the Next Administration," *Foreign Affairs* 55 (October 1976): 20–37; Victor H. Li and John W. Lewis, "Resolving the China Dilemma: Advancing Normalization, Preserving Security," *International Security* 2 (Summer 1977): 11–23.
26. See testimony of Ray S. Cline in *United States-Soviet Union-China: The Great Power Triangle,* pp. 217–218.

But PRC leaders clearly would reject the German formula. For them to agree to so explicit a "one China, one Taiwan" arrangement would be tantamount to giving up their claim to sovereignty over Taiwan and their hope of "liberating" the island. If the United States were to make such a proposal, the improvement in relations between Washington and Peking that has occurred since 1972 as a result of the understanding reached at that time would probably be reversed. The possibility of an improvement in Sino-Soviet relations would be enhanced and the risk of an eventual military confrontation between the United States and the PRC over Taiwan would increase. In order to make a continued separate existence for Taiwan compatible with improving relations between the United States and the PRC, the United States must seek a genuine compromise with the PRC rather than advance a proposition so patently unacceptable to the PRC as the German formula.

Officials of the PRC have indicated that they would find the Japanese formula acceptable. In essence, this would mean that if the United States broke diplomatic relations with the ROC, ended the security treaty, and withdrew its military personnel from Taiwan, it could continue its trade with Taiwan and its investment there. The United States and the ROC could also set up "unofficial" missions in Taipei and Washington after the pattern of Taiwan's relations with Japan, staffed by officials of the two countries on temporary leave from their official positions. The Japanese formula, however, fails to provide for Taiwan's security. The United States has had a mutual defense treaty with the ROC since 1955, whereas Japan had no such commitment. Both Carter and Vance have emphasized the importance of assuring the security of Taiwan as the United States proceeds toward normalizing relations with the PRC.

The German formula would be acceptable to the United States, but not to the PRC; the Japanese formula would be acceptable to the PRC, but not to the United States. A mutually acceptable compromise would require important concessions from both Washington and Peking. The United States would have to change radically the form of its relations with the ROC by severing diplomatic relations and ending the security treaty. The PRC would have to acquiesce in the continuance in substance of US economic and security relations with Taiwan.

The willingness expressed by PRC officials to follow the Japanese model in normalizing relations with the United States indicates that the PRC would not oppose the continuance of extensive economic relations between the United States and Taiwan. But the Japanese government decided that all official agreements with the ROC were terminated when diplomatic relations were broken and worked out a variety of private agreements to permit economic relations with Taiwan to continue.

United States economic relations with Taiwan are more dependent on official agreements than Japan's were, and private agreements might not in all cases be adequate substitutes for official agreements.

Most of the fifty-nine treaties and executive agreements between the United States and the ROC could be dispensed with without significant damage to economic relations between the United States and Taiwan, but some are very important.[27] The Treaty of Friendship, Commerce, and Navigation creates a framework for commerce and guarantees reciprocal rights to private businessmen. It also provides most-favored-nation treatment for Taiwan's exports to the United States. The air transport agreement establishes air routes and reciprocal landing rights. The agreement on civil uses of atomic energy, signed in 1972 and valid for thirty years, provides safeguards for the use of nuclear materials and technical data supplied to Taiwan by the United States. The agreement on investment guarantees makes it possible for OPIC to guarantee private American investment in Taiwan. Other important government-to-government agreements are the loan agreements of the Export-Import Bank and those agreements by which the ROC undertakes to limit the export of textiles and shoes to the United States.

Agreements on military matters are no less important than economic agreements. If the security treaty were terminated in order to reach agreement with the PRC on normalization, other agreements, such as those lending destroyers to the ROC, would need to be maintained if Taiwan's security were not to be weakened. Keeping Taiwan on the list of countries eligible to purchase weapons from the United States under the Foreign Military Sales Act would be particularly important. International law does not require the end of agreements between governments upon the severance of diplomatic relations; neither does it require that they remain in force.[28] But the United States would not only be severing diplomatic relations with the ROC; it would also be withdrawing recognition of the ROC as the legitimate government of China without recognizing it as the government of a separate and independent state. Hence, in order to retain in force those agreements essential to Taiwan's security and economic well-being, the US government would have to designate explicitly which agreements with the ROC should be regarded as continuing to govern relations between the United States and Taiwan. Both executive and congressional action probably would be required. Congressional action would probably also be needed to ensure that Taiwan continued to have the benefits of US laws normally denied to countries with which the United States has no diplomatic relations, such as

---

27. See US Department of State, *Treaties in Force*, 1976; Li, *De-Recognizing Taiwan*, pp. 21–35.
28. Li and Lewis, "Resolving the China Dilemma," p. 18.

statutes authorizing US government agencies to enter into agreements with foreign governments or persons concerning textile quotas or commercial communications satellites.[29]

Senator Henry M. Jackson suggested in July 1977 that the United States, instead of severing diplomatic relations with Taipei, should propose to Peking downgrading the US embassy in Taiwan to the status of a liaison office.[30] According to Vice-Premier Teng Hsiao-p'ing, Vance in fact made such a proposal during his August 1977 visit to Peking. But Teng called the proposal unacceptable because it would mean continued diplomatic links between the United States and Taiwan.[31]

A proposal to retain a consular office in Taiwan would be more likely to win the acceptance of the PRC. The presence of US consular officials in Taiwan would greatly facilitate continued economic and other relations between the two countries, including the issuance of visas to residents of Taiwan for travel to the United States and the protection of the interests of private Americans in Taiwan. The existence of a body of law and precedent governing consular relations would eliminate the legal and practical uncertainties that would inevitably attend improvisation by some kind of unofficial mission. The United States can find many precedents for maintaining consular relations with local officials in areas where it does not have diplomatic relations. There is also a precedent for retaining a consular office in Taiwan: Britain did so from 1950 to 1972, while it had a diplomatic mission in Peking headed by a chargé d'affaires. Although the PRC refused to exchange ambassadors with the United Kingdom so long as the British consulate remained in Taiwan, it would not necessarily take the same position with the United States, since it is more important to the PRC to have full diplomatic relations with the United States than with the United Kingdom. In agreeing to the exchange of liaison offices between Washington and Peking the PRC has already demonstrated the unique importance it attaches to relations with the United States.

Agreement on a modified Japanese formula could resolve the problem of assuring continued economic relations between the United States and Taiwan after normalization, but the security question poses more difficult choices to Washington and Peking. Here they would be breaking entirely new ground. Many Americans oppose ending the security treaty, arguing that it would shake confidence in Taiwan's future, increase the possibility that the PRC would use military force against Tai-

---

29. Li, *De-Recognizing Taiwan*, pp. 12–20, 33–34.
30. *The New York Times*, July 9, 1974.
31. *The New York Times*, Sept. 7, 1977.

wan, and weaken the credibility of other US defense commitments in the region, especially those to South Korea and Japan.[32] In order to defend the termination of the treaty, Carter would have to be in a position to demonstrate that termination would not weaken Taiwan's security. At a minimum, he would have to be able to point to PRC statements that show their intention of resolving the Taiwan problem peacefully, to US warnings to Peking that the use of force against Taiwan would gravely damage relations with the United States, and to retention by the United States of the right to continue to supply Taiwan with military equipment. Agreement on these issues is likely to prove difficult, for the PRC will insist on retaining its sovereign right to use force against its own territory if necessary, while the United States will take the view that it could not accept the use of force against Taiwan.

Since the Vance visit of August 1977, PRC officials have expressed views to visiting private Americans that diminish the prospects for an early agreement. Yu Chan, vice-minister of foreign affairs, reportedly told visitors that the sale to Taiwan of replacement weapons following normalization would be intolerable to Peking. He also said that the PRC could not accept any American statement that the United States had vital interests in the peace and stability of the Taiwan region. Vice-Premier Li Hsien-nien, in an interview with the same visitors, said that Mao Tse-tung had told Kissinger that "there are such a heap of counter-revolutionaries on Taiwan that it cannot be managed without a fight. Whether the fight takes place in 5 years, 10 years, or even longer, that is another matter." Li also said that it would be "inappropriate" for Taiwan to receive arms supplies from the United States, any other country, or any private company following the normalization of relations between the United States and the PRC. He rejected possible unilateral US statements concerning Taiwan's security, even one simply expressing a US expectation of the peaceful resolution of the Taiwan issue.[33]

In spite of the bleak outlook created by the statements of PRC officials since the Vance visit, an eventual compromise between Washington and Peking should not be ruled out. Both parties would gain from agreement on a normalization formula that would permit them to turn their attention from the Taiwan issue to their more fundamental long-term interests. Should a prolonged stalemate develop over normalization, resulting in a general deterioration of US-PRC relations, the United

---

32. E.g. the American Chamber of Commerce in Taipei took the view on Aug. 27, 1976, that "abrogation of the mutual defense treaty is totally unacceptable to the protection of American economic interests with the Republic of China." *Asia Mail*, Nov. 1976, pp. 8, 20.
33. *Wall Street Journal*, Oct. 3, 4, 1977.

States and the PRC would find it difficult to follow mutually supportive policies that would strengthen the position of each relative to the Soviet Union.

The use of military force by the PRC against Taiwan is improbable for a number of years to come, even in the absence of the US security treaty. The costs, both in military losses and in damage to PRC relations with the United States and Japan, would be extremely high. Despite statements by officials concerning Peking's willingness to use force, the PRC would undoubtedly prefer an eventual peaceful resolution of the Taiwan problem to incurring the high costs and risks of imposing a solution by force and would regard US concessions in principle in the course of negotiations on normalization as important steps toward some long-term solution.[34] Moreover, failure to arrive at an agreement on normalization would pose risks to the PRC as well as to the United States. Peking has an important vested interest in Taipei's "one China" policy and the US endorsement of that policy in the Shanghai communiqué. The US acceptance of the PRC's three conditions, even at the price of PRC concessions about US security and economic relations with Taiwan, would strengthen Washington's commitment to the "one China" principle and would reduce the risk that the United States might some day back formal independence for Taiwan.

Like Japan, Canada, the United Kingdom, and many other countries, the United States should avoid taking the position that Taiwan is legally a part of the PRC. Doing so would place Peking in a stronger position if it wanted to challenge future security and economic relations between the United States and Taiwan. The United States could simply reiterate the position it took in the Shanghai communiqué, thereby leaving the door open to the reunion of the two parts of China should the Chinese on both sides of the strait agree on a peaceful means of doing so.

The Impact on Taiwan

From the viewpoint of the ROC, the ideal result of a US effort to negotiate the normalization of relations with the PRC would be for the United States to make a proposal that the PRC would reject, thus leaving relations between the United States and Taiwan unchanged. Hints

---

34. Teng Hsiao-p'ing stated to a delegation of American specialists in world affairs headed by Vance in fall 1975 that China was willing to wait "five, ten, or a hundred years, if necessary" to reunite Taiwan with the mainland. Whiting, *China and the United States*, p. 28.

from some ROC officials that the ROC could tolerate full US diplomatic relations with both Peking and Taipei probably are based on an assumption that the PRC would reject such a proposal, but in the unlikely event that the PRC accepted it, the ROC could readily adjust.

If the United States severed diplomatic relations and ended the security treaty, the effect on the people of Taiwan would inevitably be depressing, even though the US government took prompt action to demonstrate its intention to continue the substance of relations unchanged. Most of the small number of countries still maintaining diplomatic relations with the ROC would probably follow the US example, leaving the people of Taiwan feeling isolated and lacking dignity and respect from the rest of the world. Their confidence in the future would decline.

The government would almost certainly tighten security measures and devote more resources for defense. For a time, at least, the influence of hard-liners in the government would probably increase, and the views of US-trained proponents of more liberal and flexible policies would carry less weight. Resentment toward the United States would be widespread, although ROC leaders would recognize that continued cooperation with the United States offered the best hope of survival as an independent political entity. Public demonstrations of resentment would be restrained, as they were when Japan broke diplomatic relations.

The security treaty is probably regarded by most people in Taiwan as a more important symbolic link with the United States than formal diplomatic relations. It would be difficult to convince people that Taiwan's security was not threatened by an end of the treaty. Assurances by the PRC that it intended to resolve the Taiwan problem peacefully would be suspect, especially if they were tacit or vague. US assurances of continued concern with the security of Taiwan would carry more weight but would not be regarded as a satisfactory substitute for a formal treaty approved by the US Senate. The more sophisticated observers on Taiwan would recognize that even a security treaty does not guarantee US military intervention in the defense of Taiwan, but they would place more confidence in it than in less formal assurances. The withdrawal of the remaining US military personnel from Taiwan, as the United States pledged in the Shanghai communiqué, would add to the impression that the United States was disengaging from responsibility for helping to defend Taiwan—even though US military personnel now in Taiwan are not combat forces and their presence is not essential to the defense of Taiwan. The United States could intervene effectively in the Taiwan Strait from naval and air bases outside Taiwan, but the probability that it would do so would inevitably seem less once the Taiwan Defense Command had been dissolved.

For these reasons, the announcement that the United States was ending the security treaty would have an unsettling impact on Taiwan. It is hard to judge in advance how serious an impact it would be, for much would depend on the circumstances and the actions taken by the United States to soften the blow. A convincing demonstration that the United States was prepared to continue sales of military equipment to the ROC and congressional or executive branch declarations of the US determination to oppose any attempt to resolve the Taiwan problem by force would help. The effect of the initial shock would gradually diminish, if the PRC made no militarily threatening moves and economic relations with the United States continued substantially unchanged. If the PRC did make militarily threatening moves, then the US response to those moves would be critical to morale in Taiwan.

The form of state-to-state relations between the United States and Taiwan is relatively unimportant to the Taiwanese man-in-the-street, particularly if the harsh term "breaking diplomatic relations" is avoided when the change in political relationship is mentioned. Most people would take the news that the US embassy in Taiwan was being replaced by a liaison office, a consulate, or even an unofficial mission of some kind calmly, if both the United States and the ROC took pains to demonstrate that other ongoing relations between the United States and Taiwan were continuing with little change. It would be in the ROC's interest to play down the significance of the change in official relations. It would be particularly important to avoid any hiatus in the issuance of US visas to officials, businessmen, or students. Suspension of the opportunity to travel to the United States, even for a short time, would give rise to wild rumors and panicky reactions that the government would have difficulty countering.

The form of future relations between the United States and Taiwan is far more important to government officials and to intellectuals informed on foreign affairs than it is to the general public. First, they would want to know whether the US action automatically made legally invalid all government-to-government treaties and agreements between the United States and the ROC, as Japan's severance of diplomatic relations did to all such treaties and agreements between the ROC and Japan. Prompt congressional action to maintain in force the essential treaties and agreements would reassure them on this point.

From the viewpoint of ROC officials, the maintenance of some form of official relations between the United States and the ROC is very important, in order to provide a basis in international law for managing US-Taiwan relations that would be lacking under the Japanese formula. Although the United States would no doubt take legislative action in either case to make possible continued travel, trade, and investment between the United States and Taiwan, the lack of an accepted framework in international law would raise innumerable technical problems. Hence, ROC officials see a great difference between maintaining a US consulate in Taiwan and a US "unofficial" office. They assert, and some well-informed Japanese scholars on international affairs concur, that US adoption of the Japanese formula would make it much more difficult for Japan to maintain its relations with Taiwan, because once the PRC had persuaded the United States to take the step, it would no longer be inhibited from putting pressure on Japan to end its relations with Taiwan. Officials of the ROC also predict that lowering US relations with Taiwan to this level would greatly complicate Taiwan's economic relations with other countries. Consequently, US adoption of the Japanese formula would be discouraging to ROC leaders. They would adjust to it as best they could, as they have to similar action by Japan, but the uncertainties and technical problems of such a relationship probably would have a dampening effect on economic growth.

ROC leaders, with substantial assistance from the United States, have developed an effective political system and a dynamic economy from which the great majority of the people of Taiwan have gained notable material benefits. Although Taiwan's dependence on the United States has declined and its form has changed, the connection remains very important to the government and people of Taiwan. Consequently, even though Taiwan's political system and economy have demonstrated considerable resilience over the years, the shock of US severance of diplomatic relations and the ending of the security treaty would be severe, unless mitigated by other actions.

The ROC has reached important turning points in its agricultural and industrial policies. Continued access to the US market, to US capital and technology, and to US supplies of enriched uranium are essential to the resolution of the problems attending Taiwan's effort to rise to a new level of economic development. So long as the existing framework of government-to-government treaties and agreements remains unchanged, Taiwan's access to the US economy will be assured. But if these treaties and agreements should be terminated, adequate legal replacements would have to be provided promptly or Taiwan's economy and planned future economic growth would suffer badly. Moreover, the change in US political relations with Taiwan would inevitably affect the confidence of private entrepreneurs, foreign investors, and international bankers in the future of the island. Japanese investment in Taiwan dropped to a trickle for a year after the Japanese established diplomatic relations with the PRC, although Japanese trade with Taiwan and tourist travel there continued to increase. The implication inherent in a US change in political relations with Taiwan would be more serious, and the effect on Taiwan's economy could range from a pause to a prolonged slowdown or even a decline, depending on how promptly and resolutely the US government demonstrated its intention and capability to continue economic relations with Taiwan essentially unchanged.

Political stability on the island probably would not be seriously shaken by an agreement on normalization between Washington and Peking, provided the US government continued to express interest in Taiwan's security and took steps to reassure the people of Taiwan that economic relations would continue unchanged and access to US military equipment would not be cut off. People would be worried at the implications of the ending of the security treaty, some of the more nervous would leave, and there would be some flight of capital. But the principal effect, as in 1971–1972, probably would be a tendency to unite more closely to cope with the uncertainties of the future. The government, under Chiang Ching-kuo's leadership, would remain firmly in control; ROC leaders would feel a strong motivation to adjust to the new situation as smoothly as possible, to avoid overreaction, and to continue to seek ways of strengthening ties with the United States and Japan. If the political change occurred during an upturn in the world economy and Taiwan's economy was therefore also expanding strongly, its impact would be further blunted.

Choices for the United States

The normalization issue has become a hindrance to further improvement of relations between the United States and the PRC. The shared interests that enabled the two governments to put the Taiwan problem to one side temporarily and proceed with improving relations between them have not essentially changed. But the formula agreed on for that purpose in the Shanghai communiqué did not contemplate the indefinite continuance of the form of relations that the United States then had with the PRC and the ROC. It looked forward to the normalization of relations between the United States and the PRC, the gradual withdrawal of US military personnel from Taiwan, and eventually, at some unspecified time, the peaceful resolution of the Taiwan problem between the Chinese on the mainland and in Taiwan. The Carter administration has pledged to carry the normalization process forward in accord with the principles of the Shanghai communiqué.

The establishment of full diplomatic relations between the United

States and the PRC will almost certainly require acceptance of the three conditions long put forward by the PRC: the severance of diplomatic relations with Taipei, an end to the security treaty, and the withdrawal of all US military personnel from Taiwan. From the PRC's viewpoint these formal steps are necessary if the United States is to join most of the other nations in the world in fully and formally accepting the PRC's claim to be the sole legitimate government of China. It is difficult to imagine any PRC leader, particularly those in the newly-formed post-Mao government in Peking, backing down on any of these points.

But President Carter could not agree to these conditions unless he was satisfied that the security of the people of Taiwan and their economic well-being were protected. To this end, he will need the PRC's acquiescence in the continuation of the substance of US relations with Taiwan, even though the form of these relations changes. He will also have to take steps to reassure the people of Taiwan and to convince the majority of the American people that the agreement with the PRC on the normalization of diplomatic relations does not constitute an abandonment of Taiwan. Maintenance of consular relations with Taiwan would help greatly in these respects. Moreover, following the precedents established by the Japanese, the British, the Canadians and others, Carter should avoid explicitly acknowledging that Taiwan is part of the PRC.

A US offer to meet the PRC's three conditions for normalization would be a strong incentive for PRC leaders to make the reciprocal concessions needed by Carter, although they probably would balk initially at US proposals for the continuance of consular relations and the sale of weapons to Taiwan. Yet the PRC has shown itself to be flexible in the past on the implementation of what it considers to be matters of principle, once the principles themselves have been accepted. A compromise acceptable to both sides is possible. Because of the continuing differences over Taiwan, the compromise could not take the form of a written agreement specifying each party's future policies toward the island. Like the Shanghai communiqué, the written statement announcing the compromise would leave much unsaid. It could not include explicit statements which would be unacceptable to either side, such as that the PRC reserved the right to use force against Taiwan or that the United States reserved the right to supply Taiwan with arms. It would have to be in part an agreement to disagree, in part a reaffirmation of the principles of the Shanghai communiqué, and in part an indication to the world that Washington was satisfied that Peking would not use force against Taiwan and that Peking was satisfied that the United States would not encourage the establishment of an independent state of Taiwan. The written statement would reflect but not spell out an understanding worked out in the course of the negotiations as to the kind of relations the United States would continue to have with Taiwan after normalization. Such a compromise would establish the ground rules for setting the Taiwan issue aside once again, perhaps for many years, and would allow the United States and the PRC to proceed with the strengthening of relations that is in their long-term interests.

The costs and risks for the United States in reaching agreement on normalization with the PRC are substantial. There would be domestic political opposition, criticism from some US allies, and uncertainty with regard to future PRC policies toward the United States and toward Taiwan. But the potential long-term advantages to the United States make the risks worth taking. The normalization of relations with the PRC would reduce the danger that the powerful force of Chinese nationalism could propel Peking some years hence into a military confrontation with the United States over Taiwan. It would further the expansion of bilateral relations, enhance the ability of the United States to influence the Soviet Union, reduce the possibility of a Sino-Soviet rapprochement, and improve communication and understanding between Washington and Peking and consequently their ability to pursue mutually supportive policies based on shared interests. The PRC's vested interest in the "one China" position maintained by the government on Taiwan will tend to inhibit it from exerting excessive pressure on Taiwan or on the relations of the United States and Japan with Taiwan.

Because of the substantial concessions that each side is being asked to make to achieve agreement on normalization, the negotiations are likely to be difficult and lengthy. The Canadians took two years to reach agreement with the PRC on how to deal with the Taiwan issue; the United States has a far more difficult problem. American negotiators should press ahead in search of a mutually acceptable compromise based on reciprocal concessions, for there is danger in delay. A prolonged stalemate could lead to a deterioration in US relations with the PRC and a declining prospect for the successful conclusion of the negotiations. Public debate on the issue in the United States might become increasingly polarized between extreme views, making a compromise on the middle ground more difficult for the administration.

The alternatives to seeking a compromise with the PRC are unpalatable. One would be to settle for the Japan formula, abandoning the effort to continue military sales to Taiwan after normalization and to ensure in other ways that Taiwan's security would be protected. But this is not a practicable course of action for the Carter administration, given the concern it has already voiced for Taiwan's security, the public and congressional opposition to abandoning Taiwan, and the damage that such a policy would do to US relations with Japan and its position elsewhere in East Asia. Another proposed alternative is the German formula. But such a proposal would be unacceptable to PRC leaders, to whom it would seem to retreat from the US determination, as expressed in the Shanghai communiqué, to work toward normalization and to envisage an ultimate resolution of the Taiwan problem by the Chinese themselves. The formula would appear to be a long step by the United States toward a "two Chinas" policy and would almost certainly result in the deterioration of relations between Washington and Peking.

Still another alternative, and the one most likely to be adopted if efforts to reach a compromise on normalization within the next three years fail, is to maintain relations with Peking and Taipei in their present form, deferring another attempt to normalize relations with the PRC to some future time when circumstances might be more propitious. But such a policy would be likely, at best, to freeze relations between Washington and Peking at their present level or, at worst, to initiate a period of steadily deteriorating relations. The policy would have the advantage over the German formula of maintaining the position taken by the United States in the Shanghai communiqué, and it would keep the door ajar to possible eventual normalization. Nevertheless, the failure to reach agreement on normalization would have a depressing impact, the prospects for improvement of relations would not be bright, and the danger of an ultimate military confrontation over Taiwan would rise.

In short, during the next several years, the Carter administration should proceed with a serious and sustained effort to reach agreement with the PRC on the normalization of diplomatic relations. It should be prepared to make concessions on the form of future US relations with Taiwan in exchange for PRC concessions regarding the substance of these relations. The costs and risks involved in reaching agreement on such terms are less than the costs and risks that would result from failure to try to reach agreement.

Long-Term China Policy

9

A compromise agreement making possible the establishment of full diplomatic relations between the United States and the PRC would, as in 1972, set the Taiwan issue to one side for some time and permit the two governments to go forward with the expansion of their bilateral relations, but it would not resolve the Taiwan problem. A separate Taiwan, which had extensive relations with both the United States and Japan, would continue to exist. The PRC would not give up its goal of ultimately incorporating Taiwan.

Nevertheless, the United States and the PRC have much to gain from preventing the Taiwan issue from hampering their efforts to strengthen their respective positions relative to the Soviet Union or causing a military confrontation between them. The more valuable the US connection becomes to the PRC, in terms of both the triangular relationship involving Moscow and fruitful US-PRC bilateral relations, the less PRC leaders will be inclined to jeopardize these advantages by forcing a showdown over Taiwan. So long as the United States and the ROC took no action that would foreclose the possibility of an eventual reunification of Taiwan with the mainland, PRC leaders would be unlikely to feel an urgent need to resolve the Taiwan issue.

Although no peaceful solution of the Taiwan problem can be foreseen today, it is conceivable that a new generation of leaders in Peking and Taipei would begin to talk to each other. Some form of loose association beneficial to both the PRC and Taiwan that would permit trade and an exchange of persons to take place between them might then evolve. But much patience will be required if the way is to be kept open for that possibility—forbearance by the PRC in not using force against Taiwan, patience by Taiwan in adjusting to a prolonged existence as a state lacking diplomatic relations with most countries of the world, and patience by the United States in managing an anomalous and uneasy relationship with the two parts of China.

Triangular Relations

Washington and Peking were motivated to overcome their differences in 1972 mostly by their desire to strengthen their respective positions relative to the Soviet Union; that need remains their most important motivation. For the indefinite future, the Soviet Union, more than any other nation, will have the ability to damage the interests of either the United States or China. Their triangular relationship will require delicate handling, however, because the purpose of the United States is not simply to tilt toward Peking and against Moscow, as the PRC wishes.[1] The PRC would like to heighten the confrontation between Washington and Moscow and weaken the element of détente, but Washington's objectives are more complex. On the one hand, it is essential that the United States and its allies maintain a strong military position to deter the Soviet Union from seeking advantage by military force. But on the other hand, it is essential that the United States pursue arms limitation agreements and many forms of peaceful interaction with the Soviet Union in order to lessen tension and improve the chances of resolving potentially dangerous differences.

The Soviet Union's willingness to improve relations with the United States in a variety of ways was encouraged by the opening to China in 1971–1972, and a further consolidation of Sino-American relations would probably have a similar effect, if it were not carried too far too fast. The interests of the United States would be best served by persistent, long-term efforts to improve relations with both the Soviet Union and China. A steady, balanced forward movement on both fronts would tend to be reciprocally reinforcing, provided that crude efforts to manipulate one against the other were avoided. For some time to come, a more intensive effort than has so far been attempted in improving relations with China would be justified, for the process of constructing a network of interlocking interests with the Soviet Union is considerably more advanced than is construction of such a network with the PRC. Failure to go forward with the improvement of rela-

---

1. See Barnett, *China Policy.*

tions with the PRC not only would diminish pressures on the Soviet Union to improve relations with the United States but might also strengthen the hands of those in Moscow and Peking who would like to see Sino-Soviet relations improved. Not that it will be easy to overcome the many obstacles to a Sino-Soviet rapprochement, but the deterioration of relations between the United States and the PRC would create a better atmosphere for advocates of that course of action.

From the PRC's viewpoint, the incentive for strengthened relations with the United States as a means of countering Soviet pressures may be stronger than the incentive on the US side, for the PRC is weaker and more directly exposed to Soviet military forces. The PRC does have the alternative of seeking safety through lessened tensions with the Soviet Union. In the past, some of the PRC's military leaders have been attracted by this option. Moreover, if Peking could attain a more balanced position between Washington and Moscow, it might gain greater leverage on both. But so long as Washington pursues a policy of seeking better relations with Peking, it will be difficult for Moscow to develop the combination of pressures and inducements that would produce the necessary concessions from Peking.

Heightened tension between the United States and the PRC over Taiwan would benefit the Soviet Union. Washington and Peking would find it harder to identify and act on common interests. Rising emotions on both sides would tend to obscure true long-term interests and to make their pursuit more difficult. Consequently, it would be advantageous to both the United States and the PRC in their relations with the Soviet Union to continue to set the Taiwan issue to one side.

The Japan Factor

The relationship between the United States and Japan is fundamental, not only to the US position in East Asia but also to US interests elsewhere in the world. The largest of the industrial democracies next to the United States itself, Japan is a vital collaborator in furthering the kind of economic and political world order most compatible with the interests of the American people. The economic and security relations that have developed between the United States and Japan during the past twenty-five years place both countries in a strong position from which to deal with the Soviet Union and China. Washington and Tokyo can cooperate in many ways, while it is almost impossible for the two Communist powers to do so. The determination of the Japanese people to keep Japan lightly armed and without nuclear weapons, a condition made possible to a large extent by the US commitment to Japan's defense, contributes importantly to the stability of East Asia. Were Japan to drift away from its close alliance with the United States, rearm heavily, and begin relying on its military power to accomplish objectives in the region, East Asia would become much less peaceful and stable.

Japanese policies toward the PRC and the Soviet Union are compatible with those of the United States. Japan tries to maintain a balance in these policies, not tilting toward one or the other. It has minor territorial disputes with both, more severe with the Soviet Union than with China, but treats them in a low-keyed fashion. Japan poses no military threat to the Soviet Union or China and is an important nearby source of capital equipment and a potentially important supplier of capital for both. Thus, the United States and Japan are in fundamental agreement on pursuing policies aimed at a balanced improvement of relations with both of the Communist states.

Moderate improvement or deterioration of US relations with the PRC would not significantly injure US-Japanese relations. But a rapid and extensive improvement of US relations with Peking, especially if it involved the supply of military equipment to the PRC and resulted in a deterioration of US relations with the Soviet Union, would worry the Japanese and strain US-Japanese relations. Many Japanese would wonder, as some did after the "Nixon shock" of 1971, whether the United States was moving to make China rather than Japan its principal partner in East Asia. Severe deterioration of US-PRC relations would also disturb the Japanese, particularly if it involved a military confrontation over Taiwan. The question of whether Japan would permit the United States to use military bases in Japan in a conflict with the PRC would immediately arise. The issue would be a divisive one in Japan and would place the US-Japanese security treaty under great strain. Thus, healthy relations between the United States and Japan require relatively stable relations between Washington and Peking.

Since 1972, US and Japanese policies toward the PRC have tended to move in tandem. Although the sudden change in US policy toward China in 1972 without adequate consultation disturbed the Japanese, the direction of the change was welcome. It made possible the early normalization of relations between Tokyo and Peking. It brought Washington and Tokyo much closer together in their evaluation of China and in their policies toward that country. It put an end to PRC attacks on the alleged revival of militarism in Japan and produced in their place acknowledgment by PRC leaders of the need for Japan's defense forces and for the US-Japanese security treaty in the face of the Soviet threat. The normalization of relations between Peking and

Tokyo eliminated from Japanese domestic politics the highly divisive debate on this issue and made it more difficult for the PRC to exploit domestic divisions to its advantage. Trade between Japan and the PRC grew substantially.

The improvement of both Sino-Japanese and Sino-American relations from 1972 was greatly facilitated by the Washington-Peking agreement to set the Taiwan issue to one side. It opened the way to agreement between Tokyo and Peking on the Japanese formula for continuing economic and other relations between Japan and Taiwan. The long-term interests of all three powers lie in continuing to relegate the Taiwan issue to a subordinate position. Otherwise, the Taiwan issue would not only become an obstacle to further improvement of Sino-American and Sino-Japanese relations but could also adversely effect US-Japanese relations.

The Japanese have been well satisfied with the state of US relations with the PRC and Taiwan since 1972. It would suit their interests if the PRC would tolerate indefinitely the present US diplomatic relationships with Peking and Taipei. The Japanese government would be concerned, however, if the Taiwan issue threatened to cause a serious deterioration of relations between Washington and Peking that might end in conflict. Consequently, the Japanese would not object if the United States and Peking should devise a new formula to keep the Taiwan issue from heating up, provided Taiwan's security and freedom to trade with the United States and Japan were protected.

Other East Asian States

During the era when the central purpose of US policy in East Asia was containment of the PRC's influence, most of the smaller states of the region lined up on one side or the other. With the opening to China and the collapse of US policy in Vietnam, these states began readjusting their foreign relations to the more complicated international environment. Most now have diplomatic relations with all four big powers active in East Asia.

The objectives of the United States in the region continue to be the preservation of international peace and stability, the promotion of economic and political development in individual countries, and economic access for American citizens to markets and resources. The United States continues to maintain a strong military force in the region, but its principal purpose is no longer to contain the PRC's military power and influence.

Since the late 1960s, the military power of China and the Soviet Union has been deployed primarily against each other, rather than against US forces or Japan. Sino-Soviet rivalry, especially in Southeast Asia, has intensified since the fall of Saigon. It is probably most intense in the contest for influence with the Communist governments of East Asia: North Korea, Vietnam, Laos, and Cambodia. Consequently, the atmosphere has improved for the United States to increase the emphasis on political, economic, and diplomatic measures to achieve its objectives and to reduce its emphasis on military force.

The rhetoric of the PRC continues to support Peking-oriented Communist parties in Southeast Asia, which direct small-scale insurgencies that seek to overthrow local governments. Some material support also goes to these movements, especially in Burma. But in recent years, the PRC has increased its emphasis on state-to-state relations and toned down its revolutionary rhetoric. Its rivalry with the Soviet Union takes place predominantly in the realm of state-to-state relations. The importance of Southeast Asian countries as markets for PRC products also has increased. Thus, while the PRC holds in reserve its ability to place pressure on local governments by supporting armed rebellions against them, at the present time its main concern is to have friendly and stable relations with those local governments.

Korea, an area where two heavily armed governments face each other with unabated hostility, is also the area where renewed conflict would be most damaging to the interest of all four big powers. Yet the rivalry between China and the Soviet Union for influence in Pyongyang makes it extraordinarily difficult for the big powers to agree on measures that would lower the tension and reduce the risk of war on the peninsula. The greater the stake that Peking and Moscow have in improving relations with the United States, the greater the cost to them of renewed conflict in Korea and the better the chances of finding ways to prevent it. On the other hand, the deterioration of relations between the United States and the PRC or the Soviet Union would tend to reduce the incentive for those states to cooperate in reducing tension in Korea.

Improving relations between the United States and the PRC would make it easier for them to take mutually reinforcing actions to ease crises in East Asia. Trends in PRC domestic and foreign policy suggest that occasions when both Washington and Peking would prefer peace and stability to turbulence and uncertainty will occur more frequently in the future than in the past. Circumstances in which the United States and the PRC have more interests in common then either has with the Soviet Union will also occur occasionally. Improved relations between Washington and Peking would facilitate dealing with such situations in ways consonant with US objectives. Deteriorating relations between the United States and the PRC, would reduce incentives for the two countries to work toward common ends in East Asia and would possibly augment the influence of those within the PRC who favor an increased emphasis on backing revolutionary movements in East Asia.

The way in which the United States handles its differences with the PRC concerning Taiwan will thus affect the ability of the United States to protect its interests elsewhere in East Asia. A drift toward the renewal of confrontation between Washington and Peking over Taiwan would not only make it more difficult to deal effectively with crises and tension in East Asia but also on occasion probably force the smaller nations to make difficult and unwanted choices between policies favored by the United States and those favored by China. Yet were the United States to normalize relations with the PRC at the cost of sacrificing Taiwan, many small states, made uneasy by China's size, power, and revolutionary rhetoric, would see in that action confirmation that the United States was continuing the withdrawal from the western Pacific set in motion by its failure in the Vietnam war. Their confidence in the United States and their willingness to cooperate with it would suffer. Hence, to pursue effectively US objectives throughout East Asia, a course of action is needed that would result in an improvement of US relations with the PRC, while avoiding the abandonment of Taiwan.

Bilateral Relations

The ability of the United States and the PRC to act in mutually beneficial ways when dealing with problems involving other countries rests on their success in promoting their bilateral relations. Moreover, the direct and intrinsic benefits from improving bilateral relations are not inconsiderable.

Trade is the most tangible aspect of US-PRC relations. It rose from virtually nothing in 1971 to $934 million in 1974, but dropped to $336 million in 1976. Since the PRC is a largely self-sufficient continental country and is also a developing country at an early stage, its foreign trade, increasing at a moderate pace, probably will continue to be only a small fraction of its gross national product, not exceeding 6 to 8 percent. The PRC's trade with the United States will remain a small proportion of total US trade even though the political constraints imposed by the lack of full diplomatic relations are removed. Trade could increase more rapidly for a time than it has in the past if the PRC should decide to accept long-term loans from abroad, but loans would eventually have to be repaid, and the PRC cannot rapidly increase its export capacity. Thus, for a number of years to come, PRC trade with the United States probably will be less than Taiwan's trade with the United States, which reached $4.8 billion in 1976. The political consequences of trade between the United States and the PRC are likely to be more important in the long run than the purely economic gains. Trade will create a network of contacts and interlocking interests that will help in a variety of ways to improve understanding and to better overall relations.

Travel and observation in each other's countries and the opportunities thus presented for intercommunication and increased understanding between Americans and the Chinese of mainland China are among the most valuable results of the 1972 agreement. But the visitors are too few, and their visits far too short, to penetrate effectively the enormous cultural barriers that exist between the two societies after more than two decades of almost total isolation from each other. Soviet-US exchanges of individuals and groups, although still far from ideal, are much more extensive than are those between the United States and the PRC. The normalization of relations between Washington and Peking would remove some of the barriers to greater exchanges. Although the size of the flow and the extent to which conversations can penetrate beneath a superficial level will be strictly limited by the nature of the PRC's political system, in time, better mutual understanding should result. Better understanding will not necessarily lead to more friendly or cooperative relations. Experience with the Soviet Union has demonstrated the fragility of détente even where the network of bilateral relations is far more extensive than that between the United States and the PRC. Nevertheless, with better understanding there is hope for easier and more constructive relations; without it, there is no such hope.

The strongest potential ties, but also those involving the highest risk, lie in the military field. Because of its military weakness relative to the Soviet Union, the PRC would gain important advantages from acquiring advanced military technology from the United States. The United States is likely to be cautious, however, in becoming a military supplier of the PRC, because to do so might block progress in reaching arms limitation agreements with the Soviet Union and set back rather than support the efforts to create a more stable and fruitful détente between Washington and Moscow. The Japanese government today would be deeply troubled by a Washington decision to strengthen China militarily, and other East Asian governments would be skeptical of the advantages of this course of action.

Despite the obvious problems, it would be prudent to keep an open mind on this subject. The US willingness to exercise restraint in supplying military technology to the PRC should be reciprocated by a greater Soviet willingness to reach agreements on arms limitation and to move ahead constructively with respect to other aspects of détente. The United States should reserve the option of helping the PRC to strengthen itself militarily if obstructive Soviet behavior justifies such action in the eyes of Washington and Tokyo. The calculation of costs and benefits should include a judgment whether the military technology supplied would increase the PRC's capability to attack Taiwan and, if so, whether this disadvantage was outweighed by a reduced probability of such an attack because of Peking's continuing reliance on access to US military technology to strengthen its position against the Soviet Union.

A related area where negotiation and agreements between Washington and Peking will become more important in the future is that of arms control. Although the PRC has denounced most existing arms control agreements as designed to perpetuate the military dominance of the superpowers rather than to limit nuclear arms, it has supported certain arms control measures, such as the Latin American nuclear-free zone. The prevention of the proliferation of nuclear weapons to countries such as Japan, South Korea, or Taiwan is clearly in the common interest of the United States and the PRC, even though the PRC refuses to sign or support the nuclear nonproliferation treaty. At some point in the future, as the PRC's nuclear arsenal grows, it will have to be brought into arms control negotiations. Otherwise, it would become increasingly difficult for the United States and the Soviet Union to reach nuclear arms limitations agreements. Thus, taking the long-term view, improved relations between Washington and Peking will be essential if a way to limit nuclear arms in the world is to be found.

Living with the Taiwan Problem

Normalizing diplomatic relations with the PRC clearly would enable the United States to pursue its broad policy objectives in East Asia more effectively. The willingness of the United States at last to recognize the PRC as the sole legitimate government of China and to withdraw that recognition from the ROC would significantly change the climate surrounding relations between Washington and Peking and remove constraints hampering the improvement of those relations. The two governments would be better able to proceed with the expansion of both their bilateral relations and their efforts to identify areas of common interest where mutually supportive policies might be followed. The prospects for finding a long-term solution for the Taiwan problem, or at least for working out ways of living with it indefinitely without coming to blows, would also improve. Although normalization would not resolve the differences between Washington and Peking over the future of Taiwan, the compromise would make it easier, as did the Shanghai communiqué, to put the Taiwan issue to one side and concentrate on the broader, more important objectives of the United States and the PRC in the region.

As the years pass, the PRC's industrial and military strength will grow. The advantages to the United States of being able to pursue common interests with the PRC will increase, as will the risks associated with deteriorating relations. Differences over Taiwan will pose a continuing threat to good relations between Washington and Peking. The PRC is unlikely to abandon the goal of absorbing Taiwan, whether or not it succeeds in normalizing relations with the United States. To disengage completely from Taiwan as a means of resolving the issue once and for all is unlikely to be acceptable to the United States. The American people would strongly oppose abandoning the people of Taiwan, and abandonment would severely strain the vital connection with Japan. The costs to the United States in both credibility abroad and self-respect at home would be very high.

Since no way of finally resolving the Taiwan problem that would be acceptable to Washington, Peking, and Taiwan can be foreseen today, the problem must be managed so that all three parties can somehow live with it. As the PRC's power increases, it must be discouraged from eventually pressing for a military showdown over Taiwan, especially if tension with the Soviet Union should decline. The key to living with the Taiwan problem lies in three propositions: keeping high the potential loss to the PRC in men and equipment if it resorts to military force against Taiwan; expanding relations between the United States and the PRC so that the potential gains to the PRC from continuation of this process and the potential losses from its interruption will be high; and keeping open the possibility of an eventual reunification of the PRC and Taiwan. Carrying out these three propositions simultaneously will not be easy, for they are contradictory. For example, even though a means is found in the course of normalization negotiations for glossing over the differences concerning US security relations with Taiwan, the PRC will probably continue to oppose measures to strengthen Taiwan's defenses, and persistence by the United States in

237

taking such measures may hinder the improvement of relations between Washington and Peking. Nevertheless, if a careful balance is maintained among policies based on these propositions, it should be possible to prevent the Taiwan issue from dominating US relations with the PRC, as it did before 1972.

Although it will be necessary to strengthen Taiwan's defenses as the PRC's military power grows, the United States should not rely almost exclusively on the deterrence of the PRC by military power, as it did before 1972. It is likely to be increasingly difficult for little Taiwan itself to maintain an adequate defense. Intervention by the United States with sea and air power could provide the margin needed for a reliable defense, but it is not wise to rely so heavily on the willingness of the American people to support military intervention with US forces in the Taiwan Strait ten, fifteen, or twenty years hence. A 1977 poll showed a majority opposing military intervention by the United States in defense of Taiwan, although views on this question admittedly can change quickly depending on circumstances.[2] But in order to reduce the risk that the United States would be called on to intervene militarily in the Taiwan Strait, increasing emphasis should be placed on propositions that would induce the PRC to base its Taiwan policy judgments predominantly on potential political gains and losses from particular courses of action rather than on the military option.

Progress in expanding relations with the PRC, which would be advantageous to the United States for various reasons unrelated to Taiwan, would also make the Taiwan problem easier to live with. To the extent that the PRC profits from the expansion of relations with the United States, it will be reluctant to jeopardize present benefits and potential gains by pressing too hard on the Taiwan issue. Ultimately, the advantages to the PRC of a broad range of ongoing relations with the United States may become so firmly institutionalized that it would be no more willing to forgo those advantages by resorting to force against Taiwan than it is today to forgo the advantages derived from eschewing force against Hong Kong and leaving it under British rule.

In pursuing a policy of expanding relations with the PRC, the most difficult decisions for the United States would lie in the supply of military technology to the PRC and its potential effect on the defensibility of Taiwan. Outside the military field, the expansion of US relations with the PRC would rarely pose such difficult choices. It would not be a zero-sum game in which progress in US-PRC relations in-

---

2. In the poll taken by Gallup for Potomac Associates in April 1977, 36 percent of the respondents favored military intervention by US naval and air forces if Taiwan were attacked by the PRC, 40 percent were opposed, and 24 percent were undecided. Clough, Oxnam, and Watts, *The United States and China*, p. 34.

evitably resulted in damage to Taiwan or to US relations with Taiwan. On the contrary, Taiwan would in general benefit from any expansion of US relations with the PRC that gave the PRC a greater stake in maintaining those relations.

Keeping the door open to the eventual reunification of Taiwan with the mainland is also essential if the Taiwan problem is not to provoke another dangerous confrontation between the United States and the PRC. The PRC's willingness to put the issue to one side resulted in considerable measure from the attitude expressed on this point by the United States in the Shanghai communiqué. Not only did the United States not challenge the view of the Chinese on both sides of the Taiwan Strait that Taiwan was a part of China, but it also looked forward to the day when the Taiwan problem might be resolved peacefully by the Chinese themselves. So long as the eventual reunification of Taiwan with the mainland is not foreclosed by some irrevocable action by the United States or by the authorities on Taiwan, pressure on PRC leaders to use force to settle the matter quickly will probably not be strong. The policy followed by the United States should seek to strengthen the hands of those in the PRC who advocate patience and political methods for dealing with the Taiwan issue and should avoid giving ammunition to those who would suport attempting an early settlement by the use of force.

Keeping the door open to ultimate unification also preserves a potent weapon in the hands of the authorities in Washington and Taipei: the threat that, if Peking presses too hard on the Taiwan issue, Washington will recognize Taiwan as an independent state. The existence of this option exerts a subtle pressure on Peking to agree to a compromise on normalization that would reaffirm Washington's commitment to the "one China" principle as expressed in the Shanghai communiqué. The option would continue to exist even after normalization, provided the United States avoided an express acknowledgement that Taiwan was a part of the PRC, but the chances that Taipei would exercise the option would tend to decline if relations between the United States and the PRC continued to improve. For as each power's stake in this continued improvement grew, Peking would be less likely to threaten force against Taiwan and thus provoke a declaration of independence, while Washington would be less willing to jeopardize its relations with the PRC by recognizing Taiwan's independence.

The need to cultivate the native Taiwanese in order to preserve the commitment of the ROC to the "one China" position would also tend to inhibit Peking from pressing too hard. The PRC has a stake in the kind of education being given the children and young people of Taiwan. Although more than 80 percent of the children speak their local *hokkien* or *hakka* dialects at home, all children are taught in Mandarin, the same standardized dialect of Chinese which the PRC has made the *lingua franca* on the mainland. Through their courses in Chinese history and literature, they are taught to regard themselves as part of the great Chinese people, intimately linked to their compatriots on the mainland. But if the pressure from the mainland became too great, it is not inconceivable that the result would be to provoke a Taiwanese nationalism. The desire to make greater use of *hokkein,* the Amoy dialect most widely spoken among Taiwanese, would overcome the present restraints on the use of that dialect on radio or TV and in motion pictures and schools. Emphasis would be placed on the history of Taiwan rather than the history of China. The cultural bonds between Taiwan and the mainland would be weakened. The people of Taiwan might come to look on Singapore as a model for their political future, rather than wishing to continue in principle as part of China.

Communications between Peking and Taipei probably would make the continuing state of civil war less explosive and more tolerable for both parties. A dialogue could reassure Peking that Taiwan's leaders were not about to set up an independent state and reassure Taiwan that Peking did not intend to seek an early resolution of the problem by military force. It could reinforce the tacit understandings that for many years have minimized the risk of military clashes in the Taiwan Strait. Although a dialogue could be used to make threats as well as to offer reassurances, in either case it would make possible a more accurate reading of each other's intentions.

The government of the ROC has been adamantly opposed to talking with the PRC. Whereas no early change in this position is likely, the normalization of US relations with the PRC may cause some influential people in Taiwan to begin seriously to assess the possible advantages of a dialogue. The growth of indirect communication by means of increased visits of Chinese from the United States or Japan to the China mainland and Taiwan will in any case gradually give leaders in the PRC and the ROC a more accurate understanding of conditions and attitudes on the other side of the Taiwan Strait. The disguised trade between Taiwan and the China mainland via Hong Kong, already of significant proportions, will probably increase. In time as the ROC adjusts with greater confidence to its unique international status as an autonomous political entity lacking formal recognition as a separate state, it may well come to see advantages in talking to its adversary. A desire for dialogue on the part of the ROC should be allowed to ripen without US pressure.

While talks probably would make the separation of Taiwan from the mainland easier for both parties to live with, they would be unlikely to lead to the peaceful integration of Taiwan into the PRC, because recent trends in Taiwan indicate that obstacles to unification are likely to grow rather than diminish. Ties with the mainland will erode as the political influence of the Taiwanese increases and as the gap in living standards between Taiwan and the mainland expands further. The ROC has demonstrated its ability to expand its flourishing economic relations with many nations of the world despite the loss of diplomatic relations with those nations. If the United States maintains its economic relations with Taiwan and does not shut off access to military spare parts and equipment, Taiwan's resilient political and economic system should enable it to continue to function successfully as a separate political entity despite temporary difficulties imposed by the normalization of relations between Washington and Peking.

As the modern industrial sectors on the China mainland and in Taiwan expand, the advantages of trade between them will become increasingly evident. Japanese trading companies, which trade extensively with both the PRC and Taiwan, could serve initially as middlemen. If the PRC's current policies of increasing the emphasis on science and technology and easing the political pressure on intellectuals are continued for a number of years, they probably will result in a growing tendency to draw on the skills of Chinese trained in the United States. Similarly, the PRC could benefit from the knowledge acquired by Chinese working in the new, high-technology industries being established in Taiwan, and Taiwan could benefit from visits by scientists in fields in which mainland China is more advanced. Such exchanges, visionary today, are not beyond the bounds of possibility for pragmatic leadership on both sides of the Taiwan Strait.

Gradually, it may become apparent to new generations of leaders in Peking and Taipei that they stand to benefit more in the long run from a moderation of hostility between them and some limited exchange of goods and people than from policies and actions that highlight differences and increase tension between Washington and Peking over Taiwan. Only then will it become possible for Peking and Taipei to work out some form of loose association that preserves the principle of one China and fosters mutually beneficial interchange, but allows Taiwan to continue to function as an autonomous political entity in control of its own political and economic systems and foreign relations.

Conclusions for US Policy

Maintaining the proper balance in US policies based on the three propositions suggested will demand diplomatic dexterity and attentiveness to the sensitivities of PRC and ROC leaders: PRC leaders must be accorded respect and treatment appropriate to the rulers of the world's most populous state; and ROC leaders must be reassured of the US determination to protect Taiwan's security and economic health, but the reassurance ought to be provided in ways not needlessly provocative to the PRC. At times, the policy choices will be difficult. If the PRC should press the United States to take actions that would damage Taiwan's security or undermine its economy, the United States would have to refuse, even at the cost of injuring Washington-Peking relations. The United States will also at times have to take actions resented by the ROC, even though they do not seriously endanger Taiwan's security or economic health. The Taiwan issue will continue to be a frustrating problem in US relations with the PRC, but with careful handling, the injury it does to those relations probably can be kept at a tolerable level.

Despite the PRC's dissatisfaction over US policies toward Taiwan, PRC leaders may come to recognize that the US connection with Taiwan can be of use to them in several ways. During the period, perhaps of many years, pending a peaceful settlement of the Taiwan problem, the US connection can reduce the risk that Taiwan's leaders will feel compelled to declare independence, manufacture nuclear weapons, or develop relations with the Soviet Union out of desperation. The United States should seek to convince PRC leaders that, in order to preserve this degree of influence on the ROC, it must follow policies fostering confidence on the part of the people of Taiwan that their security and standard of living are reasonably secure.

These judgments may be overly optimistic. Governments frequently fail to act in what may seem to a rational observer to be in their long-term interests. The pressures of domestic politics foreclose options and emotions cloud judgment. It may prove impossible for the United States and the PRC to reach agreement on normalizing their relations within the coming two or three years. Or even if that hurdle is surmounted, a series of subsequent misjudgments and miscalculations could sharpen the continuing differences over Taiwan until they became unmanageable and resulted in a military confrontation. Such a confrontation might be precipitated by ROC actions if the United States or the PRC failed to give adequate weight to its needs and options. Thus, there can be no assurance that the United States will not be faced some day with the hard choice of abandoning Taiwan or intervening with military force to help defend it.

But the point is that it need not come to that. By concentrating on their fundamental long-term interests, the United States and the PRC should be able to arrive at a workable and lasting compromise regarding

Taiwan that would keep the door open to a peaceful settlement between Peking and Taipei. Living with the problem of Taiwan without coming to blows need not be an impossible dream. The costs, risks, and uncertainties associated with attempts by Washington, Peking, or Taipei to impose its own final solution will remain high. The aim of US policy should be to maintain a situation which, while not entirely satisfactory to any of the parties, is easier for each to tolerate than the probable consequences of forcing a showdown. The interests of the United States can be protected by holding firmly to the principle that a final solution of the Taiwan problem must be worked out peacefully by the Chinese themselves, without the threat or use of force.

APPENDIX
BIBLIOGRAPHY
INDEX

Appendix. Joint Communiqué Issued at Shanghai, 1972

President Richard Nixon of the United States of America visited the People's Republic of China at the invitation of Premier Chou En-lai of the People's Republic of China from February 21 to February 28, 1972. Accompanying the President were Mrs. Nixon, U.S. Secretary of State William Rogers, Assistant to the President Dr. Henry Kissinger, and other American officials.

President Nixon met with Chairman Mao Tse-tung of the Communist Party of China on February 21. The two leaders had a serious and frank exchange of views on Sino-US relations and world affairs.

During the visit, extensive, earnest and frank discussions were held between President Nixon and Premier Chou En-lai on the normalization of relations between the United States of America and the People's Republic of China, as well as on other matters of interest to both sides. In addition, Secretary of States William Rogers and Foreign Minister Chi Peng-fei held talks in the same spirit.

President Nixon and his party visited Peking and viewed cultural, industrial and agricultural sites, and they also toured Hangchow and Shanghai where, continuing discussions with Chinese leaders, they viewed similar places of interest.

The leaders of the People's Republic of China and the United States of America found it beneficial to have this opportunity, after so many years without contact, to present candidly to one another their views on a variety of issues. They reviewed the international situation in which important changes and great upheavals are taking place and expounded their respective positions and attitudes.

The US side stated: Peace in Asia and peace in the world requires efforts both to reduce immediate tensions and to eliminate the basic causes of conflict. The United States will work for a just and secure peace: just, because it fulfills the aspirations of peoples and nations for freedom and progress; secure, because it removes the danger of foreign aggression. The United States supports individual freedom and social progress for all the peoples of the world, free of outside pressure or intervention. The United States believes that the effort to reduce tensions is served by improving communication between countries that have different ideologies so as to lessen the risks of confrontation through accident, miscalculation or misunderstanding. Countries should treat each other with mutual respect and be willing to compete peacefully, letting performance be the ultimate judge. No country should claim infallibility and each country should be prepared to re-examine its own attitudes for the common good. The United States stressed that the peoples of Indochina should be allowed to determine their destiny without outside intervention; its constant primary objective has been a negotiated solution; the eight-point proposal put forward by the Republic of Vietnam and the United States on January 27, 1972 represents a basis for the attainment of that objective; in the absence of a negotiated settlement the United States envisages the ultimate withdrawal of all US forces from the region consistent with the aim of self-determination for each country of Indochina. The United States will maintain its close ties with and support for the Republic of Korea; the United States will support efforts of the Republic of Korea to seek a relaxation of tension and increased communication in the Korean peninsula. The United States places the highest value on its friendly relations with Japan; it will continue to develop the existing close bonds. Consistent with the United Nations Security Council Resolution of December 21, 1971, the United States favors the continuation of the ceasefire between India and Pakistan and the withdrawal of all military forces to within their own territories and to their own sides of the ceasefire line in Jammu and Kashmir; the United States supports the right of the peoples of South Asia to shape their own future in peace, free of military threat, and without having the area become the subject of great power rivalry.

The Chinese side stated: Wherever there is oppression, there is resistance. Countries want independence, nations want liberation and the people want revolution—this has become the irresistible trend of history. All nations, big or small, should be equal; big nations should not bully the small and strong nations should not bully the weak. China will never be a superpower and it opposes hegemony and power politics of any kind. The Chinese side stated that it firmly supports the struggles of all the oppressed people and nations for freedom and liberation and that the people of all countries have the right to choose their social systems according to their own wishes and the right to safeguard the independence, sovereignty and territorial integrity of their own countries and oppose foreign aggression, interference, control and subversion. All foreign troops should be withdrawn to their own countries.

The Chinese side expressed its firm support to the peoples of Vietnam, Laos and Cambodia in their efforts for the attainment of their goal and its firm support to the seven-point proposal of the Provisional Revolutionary Government of the Republic of South Vietnam and the elaboration of February this year on the two key problems in the proposal, and to the Joint Declaration of the Summit Conference of the Indochinese Peoples. It firmly supports the eight-point program for the peaceful unification of Korea put forward by the Government of the Democratic People's Republic of Korea on April 12, 1971, and the stand for the abolition of the "U.N. Commission for the Unification and Rehabilitation of Korea." It firmly opposes the revival and outward expansion of Japanese militarism and firmly supports the Japanese people's desire to build an independent, democratic, peaceful and neutral Japan. It firmly maintains that India and Pakistan should, in accordance with the United Nations resolutions on the India-Pakistan question, immediately withdraw all their forces to their respective territories and to their own sides of the ceasefire line in Jammu and Kashmir and firmly supports the Pakistan Government and people in their struggle to preserve their independence and sovereignty and the people of Jammu and Kashmir in their struggle for the right of self-determination.

There are essential differences between China and the United States in their social systems and foreign policies. However, the two sides agreed that countries, regardless of their social systems, should conduct their relations on the principles of respect for the sovereignty and territorial integrity of all states, non-aggression against other states, non-interference in the internal affairs of other states, equality and mutual benefit, and peaceful coexistence. International disputes should be settled on this basis, without resorting to the use or threat of force. The United States and the People's Republic of China are prepared to apply these principles to their mutual relations.

With these principles of international relations in mind the two sides stated that:

- progress toward the normalization of relations between China and the United States is in the interests of all countries;
- both wish to reduce the danger of international military conflict;

249

- neither should seek hegemony in the Asia-Pacific region and each is opposed to efforts by any other country or group of countries to establish such hegemony; and
- neither is prepared to negotiate on behalf of any third party or to enter into agreements or understandings with the other directed at other states.

Both sides are of the view that it would be against the interests of the peoples of the world for any major country to collude with another against other countries, or for major countries to divide up the world into spheres of interest.

The two sides reviewed the long-standing serious disputes between China and the United States. The Chinese side reaffirmed its position: The Taiwan question is the crucial question obstructing the normalization of relations between China and the United States; the Government of the People's Republic of China is the sole legal government of China; Taiwan is a province of China which has long been returned to the motherland; the liberation of Taiwan is China's internal affair in which no other country has the right to interfere; and all US forces and military installations must be withdrawn from Taiwan. The Chinese Government firmly opposes any activities which aim at the creation of "one China, one Taiwan," "one China, two governments," "two Chinas," and "independent Taiwan," or advocate that "the status of Taiwan remains to be determined."

The US side declared: The United States acknowledges that all Chinese on either side of the Taiwan Strait maintain there is but one China and that Taiwan is a part of China. The United States Government does not challenge that position. It reaffirms its interest in a peaceful settlement of the Taiwan question by the Chinese themselves. With this prospect in mind, it affirms the ultimate objective of the withdrawal of all US forces and military installations from Taiwan. In the meantime, it will progressively reduce its forces and military installations on Taiwan as the tension in the area diminishes.

The two sides agreed that it is desirable to broaden the understanding between the two peoples. To this end, they discussed specific areas in such fields as science, technology, culture, sports and journalism, in which people-to-people contacts and exchanges would be mutually beneficial. Each side undertakes to facilitate the further development of such contacts and exchanges.

Both sides view bilateral trade as another area from which mutual benefit can be derived, and agreed that economic relations based on equality and mutual benefit are in the interest of the peoples of the two countries. They agree to facilitate the progressive development of trade between their two countries.

The two sides agreed that they will stay in contact through various channels, including the sending of a senior US representative to Peking from time to time for concrete consultations to further the normalization of relations between the two countries and continue to exchange views on issues of common interest.

The two sides expressed the hope that the gains achieved during this visit would open up new prospects for the relations between the two countries. They believe that the normalization of relations between the two countries is not only in the interest of the Chinese and American peoples but also contributes to the relaxation of tension in Asia and the world.

President Nixon, Mrs. Nixon and the American party expressed their appreciation for the gracious hospitality shown them by the Government and people of the People's Republic of China.

Bibliography

Barnds, William J., ed. *China and America: The Search for a New Relationship*. New York: New York University Press (Council on Foreign Relations), 1977.

Barnett, A. Doak. *China and the Major Powers*. Washington, D.C., Brookings Institution, 1977.

————. *China Policy*. Washington, D.C., Brookings Institution, 1977.

Bueler, William M. *U.S. China Policy and the Problem of Taiwan*. Boulder: Colorado Associated University Press, 1971.

Chaffee, Frederick H., and others. *Area Handbook for the Republic of China*. Foreign Area Studies. Washington, D.C., The American University, 1968.

Chen, Lung-chu, and Lasswell, Harold D. *Formosa, China, and the United Nations*. New York: St. Martin's Press, 1967.

Chiu, Hungdah, ed. *China and the Question of Taiwan: Documents and Analysis*. New York: Praeger, 1973.

Clough, Ralph N.; Oxnam, Robert B.; and Watts, William. *The United States and China: American Perceptions and Future Alternatives*. Washington, D.C.: Potomac Associates, 1977.

Cohen, Jerome; Friedman, Edward; Hinton, Harold; and Whiting, Allen S. *Taiwan and American Foreign Policy*. New York: Praeger, 1971.

Davidson, James W. *The Island of Formosa: Historical View from 1430 to 1900*. London: privately published, 1903.

Gallin, Bernard. *Hsin Hsing, Taiwan: A Chinese Village in Change*. Berkeley: University of California Press, 1966.

Goddard, W. G. *Formosa: A Study in Chinese History*. London: MacMillan, 1966.

Hsieh, Chiao-min. *Taiwan-Ilha Formosa: A Geography in Perspective*. Washington, D.C.: Butterworths, 1964.

Jacoby, Neil H. *U.S. Aid to Taiwan: A Study of Foreign Aid, Self-Help, and Development*. New York: Praeger, 1966.

Jo, Yung-hwan, ed., *Taiwan's Future?* Hong Kong: Union Research Institute, for Arizona State University, 1974.

Kerr, George H. *Formosa: Licensed Revolution and the Home Rule Movement, 1895–1945*. Honolulu: The University Press of Hawaii, 1974.

————. *Formosa Betrayed*. Boston: Houghton Mifflin, 1965.

Bibliography

Koo, Anthony Y. C. *The Role of Land Reform in Economic Development: A Case Study of Taiwan.* New York: Praeger, 1968.

Li, Victor H. *De-recognizing Taiwan: The Legal Problems.* Washington, D.C.: Carnegie Endowment for International Peace, 1977.

Mancall, Mark, ed. *Formosa Today.* New York: Praeger, 1968.

Mendel, Douglas. *The Politics of Formosan Nationalism.* Berkeley: University of California Press, 1970.

Moorsteen, Richard, and Abramowitz, Morton. *Remaking China Policy: U.S.–China Relations and Governmental Decisionmaking.* Cambridge: Harvard University Press, 1971.

Morello, Frank P. *The International Legal Status of Formosa.* The Hague: Martinus Nijhoff, 1966.

Oksenberg, Michel, and Oxnam, Robert B. *China and America: Past and Future.* Headline Series. New York: Foreign Policy Association, April 1977.

Peng, Ming-min. *A Taste of Freedom.* New York: Holt, Rinehart and Winston, 1972.

Rankin, Karl L. *China Assignment.* Seattle: University of Washington Press, 1964.

Riggs, Fred W. *Formosa under Chinese Nationalist Rule.* 1952. Reprint. New York: Octagon Books, 1972.

Rowe, David Nelson. *Informal "Diplomatic Relations": The Case of Japan and the Republic of China, 1972–1974.* Hamden, Conn.: Shoe String Press, 1975.

Schreiber, Jordan C. *U.S. Corporate Investment in Taiwan.* New York: Dunellen, 1970.

Shen, T. H., ed. *Agriculture's Place in the Strategy of Development: The Taiwan Experience.* Taipei: Joint Commission on Rural Reconstruction, 1974.

Sih, Paul K. T., ed. *Taiwan in Modern Times.* New York: St. John's University Press, 1973.

Tsou, Tang. *Embroilment over Quemoy: Mao, Chiang, and Dulles.* Salt Lake City: University of Utah Press, 1959.

U.S. Congress, House, Special Subcommittee on Investigations of the Committee on International Relations. *United States–China Relations: The Process of Normalization of Relations.* 94th Cong., Nov. 18, Dec. 8 and 17, 1975; Feb. 2, 1976.

U.S. Congress, House, Subcommittee on Asian and Pacific Affairs of the Committee on International Relations. *Normalization of Relations with the People's Republic of China: Practical Implications.* 95th Cong., 1st sess., September–October 1977.

U.S. Congress, Senate, Committee on Foreign Relations. *U.S. Relations with the People's Republic of China.* 92nd Cong. 1st sess., July 1971.

Whiting, Alan S. *China and the United States: What Next?* Headline Series. New York: Foreign Policy Association, April 1976.

Wilson, Richard W. *Learning to Be Chinese: The Political Socialization of Children in Taiwan.* Cambridge: M.I.T. Press, 1970.

Yang, Martin M. C. *Socio-Economic Results of Land Reform in Taiwan.* Honolulu:University Press of Hawaii, for East-West Center, 1970.

Yen, Sophia Su-fei. *Taiwan in China's Foreign Relations, 1836–1874.* Hamden, Conn.: Shoe String Press, 1965.

Index

Index

Geographic features, 69
Geological Society, 159
German formula, 215–216, 227
Government. *See* Political system
Government Information Office, 50, 64
Great Leap Forward (1958), 17, 21, 179, 182
Green, Marshall, 202–203
Green, Theodore, 19
Gross National Product: aid as percent of (1951, 1965), 24; in 1953–1962, 70; housing investment as percent of, 71; exports as percent of (1973), 81; military budget as percent of, 121. *See also* Net domestic product
Gulf Oil Corporation, 86, 213
Guyana, 151

Hainan Island, 96–97
Hakkas, 38
Harris, Townsend, 5
Hawaii, US annexation of (1898), 6
Ho Ying-ch'in, Gen., 193
Holy See, 162
Hong Kong, 123
Horikoshi, Teizo, 190
Housing, investment in (1952–1974), 71
Hsieh Tung-min, 62, 144
Hua Kuo-feng, 26, 141, 143, 145
Hughes Aircraft Corporation, 104
Huntington, Samuel, 51, 54

Ichiang Shan Island, 99
Ikeda, Hayato, 180, 181
Imports: from US (1960s), 24; of foodstuffs, 75–76; principal market, 79–80; of crude oil and petroleum products, 85–86; from US and Japan (1975), 161; from Middle East and Europe, 162
Income: inequality in Mexico and Taiwan, compared, 52; distribution, 70; decline of farm, 76–77, 87; savings as percent of national, 82, 93; mechanization of agriculture and increase in farm, 88, 91. *See also* Per capita income
Independence, as goal, 170–171, 239, 240
India, 153
India-China conflict (1962), 108, 124
Indonesia, 132, 133, 153
Industry: percent of domestic production (1952), 72; financing, 75, 76; development of, 75–80, 84; rate of increase of production, 77; expanding private, 77–78; problems and policies, 80–87; heavy, 83–85; shift from labor-intensive to technology-intensive, 84–85; labor and expansion of, 88; expected growth rate to 1981, 92; producing military equipment, 105
Inflation: experience of, 75, 78; rate to 1981, 92; policy of avoiding, 94
Information and cultural centers, 166–167
Institute of Nuclear Energy Research, 118
Intelligence operations, 16, 99, 130–131
Interchange Association (ICA), 164, 190–192, 195, 197
Intergovernmental Civil Aviation Organization, 156, 158
International Atomic Energy Agency (IAEA), 119, 156
International Badminton Federation, 160
International Basketball Federation, 159
International Civil Aviation Organization, 197
International Council of Scientific Unions (ICSU), 158–159
International Federation of Football Associations, 160
International Hydrographic Organization, 156
International Labor Organization, 156
International Maritime Consultative Organization, 156
International Monetary Fund (IMF), 156–157
International Olympic Committee (IOC), 155, 159
International status: UN seat issue, 148–153; bilateral diplomatic relations, 153–154; representation in international organizations, 155–160; informal methods of intercourse, 161–168; and Japan, 187–194
International Telecommunications Satellite Organization (INTELSAT), 159
International Telecommunications Union, 156
Inter-Parliamentary Union, 183
Investment: by US, 24, 27–28, 161; improving climate for, 78; foreign capital, 80; in transportation, 82; in integrated steel mill, 83; in further economic development, 84; maintaining favorable climate of, 85; capital, as percent of growth, 93; and overseas Chinese, 133; by Japan, 161, 183, 193–194; by Saudi Arabia, 162; by Japan, 185–186